SOUTHERN
HYPERBOLES

Southern Literary Studies
Scott Romine, Series Editor

SOUTHERN HYPERBOLES

Metafigurative Strategies of Narration

Michał Choiński

LOUISIANA STATE UNIVERSITY PRESS

BATON ROUGE

Published by Louisiana State University Press
Copyright © 2020 by Louisiana State University Press
All rights reserved
First printing

Designer: Laura Roubique Gleason
Typeface: Minion Pro

Library of Congress Cataloging-in-Publication Data

Names: Choiński, Michał, 1983– author.
Title: Southern hyperboles : metafigurative strategies of narration / Michał Choiński.
Description: Baton Rouge : Louisiana State University Press, 2020. | Series: Southern
    literary studies | Includes bibliographical references and index.
Identifiers: LCCN 2019050596 (print) | LCCN 2019050597 (ebook) | ISBN 978-0-8071-
    7298-8 (cloth) | ISBN 978-0-8071-7379-4 (pdf) | ISBN 978-0-8071-7380-0 (epub)
Subjects: LCSH: American literature—Southern States—History and criticism. | American
    literature—20th century—History and criticism. | Hyperbole in literature.
Classification: LCC PS261 .C47 2020 (print) | LCC PS261 (ebook) | DDC 810.9/8975—
    dc23
LC record available at https://lccn.loc.gov/2019050596
LC ebook record available at https://lccn.loc.gov/2019050597

To my parents

CONTENTS

ACKNOWLEDGMENTS

This book has been a labor of love for the last six years. During that time, I have been fortunate enough to receive support and assistance from a number of people to whom I feel deeply indebted.

First, I would like to thank Robert Brinkmeyer Jr., who first introduced me to Lillian Smith and Katherine Anne Porter, and with whom every conversation quickly turned into a laboratory for new ideas about American culture and literature. The genesis and completion of this book would not have been possible without those illuminating conversations.

I am deeply grateful to Marta Gibińska-Marzec, who first taught me rhetoric and Shakespeare's drama during my undergraduate studies at the Jagiellonian University and who has offered me astute guidance on how to read literature ever since. Her insightful suggestions regarding the content and the organization of the manuscript have been invaluable.

I wish to thank Elżbieta Chrzanowska-Kluczewska, head of the Institute of English Studies at the Jagiellonian University, for her excellent advice on how to develop the figurative methodology used in this study and how to organize the methodological chapter of the book. Her expertise on the figurative aspects of language is unsurpassed.

Zygmunt Mazur, head of the Department of American Literature and Culture at the Institute of English Studies, remained invariably supportive and understanding over these six long years, always doing his best to facilitate the writing process. I am grateful for his help and encouragement.

Nancy Schultz from Salem State University and Aeddan Shaw, my colleague from the Institute of English Studies, were kind enough to provide me with insightful comments on the manuscript of *Southern Hyperboles*. I am deeply grateful for their feedback and for saving me from the embarrassment of a number of silly typos. Needless to say, any mistakes which may remain are my responsibility.

I wish to thank my colleagues and friends Małgorzata Cierpisz, Maciej Eder, Jeremiasz Jagiełła, Alicja Kowalczewska, Urszula Niewidomska-Flis, and Jan Rybicki for their tireless support and kind words of encouragement, especially when the final stages of my work on the manuscript became a time of personal struggle.

The book also would not have been possible were it not for the OPUS research grant awarded by the Polish National Science Centre (OPUS 2016/23/B/HS2/01207, "Hyperbole in the Writings of American Southern Authors"). The funds provided by the grant allowed me to travel to libraries and research centers outside of Poland and to participate in a number of academic conferences between 2017 and 2020. I am deeply grateful to the Polish National Science Centre for sponsoring my research.

Over these six years, I was lucky enough to enjoy the hospitality of a number of academic institutions, which kindly allowed me to use not only the excellent resources of their libraries but also comfortable desks where I could pile up my carefully hoarded books: the John F. Kennedy Institute at Freie Universität, Berlin; the Jonathan Edwards Center at Yale University; and the Institute of Southern Studies at the University of South Carolina. It was a delight to be able to work in those libraries, and the oases of tranquillity that they afforded played a large part in seeing this project come to fruition.

Last, but not least, I wish to thank my parents, Janusz Choiński and Krystyna Choińska, for their unquestionable and loving support. They have always encouraged me to reflect on the surrounding world—I remain grateful for that lesson. This book is dedicated to them.

SOUTHERN HYPERBOLES

INTRODUCTION

This book springs from my enduring fascination with the literature of the American South. Ever since I started teaching southern fiction almost a decade ago, I have been increasingly preoccupied with its distinctiveness as well as with what one of my students once described as southern "exotic rhetoric." Certainly, part of my growing interest was connected to my own regional background. I was brought up in Galicia, in the southern part of Poland, which is notorious for its dedication to social propriety and religious traditions and a propensity for nostalgic mythmaking, especially in the context of Poland's troubled history. Thus, I have felt an understandable affinity with the tensions rooted in the literature of the American South. And I wanted to learn more, particularly in terms of understanding the language principles behind the southernness I intuitively saw in the various texts I so much enjoyed teaching.

In this context, I cannot resist evoking a well-known analogy from *Sophie's Choice*, by William Styron:

> Poland is a beautiful, heart-wrenching, soul-split country which in many ways [. . .] resembles or conjures up images of the American South—or at least the South of other, not-so-distant times. It is not alone that forlornly lovely, nostalgic landscape which creates the frequent likeness—the quagmiry but haunting monochrome of the Narew River swampland, for example, with its look and feel of a murky savanna on the Carolina coast, or the Sunday hush on a muddy back street in a village of Galicia, where by only the smallest eyewink of the imagination one might see whisked to a lonesome crossroads hamlet in Arkansas these ramshackle, weather-bleached little houses, crookedly carpentered, set upon shrub less plots of clay where scrawny chickens fuss and peck. (246–247)

This description helped me to comprehend the drive behind my enduring interest and an intuitive sense of affinity, but the issue of the stylistic denominator of "southernness" returned to haunt me, as it were, and properly addressing it required more than just a single quote, even by such a writer as Styron.

Thus, in my research for this book, my ambition was to try to study texts by various southern authors in search of their common rhetorical trait. I came to believe that this characteristic element is not connected only with how particular words, figures of speech, and sentences are put together on the surface of the text, nor does it spring solely from the selection of themes and motifs, or even from the notorious southern aesthetics of the grotesque. In *Southern Hyperboles*, I wish to argue that the answer to my research inquiry stems from how the texts in question are formed on a more tacit, figurative level and how they are framed by metaliterary patterns that often remain hidden but nonetheless govern the overall artistic rules of engagement. My analysis aims to demonstrate how the thoughts of the southern authors operate throughout the texts and to describe the kind of figurative processes of comprehension that are triggered by a nexus of interlocking regional and social factors.

The metafigurative methodology selected here for the study of the seven authors—Katherine Anne Porter, William Faulkner, Lillian Smith, Katharine Du Pre Lumpkin, Tennessee Williams, Flannery O'Connor, and Harper Lee—seems inviting, given the rhetorical nature of southern prose. In "An Introduction to *The Sound and the Fury*," Faulkner, assuming the collective voice of the South, declares, "We need to talk, to tell, since oratory is our heritage" (413). His insistence on the importance of oral tradition, and on the potent, emphatic use of language, remains visible in the metalinguistic character of southern writings. The unique idiom of language use discussed in this book highlights the very fact of artistic communication taking place, inviting the readers to participate in perpetual "storytelling," a prolonged dialogue within and without. As Richard Gray stipulates in *The Life of William Faulkner*, Faulkner habitually used this "productive relation between voices: not just the possibility but the fact of genuine dialogue within communities and between generations" in the South (3). Gray's Bakhtinian readings of Faulkner, as well as the entirety of southern literature he describes in *A Web of Words: The Great Dialogue of Southern Literature*, points to the metadiscursive nature of southern fiction, one figurative aspect of which I place under scrutiny in this book.

In the opening chapter of *Southern Hyperboles*, I look into how the figurative organization of a text remains indicative of its author's mode of cognition.

Reporting on various takes on tropology and a variety of functions that figuration may perform in texts, I differentiate between tropes that encompass words or clusters of words (microtropes), those that organize larger sections of a text (macrotropes), and those that provide framework for its overall design (metafiguration). This last level of figuration is where I intend to anchor my analysis here, also demonstrating how particular tropes and figures at lower levels build up the metafigurative framework of the entire text. In the second part of the opening chapter, I discuss the discursive aspects of metafiguration, paying particular attention to Hayden White's concept of tropology, of how the four Vichian master tropes of metaphor, metonymy, synecdoche, and irony come to represent different modes of cognition.

The underlying argument behind *Southern Hyperboles* is that a number of novels, short stories, and dramas written by various contemporary authors of the American South are, to a large extent, governed by the figurative metalogic of yet another trope, hyperbole. This hyperbolic mode relies on a clash of opposites and on the rapid intensification of disharmonious ideas that are pushed to the extreme, disrupting the established decorum. Through hyperbole, the contrasts are escalated and the sense of the normal is disrupted. At that moment of the merger of impossibility and possibility, the triggered recipient experiences a discordant shock. But this state of confusion is only momentary. Once the mind of the recipient recovers from the disjunctive jolt, hyperbole allows him or her to reach a new understanding of the surrounding world. Ultimately, as Goran Stanivukovic stresses, the hyperbolic metalogic can become a constructive "generator of thought and meaning," whose metalogic relies on the transition from disruption and escalating conflicts to new sets of ideas and a fresh perspective on the discussed phenomena (17).

Hence, my study of the seven southern authors in this book does not focus on hyperbole alone as an ornament on the surface of the text. I am interested in the southern figurative "mode of writing," to borrow David Lodge's term, that is, in metahyperbole as a grid that organizes the studied texts in terms of diverse aspects, such as the figurative, the narrative, or the symbolic. In my analysis, I aim to look into how individual, small figures, as well as macro figures that organize larger sections of texts, ultimately constitute the tacit metafigurative layer, and become the overall "mode of comprehension."

In southern writings from the beginning of twentieth century, this hyperbolic mode of comprehension springs naturally from the tensions of a segregated, patriarchal society and the presence of racial and social decorums.

Little wonder, then, that in his essay "The Southerner as American Writer," Hugh Holman looks at southernness exactly as a "reconciliation of opposites," arguing that one can find "at the heart of the southern riddle, a union of opposites, a condition of instability" (1). This merger of opposites, of repelling forces, requires a violent push to overcome that natural "instability" as well as a trained selectiveness of mind to cope with the concurrence of opposites. So, in the next section of the book, attempting to build a bridge between the metafigurative approach and the main analytical chapter, I survey a handful of selected publications that explore "southernness" and focus, in particular, on its penchant for myth making and the dedication to social decorum and grotesque aesthetics. I want to show how some of these notions pervade the literature on the region and how they generate and escalate conflicts, forming the substratum for the hyperbolic mode.

At an initial stage of research, I had to make a decision regarding the selection of texts I planned to put under scrutiny. Because of the level of focus I aim to maintain in my analysis, limiting the discussion to one literary period was unavoidable. Thus, all works selected for discussion in this book were written by authors from the South over the decades spanning the 1930s through the 1950s, a troubled era in the history of Dixie. Teeming with social tensions, this period was interesting for me due to its suspense between the Old South and the New South, on the one hand, and the drive toward industrialization, racial integration, or the advancement of feminism, on the other hand. My working assumption was that in this time of apprehension, hyperbolic metalogic became, for a number of southern authors, a viable means of processing the surrounding reality.

The readers will immediately notice that the authors of all the texts studied in this book are white. Obviously, this does not mean that there are no southern writers of color who employ metafigurative means to negotiate their identity with the region. On the contrary, a number of names could be provided in this context, among whom Richard Wright, would be a particularly promising object of literary discussion. In *Southern Hyperboles,* however, I have decided to limit my analyses to white male and white female authors because, in short, the kind of white, paradoxical, and haunted tensions I look into in this book were conditioned by a network of factors very different from those that contextualized, for instance, how African American authors construed their linguistic relationship with the region. Including authors of different ethnic backgrounds in one study ran the risk of being reductive toward their respective complexities. The use of metafigurative modes in fiction authored by non-white authors deserves an exhaustive study of its own.

Next, I was confronted with another, even tougher choice regarding the selection of particular names that were to be discussed in the project. The frustrating decision to leave out, for instance, Eudora Welty was dictated by the imperative to include authors whose use of the hyperbolic mode is most diverse and thus to demonstrate the variety of ways in which the metatrope functions in southern literature. The order in which these novels, short stories, and plays are discussed in the book is chronological, respective of the time when they were written. Such a decision was made in the hope of capturing a diachronic image of how the southern figurative rules of engagement changed over the three decades.

In the first analytical section of the book, "Rites of Passage" (chapter 2), dedicated to Katherine Anne Porter's short stories, I study the metahyperbolic design that she appropriates as a catalyst of growth for her protagonist. The mounting tensions there radiate from the overbearing presence of the southern decorum, the "old order," embodied in Porter's stories through the character of Sophia Jane, or the Grandmother, whose figurative representation in "The Source" I first discuss in the chapter. The entire autobiographical Miranda cycle illustrates an obscure process of emancipation from the grip of decorum, yet the clearest example of Porter's hyperbolic metafiguration can be found in "The Grave," the final short story I study in chapter 2. There, each element of the plot forms a part of the hyperbolic metanarrative: against the background of the emptied graves, Miranda and her brother establish a gender decorum, which is then pushed to the extreme with the ritualistic skinning of the dead rabbit, culminating in a shocking revelation for the girl, who after many years still feels the tremors of the hyperbolic shock.

In chapter 3, "The Polyphony of the Past," I discuss William Faulkner's "Dry September" and "A Rose for Emily" as two different applications of hyperbolic metalogic. First, the fierce debate that precedes the formation of the lynching group is studied as an instance of agon, an eristic duel in which the owner of the barbershop seeks to publicly refute the accusations leveled against Will Mayes. His selection of arguments, however, cannot match the aggressive rhetoric of the future lynchers, and his defense brings about the opposite result from what he intends. Through a contrastive clash of rhetorical appeals, the agon escalates and inevitably spirals into violence. Next, Faulkner's most popular short story "A Rose for Emily" is discussed to demonstrate how the macrometaphors of spatial and temporal confinement and of death are used to characterize Miss Emily's relationship with the collective voice of Jefferson and to illustrate the region's troubled preoccupation with the past.

In the fourth chapter, "Breaking out of Hyperbole," two southern social autobiographies from the 1940s, Lillian Smith's *Killers of the Dream* and Katharine Du Pre Lumpkin's *The Making of a Southerner,* are studied to demonstrate how narratives of southern upbringing employ the metahyperbolic mode for the establishment of a troubled identity. The indictment of southern society in these two texts has profound linguistic implications, since the autobiographic act of personal recreation that both authors undertake becomes an act of metalanguage. In the case of Smith's text, I look into various micro- and macrotropes that allow her to expose the haunted traumas of her childhood. Her figurative attempts to "cut the umbilical cord" with the racist South, and the closing of the "doors" of her mind, stress the conceptual separation and the struggle with figurative tensions that escalate and allow her to deliver a new "self." In *The Making of a Southerner,* it is the myth of the Lost Cause and the religious reverence the Lumpkin family had toward it that frames the metahyperbole. The narrator of the book portrays the development of a selective southern memory, which grows out the of the myth and pushes all problematic facts and recollections into the mental limbo of a "twilight zone." In both texts, it is the unruliness of hyperbole that allows the cultural decorum to be both challenged and broken and that ultimately secures the space for Smith and Lumpkin to try to renegotiate their identities.

Chapter 5, "Hyperbolic Dissolution," discusses four of Tennessee Williams's dramas. I argue that Williams's hyperbolic design is best manifested in the characters of southern belles, who collapse under mounting social tensions and whose identity figuratively disintegrates at the moment of the excessive apex, as they are forcibly transported into an ominous hospital institution. Williams saw a similar drama at his family home, with his sister Rose, whose progressing mental disorder and the subsequent lobotomy became a lifelong, guilt-ridden obsession for him.

To demonstrate how he dramatizes these circumstances, I first look into how the macrometaphors of solidity and temperature are used in *Summer and Smoke* to represent the disparity between Alma Winemiller and John Buchanan. The figurative divergence there is the basis for the hyperbolic contrast, but whereas in *Summer and Smoke* William presents only its onset, Alma's pathway to downfall, the full-blown outcome and the destructive culmination of the excessive drama becomes visible with the female characters of *Portrait of a Madonna, Hello from Bertha,* and *A Streetcar Named Desire*—each featuring a southern belle who breaks down and disintegrates mentally as well as physically and whose nostalgic wish for a romantic happy ending is violently crushed when she is displaced to a menacing hospital ward. In Williams's case, therefore, the epitome of the hyperbolic metalogic is psychological and physical obliteration—his metahyperbole is one that dissolves the desperate self.

Next, in "Hyperbolic Epiphany," two of Flannery O'Connor's short stories ("A View of the Woods" and "Greenleaf") and one novel (*The Violent Bear It Away*) are studied to demonstrate her engagement of hyperbolic metalogic. There is an ostensible religious agenda behind O'Connor's writings, and she compulsively escalates the opposites to convert readers through her version of a religious shock therapy. The world of O'Connor's fiction is irreparably conflicted, populated by grotesque misfits and scarred with contrasts that deteriorate to the point of a violent breakage. As O'Connor systematically twists and turns the circumstances of her characters' lives, the climactic moment of the intensification is usually marked by death, as in the case of Mrs. May, impaled by a bull's horn in "Greenleaf," or the drowning of Bishop in *The Violent Bear It Away.* It is at this moment that the metafigurative hyperbole reaches its climax and forces the characters into a new, epiphanic understanding of the circumstances of their lives, usually exposing their grotesqueness and misery. Thus, in the chapter dedicated to O'Connor's fiction, I look into the hyperbolic metafiguration that brings out the revelatory potential of the trope, focusing on how O'Connor designs her stories in the grotesque aesthetics and distinguishing between various types of violence one can find in her fiction.

Finally, the sixth analytical chapter (chapter 7), "To Kill the Watchman," scrutinizes Harper Lee's two novels, *To Kill a Mockingbird* and *Go Set a Watchman.* The books share an ambiguous relationship (*Watchman* being the initial version of the former, although placed later in terms of plotline and published only recently) and constitute an interesting case study for the analysis of how the mechanisms that protected the southern decorum of prejudice can be represented. In the case of *To Kill a Mockingbird,* the failed attempt to lynch Tom Robinson and the shooting of the mad dog are studied to show how the "unruly" excess is contained. In Harper Lee's second book, the persuasive rhetorical strategies used by Uncle Jack in his conversations with Jean Louise to defend the racist views held by Atticus Finch exemplify the figurative and eristic mechanisms that protect the status quo. Thus, it is through the joint reading of the two books that one can see their common emphasis on the threat of the hyperbolic excess.

In these discussions, this book makes no pretense of capturing the epitome of literary "southernness," nor does it seek to tackle the issue of the South's literary salience against the background of American culture in its entirety. The reader who starts reading *Southern Hyperboles* in the hope of finding an attempt to define the characteristics of the rhetorical "South" is bound to return this book to the shelf in disappointment. The completion of such a goal would far exceed my competence—if it were achievable at all. In fact, even pointing to a single metafigurative denominator, one "mode of comprehension," in the context of a regional literature is a daunting task. In the South, there are layers upon layers of paradoxical semiotics of culture and troubled myths that need to be examined, all pointing to a phalanx of interlocking issues and themes— and behind the idea of a singular South we are in fact looking at a nexus of interlocking and overlapping Souths. I do believe, however, that this study may offer a useful heuristic tool for readers who experience analogous jouissance when reading Porter, Faulkner, and O'Connor and who intuitively feel that, beyond mere sentences, paragraphs, and plots, there is a figurative affinity that justifies ranking them as "southern" writers.

1

HYPERBOLE AND THE SOUTH

Figurative Modes of Cognition

The approach used in this book traces its roots back to rhetoric and various studies on figuration. However, I seek to move beyond a conventional stylistic analysis and the classical divisions into *figurae elocutionis* (figures of speech) and *figurae sententiae* (figures of thought). Such a distinction is of little value in the context of this book insofar as I assume that all figures are figures of thought and all figurative elements of a text, on some level, are emblematic of the writer's creative processes. Ostensibly, they testify to how the minds of authors process the surrounding reality and the kind of modes of thinking they assume in their artistic enterprises. In the words of Michael and Marianne Shapiro, tropology remains located "at the deepest and most general level of human interaction with the world, [while] figuration is of first importance for theories of cognition and meaning" (*Figuration* xviii). By anchoring my discussion on the metafigurative level, and by focusing on figures not as ornaments but as modes of cognition, I hope to be able to set up a framework that is helpful for a better understanding of southern fiction and for uncovering the figurative mode of comprehension within which it operates.

In his discussion of the "poetics of mind," Raymond W. Gibbs Jr. says that "the mind itself is primarily structured out of various tropes. These figures of thought arise naturally from our ordinary, unconscious attempts to make sense of ourselves and the physical world" (434). Thus, by looking into the figurative framework of a text, one also gets a chance to glimpse the mind behind the language. This kind of approach to figuration is not far removed from Kenneth Burke's theory of tropes, described in *A Rhetoric of Motives*, or from more recent proposals of cognitive metaphor theory, first laid out by George Lakoff and Mark Johnson four decades ago in *Metaphors We Live By* and then augmented by Lakoff and Mark Turner in *More than Cool Reason*. Their approach was that of the "embodied" mind that metaphorically conceptualizes different experiential domains, mapping one domain onto another and thus forming a conceptual grid that is the source of a number of metaphoric expressions in common, everyday language. For the stylists within the paradigm of cognitive metaphor theory, such as Peter Stockwell or Margaret H. Freeman, metaphor occupies a central role in figuration.

Whatever the affinities with other tropes, the figurative "move" in metaphor always requires a duality of domains—it is a conceptual movement "toward," based on likeness. The early approach to the construction of metaphor was laid out in the 1930s by English literary critic I. A. Richards. In *Philosophy of Rhetoric,* he draws a distinction between two constituents of metaphor: tenor and vehicle. Tenor signifies what the trope refers to, while the vehicle is the phrase employed—and this whole model would concern mostly the use of metaphors in the artistic context. In cognitive metaphor theory, a more dynamic and bidirectional approach, humans "live by" metaphors that are not merely linguistic or literary devices but effectually function as common modes of thought. As famously stressed by Terry Eagleton, the contemporary British literary theorist, "There is more metaphor in Manchester than there is in Marvell" (16).

Numerous commentators have been vocal in their concerns regarding the enduring hegemony of metaphor in rhetorical theory. For Gérard Genette, fixation on metaphorical tropology and its inflation has distorted the studies on figuration, contributing to their "generalization" and devaluation (103). In her recent study of figuration, tellingly entitled *Much More than Metaphor,* Elżbieta Chrzanowska-Kluczewska seeks to move beyond the metaphorical monopoly. Her approach stems from the seminal idea of four central, corresponding tropes: metaphor, metonymy, synecdoche, and irony. This figurative tetrad was set up by the eighteenth-century Italian philosopher Giambattista Vico in his most renowned work, *The New Science.* Notably, the Vichian approach goes beyond the merely ornamental potential of figures and considers the tropical quarter almost in cognitive terms, as different modes of expression whose implications are linguistic as well as mental.

Kenneth Burke's view on tropes appropriates Vico's model, placing its four constituents under one umbrella term: master tropes. The label itself is telling of the Burkian model, as it reveals the idea of figurative governmentality embedded in the core of the paradigm, the "mastery" of the four over other figurative entities. Here, each of the tropes is associated with a different mental operation, and each takes on a distinct "role in the discovery and the description of truth," as described in *A Rhetoric of Motives:* the metaphorical figuration is correlated with the assumption of a perspective, the metonymical with reduction, the synecdochical with representation, and, finally, consummating the tetrad, the ironic is correlated with the most dynamic clash of various perspectives (503). While the notion of "truth" in Burke's statement may be seen as contestable, his distinction between the "discovery" and the "description" is significant for this study. The former signifies the heuristic function of troping, as a means of cognitive engagement that allows one to process the surrounding world and its complexities, while the latter, metatropical, would provide the language of the user with the proper means to express the results of this computing.

Figures, whether they belong to the rank of the "master" or not, can realize their multifaceted functions on various textual levels. Thus, their function as well as their expressive nature varies depending on their actual size and location. In *Metaphoric Narration,* Luz Aurora Pimentel distinguishes between the tropes that remain included in lexical phrases, which she dubs "lexematic" or "phrastic," and the tropes that transcend sentences, which she calls "transphrastic." These dual divisions are augmented by Chrzanowska-Kluczewska, who places the tetrad of master tropes on three diverse levels in a text, stressing their three different functional and interpretative ranks: the micro-, the macro-, and the megafigurative.

The micro level of figuration lies within the core interest of traditional stylistic studies of literature. Here, figures fill up the space within phrases and clauses; they are singular, both petite in scale and conspicuous. Ostensibly, since they do not constitute larger clusters and patterns, their impact does not exceed the immediate textual neighborhood. In my discussion of southern fiction in *Southern Hyperboles,* I often look into numerous microfigurative phrases used by southern authors, but my intention is to demonstrate how they make up the larger patterns of figurative expression.

The macro level concerns figures that are larger in scale and that span entire sentences, paragraphs, or—in the case of poetry—texts. These tropes are as overt as the microlevel figures, and since they manifest themselves emphatically in the discourse, they remain easily perceptible to the reader. Their extended presence in the discourse and their sheer larger size allows them to function as cohesive devices, determining the figurative structure of the text. This level of figuration has been an integral part of classical rhetorical theory, and such authors as Quintilian observe that those metaphors that transcend local clauses and make up figurative series or sequences may inform the way the speaker's entire language is viewed, rendering it allegorical and enigmatic (8.6.14).

Finally, megatropes, the most abstract and elusive figurative rank, are concerned with the meta level of the text. Viewed as rhetorical strategies that may consist of diverse micro- and macrofigurative elements, the figures of the metatropical level are covert and manifest themselves in the tacit layer of the textual semantics, hidden behind two lower levels of figuration. Thus, they tend to require a more attentive reader and a more holistic approach to the entire text and its intertextual context in order to be discussed. At this metafigurative level, the discourse shows an author's creative heuristic model and the cognitive operations they adopted in order to compile the text most visibly. It is also through the megatropical figuration that the text metaphorically points to itself and its expressive rules of engagement—in deconstructive fashion, it testifies to its own inevitable, autoreflexive directionality.

Speaking about Speaking

A metafigurative discussion of various authors and groups of writers is no novelty. For instance, David Lodge's study of modernist writers, *The Modes of Modern Writing,* places emphasis on what he calls the "modes of writing" and the way they transpose between the metaphorical and metonymic figurations. The transition between these modes is exemplified by the juxtaposition of the modernist and the metaphoric, represented by James Joyce, with the antimodernist, realistic, and metonymic, represented by Philip Larkin. Lodge's analysis demonstrates how metafiguration may help us in determining the tropological underpinning of various literary groups and epochs.

Likewise, Hayden White's concept of historical metadiscourse, presented in *Tropics of Discourse,* remains of relevance for the figurative approach to southern fiction assumed in this book. White's metafiguration is essentially structuralist as its underlying assumption is that the narratives of the past are subservient to a particular "metalogic" of cognitive processing. In other words, White would argue that there is a certain prenarrative pattern, a structure of thinking that precedes discourse, which in turn may be viewed as an indicative of how ideas are generated and processed. His considerations, therefore, are placed on a deep, subconscious level, similar to Chrzanowska-Kluczewska's megatropology.

To White, with the abandonment of the ambition for a historiographic representation of past events "as they happened" and the forsaking of the ideal of a historian as a translucent glass panel, a nonexistent conductor of facts, the examination of the past ineluctably becomes an inventive act of construction. From this viewpoint, the facts of the past cannot simply be gathered and arranged in a sequence that is determined by themselves—as Nietzsche stressed, the historian's duty is an "artistic" act of processing and sequencing such facts. Hence, it becomes axiomatic that the language employed by a historian remains inescapably biased, and its verbal layer is permeated with creative subjectivity. More importantly, narration is established not to be secondary to cognition but to constitute the very means of comprehension—in essence, the phenomena are knowable and cognizable exactly through the process of a narrative. As a result, the text becomes something more than just an informative collection of signs—it yields an insight into the cognitive process of human understanding, necessarily biased and opinionated.

Each person's mind is biased toward a certain way of computing phenomena and viewing the relations among them. In *Tropics of Discourse,* White delves into the figurative modes of narration that are discernible in discourse and that constitute its core—as he puts it, "troping is the soul of discourse" (2). So, figures are unavoidable, not only on the textual level but also on the conceptual level—and they point the text to itself by their "metadiscoursive reflexiveness." As Hayden White stresses in his work, "This is why every discourse is always as much about discourse itself as it is about the objects that make up its subject matter" (4).

For our discussion of southern fiction, the analytical implications of such an observation are essential. It follows that one can discern a layer of meaning within a narrative interpretation that not only is about the subject matter but also is quintessentially about the interpretation itself. This is what I intend to discuss in *Southern Hyperboles*—the extent to which the processing of the regional world of Dixie left a distinctly metafigurative mark on a group of white writers from the South.

To White, the conceptual practices through which one renders the unknown known and builds connections among phenomena can be parsed as the process of troping, drawing on the four principal modalities of figuration identified, after Burke, as master tropes: metaphor, metonymy, synecdoche, and irony. White identifies these as consecutive stages of a cognitive process through which one arrives at a new understanding. No longer an issue of style but more a matter of communication and mental processing, troping becomes associated directly with epistemology and the subconscious patterns of comprehension one employs to process the past.

Thus, the first move of the figurative metalogic can be likened to metaphor. This ubiquitous trope, critical for poetic expression and common discourse alike, is based on the idea of "likeness" between phenomena and the transposition of one domain of experience onto another. Etymologically, the term "metaphor" originates in *metapherein,* from *meta-* (over, across) and *pherein* (to carry, to bear), and means "to carry over." The very origin of the word yields an insight into the cognitive process it entails, which is, as it were, grasping a shard of meaning and transporting it beyond the original mental area into a domain that has not been previously associated with it, thus constructing a previously nonexistent connection. In *Tropics of Discourse,* White sees this metaphorical "modality of metalogic" as constructive and dynamic—it "asserts a similarity in a difference, and, at least implicitly, a difference in similarity" (30). Thus, the move of metaphor, according to White, is a "search for similitude" (73) in which one scans the features of one phenomenon to recognize their resemblance to another phenomenon. Like a child that begins to comprehend the world by recognizing the links conjoining its constituents, a person engaged in the metaphorical move discovers and conceives connections. This bridge-building synthesizing of ideas entails, therefore, an act of characterization and a search for objects that will evoke the images associated with the phenomena of culture.

The second modality is associated with metonymy. Through the movement from the previous mode to this one, the metaphorical construal based on the recognition of likeness undergoes the process of fragmentation—such a turn is unavoidable because metonymy's core framework is based on contiguity. Roman Jakobson argues that while metaphor is associated more with the "principle of selection," metonymy is to be associated with the "principle of combination" (254). Both tropes, however, constitute key linguistic categories, and the distinction between them—as observed by the Russian formalists— has implications for all human verbal behavior, and even for all behavioral and representational modes in general. The fragmentary "combination" of metonymy is fundamentally different from the recognition of the holistic "likeness" that characterizes the metaphorical move, but at the same time it constitutes its natural consequence. The model of a narrative based on the metalogic of metonymy would draw on its reductive potential and the ability to single out constituents within a whole. Writers fitting into this mode would defragment the phenomena as complete wholes and would frame their historiographical narratives around the links that objectively join the fragments through the relationships of cause and effect.

The third mode of narrative metalogic is synecdochical. Having been disintegrated and divided into constituent elements, the studied objects and phenomena can be reintegrated and assigned to different orders, classes, and categories in terms of diverse "patterns of integration." Observably, these patterns serve a different purpose than in the case of metonymy. At this stage, the establishment of the relationship between the whole and the element aims to identify the whole as a sum that remains qualitatively equivalent to the parts that make it up. So, as Burke argues in *A Rhetoric of Motives*, while metonymy is reductive, synecdoche is more representative, and while synecdochic relationships are convertible and may function is either direction, metonymy focuses on the substitution of qualities for qualities (508). Also, as one looks at the semantic relationships among the entities constituting synecdoche, the relationship of an element to the whole often turns out to be more physical than associative, as is the case with metonymy.

Finally, the salient element distinguishing the two concerns the matter of directionality. While both metonymy and synecdoche operate within the same framework of a relationship between *pars* (part) and *totus* (whole), they differ in terms of the direction of thought, since within this third mode of narrative figuration the mind moves toward the integration of all apparently isolated phenomena into a whole. Thus, for this third figurative modality, defragmentation allows one to shed new light upon the complete phenomenon and to scrutinize it as a totality of the salient elements that constitute it.

The final metafigurative mode of comprehension involves irony, the fourth of the master tropes outlined by Vico and Burke. Defined by classical authors such as Quintilian as the "opposite of what is being said" (9.2.44), irony is a trope that has been in the spotlight in a number of academic contexts, from literature through humor studies to linguistics. Upon closer scrutiny, however, the brief definition provided by the Roman rhetorician and replicated in a number of other rhetorics offers more doubts than answers. In particular, it generates quibbles about such notions as the communicative intention and language comprehension as well as a rather nebulous opposition between literal and implied meanings.

In answer to those doubts, Peter Oesterreich stresses the distinction among three primary applications of irony. The first one, *ironia verbi*, concerns the employment of the trope in the utterances of individual people, the most intuitive and common understanding of the notion. The second one is more general and is encapsulate the manner in which one can reflect upon human life and its events; this is *ironia vitae*. The final level of irony, *ironia entis*, the most universal, involves existence in its entirety. These three modes of irony, functioning on the rhetorical, existential, and philosophical levels, and their scalar nature, testify to the complex philosophical implications of the trope.

Unlike the metaphorical move, which is based on similarity, the ironic move stems from disjunction. Thus, the addressee has to decode a message communicated by the opposite (which is then refuted by the signals of irony, nonverbal and verbal alike) and pierce the indirectness that hides the communicative intention. All this makes irony a profoundly subversive trope as the addresser purposefully seeks, as it were, to fool the addressee and to challenge the very principles of communication that allow for exchange. Ironic rumination is thus essentially revisionist in its nature. It allows for a critical comprehension of the self and the realization of the alternatives to what is expected, thus completing the journey from a credulous recognition of the metaphorical metalogic of similitude to a reflection that allows the self to judge things and reorganize the way the totalities are comprehended—in this sense, it is not dissimilar from the hyperbolic metalogic discussed extensively later in this chapter.

White's tropical path, consistent and promising as it is, may pose some difficulties in terms of its actual application for the description of the historical corpus. For instance, in his paper from 1990, Donald Ostrowski attempts to classify different Russian historians according to the tropical mode of representation they employ, but not all of the appropriations of White can be deemed successful, the main reason being that it is occasionally hard to pinpoint the operative trope and, as Richard T. Vann notes, "only the least imaginative historians (such as Ranke) line up everything according to the elective affinities" (151). Frank Ankersmit's thought constitutes perhaps one of the best examples of how White's idea may be expanded upon for the discussion of narration. In the book *Historical Representation,* this Dutch professor of intellectual history and an important voice in the contemporary reflections on historical narrativism proposed the finding of a *juste milieu,* a middle way between the linguistic innocence of the traditional theory of history and the hyperboles of some postmodern theorists (21). In particular, he comments on the alleged divide between the act of "speaking" and the act of "speaking about speaking" (30)—the former directing the attention to reality, to how the narrative denotes the elements of the extralinguistic reality, and the latter focusing on the meta level, pointing to language itself. Ankersmit argues that some narratives of the past, when taken as whole, complete "verbal representations," transcend the boundary of "speaking" and "speaking about speaking," and allow the assertion that "language can become a truth maker no less than reality" (32). The Dutch philosopher sees all elements of representation, including the periodization labels or meta-operative terms, as coalescing the issues of meaning and empirical fact. The role of the commentator on the past, in his view, would be the integration of both the actual experience and the language used to describe it into a better historical understanding. Following his reasoning, my discussion of the metafigurative aspects of southern literature may provide an insight into the functioning of the "real" regional mind-set of its authors and point to the palpable dilemmas that shaped their rules of artistic engagement.

Ankersmit (12–13) also draws a distinction between descriptions and representations. The former involves a reference that can be subject to falsification, following the understanding of truth proposed by the Polish logician Alfred Tarski, as a correspondence between a statement of language and the state of affairs in the world. Representation, on the other hand, as an object itself, shares the quality of being "opaque—as things are" and does not have to pass the falsifiability test. The epistemological notions of "reference" or "truth" do not necessarily apply in the representational context as they do in the case of descriptions. Also, for Ankersmit, representations may be compared to proper names that denote the complexity of the phenomenon they represent. They are to be considered more as operative on the meta level; consequently, "representations always bring us to the level of 'speaking about speaking' . . . the level of metalanguage fixing the relationship between object-language and the world" (291–292). Discussions about the past are thus effectively discussions about how the past is discussed and perceived—a statement that is of considerable relevance for a host of southern writings.

The metafigurative level of "speaking about speaking" is precisely where I want to anchor my discussion of southern fiction. Going beyond micro- and macrofiguration, I seek to demonstrate here how the metafigurative hyperbole reveals itself through language and the organization of the narrative in the work of such authors as Katherine Anne Porter, William Faulkner, or Flannery O'Connor. As much as these writers differ in style, in micro- and macrofigurative terms the tacit metanarrative framework of their works turns out to be similar, exhibiting the hyperbolic mode of comprehension and a specific decorum-oriented notion of excess. In essence, hyperbolic metafiguration is the quintessential manner of southern "speaking about speaking."

Hyperbolic Metafiguration

In *New Science,* which so strongly influenced Burke's and White's thought, Giambattista Vico does not grant hyperbole the status of one of the master tropes. The exclusion from this elite figurative club has impacted the status of hyperbole as a research subject for years. Indeed, when compared with the overwhelming host of studies on metaphor, there are relatively few books dedicated solely to the hyperbolic figuration. Over the past years, the trope has been predominantly studied in the context of the aesthetics of the grotesque (as in Geoffrey Harpham's *On the Grotesque*) or baroque literature (as in Christopher Johnson's *Hyperboles*). Also, as one of the most frequently occurring figures of speech, whose functioning is so dependent on the communicative context, hyperbole has been put under scrutiny by researchers dealing with linguistic pragmatics and cognitive linguistics (as in Claudia Claridge's *Hyperbole in English*). The present book seems to be the first study of hyperbole as a metatrope, a figurative mode of literary design and artistic thought that can be used to study a regional group of writings.

One would expect hyperbole to have had a more impressive academic career. Surely, this trope aligns particularly well with the modern interest in language ungovernability and excess, especially in the context of literary studies, and naming a wide array of writers, as well as critics, for whom verbal excess has become a *principium operandi* would be relatively easy. For instance, one could argue that some narrative forms of the stream of consciousness technique are inevitably hyperbolic in the way they break the discursive conventions and mimic the haphazard cognitive processes of the human mind.

Moreover, hyperbole does not belong to literary studies alone—it is, in fact, a distinctly common phenomenon of thought and communication. In everyday, rudimentary exchanges, every single one of us employs multiple overstatements, exaggerations, bloated comparatives, or superlatives. Then again, there is much more to hyperbole than such scattered occurrences in small talk. I intend to argue here that the trope of hyperbole entails a specific mode of comprehension and that a discussion of this figurative metalogic may yield an interesting insight into twentieth-century southern fiction.

The most salient component of the hyperbolic concerns upscaling reality and blowing it out of proportion. One of the founding fathers of Roman rhetorical thought, Quintilian, sees the trope of hyperbole exactly as a means of amplification (8.4.8). This rhetorical "growth" or "increase" can assume a number of forms, including an argument that pushes a thought beyond its original limitations, the accumulation or amassing of synonyms or paraphrases for emphatic effect, or a climax in which a listing of elements in increasing force or relevance is employed. All of these means of amplification remain inextricably bound to rhetorical pathos, the evocation of emotions among members of the audience that serves a persuasive purpose. The emotionality of verbal excess is perhaps one of the reasons why Christopher Johnson sees such a strong link between the hyperbolic figuration and the Romantic poets and their interest in the sublime (42).

Thus, the relationship between hyperbole and the dictates of classical decorum has always been problematic. Those whose sense of aesthetics revolves around the idea of proportion, stability, and moderation have constantly waged war against disconcerting verbal excess, arguing that the hyperbolic discourse can be highly subversive to the speaker. In *Rhetoric,* Aristotle observes that the use of hyperbole and exaggerated speech could make one seem "adolescent," and all respectable people ought to avoid it, lest they run the risk of demonstrating a deficient character (3.11.15). Both the open defiance of rationality exhibited by hyperbole and the transgression of decorum it entails antagonized the leading Roman rhetoricians. Cicero appreciates the role of hyperbole for impressive verbal ornamentation but simultaneously views the trope as a contention of rhetorical propriety and as a category that remains in opposition to the virtues of his "good" orator. In a similar fashion, Quintilian warns against the improper use of amplification that can make the speaker seem artificial, immaturely affectionate, or even foolish (8.6.73–74).

In these early approaches, it seems that, for an extraordinary excess to be embraced by the hearers, and to avoid repelling them, either the speaker had to be moved in some extraordinary manner, as through aesthetic or religious elevation, or the excessive topic itself had to impose an excessive manner of communication. Yet the use of excess was shunned by Christian rhetoricians such as Alain de Lille or Robert of Basevorn, who saw hyperbolic statements as deceitful and obstructive of the simplicity that should shape divinely inspired discourse. In the fourteenth century, Basevorn's *The Form of Preaching* warned against the perils of rhetoric and urged a restrained use of elocution. The admission of figuration in preaching was viewed as contentious and was approached with a great deal of reluctance. Such an admission could only be defended by the rationale that the divine as an infinite subject requires linguistic means that similarly gravitate toward the infinite and the inexpressible. As Ceri Sullivan argues in *The Rhetoric of the Conscience*, "It was commonplace that either saying nothing at all, or, alternatively, going to excess, are the appropriate modes of talking of, or to, an unknowable God" (34). It would seem that there is indeed a special context of religious excess, within whose controlled boundaries hyperbole allows one to roam undisturbed. In such thematic areas as religious elation, a specific decorum of excess emerges—the convention of breaking the conventions—which not only justifies the expansion of excess but also successfully regulates and nurtures it. The evangelical agenda underpinning Flannery O'Connor's fiction, which I will discuss later, follows a similar rationale of excess.

In their comprehensive corpus study "There's Millions of Them," Michael McCarthy and Ronald Carter stress that hyperbole commonly "magnifies and upscales reality" in daily exchanges (158). At the same time, this communicative escalation can only take place with hyperboles that are nonconventionalized and that bring about a shock in the hearers. To McCarthy and Carter, some hyperbolic expressions in common-language conversations remain "dead" in the sense that they lack the communicative power to attract attention and that they hardly reveal themselves as figurative. In essence, interlocutors use them and hear them without any effect of surprise or shock. Following on the study of Rukmini Bhaya Nair, Ronald Carter, and Michael Toolan, McCarthy and Carter rank such hyperbolic expressions as the "low-risk" tropes—to be contrasted with noninstitutionalized tropes, which are innovative and involve "creative risk taking" (27).

Creative risk taking and shocking contrasts constitute the pillars of the hyperbolic sense of aesthetics discussed in this book. Hyperbole, like irony, is a figure of disparity. Dan Sperber and Deirdre Wilson even argue that hyperbole is essentially nothing short of a subtype of irony. Johnson stresses that "the hyperbolist uses the disruption of literal sense to communicate what could not have been otherwise communicated" (11). However, at the end of the day, the disruptions and contrasts created by hyperbole are productive as, deep down, the trope is a creative act, a "generator of thought and meaning," as Goran Stanivukovic pointed out in "Mounting Above the Truthe" (17). Not only does it require speakers to go beyond the immediate reality and push the boundaries of concepts beyond their limits, but also it forces them to imagine what is beyond and to describe it. The moment the referentiality of the immediate breaks down and hyperbole moves beyond the literal, speakers have to rearrange their thoughts for this cognitive transition to take place and, in this way, a new meaning emerges. In a similar way, a lie has to be processed, but within the hyperbolic act of communication, no one tries to fool the interlocutor about the truthfulness of the proposition. Hyperbole does seek to challenge what is deemed truthful but it does not seek to replace it. It is a revelation through shock, rather than deceit, that is the ultimate goal of the hyperbolic mode of comprehension.

This heuristic potency of the hyperbolic relies strongly on its dynamic character. Robert J. Fogelin looks at the trope as a "moment of excessive exaggeration." In his brief definition, the American philosopher puts hyperbole in a temporal frame, thus implying that it could be seen as a move, as a transient moment of suspense and revelation, rather than as a fixed and stagnant ornament (x). Similarly, Joshua Ritter's view of hyperbole is that of a process, of an "art of becoming," since "by generating confusion through excess, hyperbole alters and creates meaning" (411). The opening stage of the hyperbolic process involves shock and a momentary suspension of reason. Hyperbole perplexes by subverting what is intuitively deemed truthful and by forming a violent disparity between the linguistic and extralinguistic reality. By forcing a hearer to process and conjoin incorrigible phenomena, hyperbole puts the mind on edge, thus causing a reflection or even a minor epiphany. In a nutshell, hyperbole illuminates through shocking deconstruction and open falsity.

The counterfactuality of the hyperbolic mode has been deemed as one of the contentious properties of the trope. In *The Arte of English Poesie*, one of the most influential Renaissance texts on rhetoric and stylistics, George Puttenham equates the hyperbolist with a "loud liar" and an "overreacher." He also expresses concerns about the epistemological status of hyperbole: "Now, when I speake that which neither I my selfe thinke to be true, nor would haue any other body beleeue, it must needs be a great dissimulation, because I meane nothing lesse then that I speake." To Puttenham, if hyperbole is defined by its counterfactuality and neither the speaker nor the addressees give credit to what is stated, then the main focus of the trope is upon itself and the very rhetorical act of communication. This would make hyperbole an essentially metalinguistic figure whose functioning forces a reflection on language and communication. Commenting on Puttenham's deliberations, Audrey Wasser proposes that hyperbole is in fact a "heightened or self-conscious mode of language," and due to its metafigurative potential, it may be considered a "sort of figure of figures" (833). Given such claims, one is left to wonder why hyperbole was not included in the original group of master tropes.

Hyperbole has the potency to entrap logical discontinuities and fuse them together despite their natural repulsion. As Ritter observes, it "dramatically holds the real and the ideal in irresolvable tension and reveals the impossible distance between the ineptitude and the infinite multiplicity of language to describe that which is indescribable" (407). This quality is instrumental to the metalogic of southern autobiographies I will discuss later, if not for the entire "mind of the South" as proposed by W. J. Cash. The amalgams of impossibility and possibility, as well as of falsity and truthfulness, render hyperbole not only a circuitous figure but also a figure of violence. This accounts for the "demonic" nature Jacques Derrida ascribes to hyperbole in *Writing and Difference* (57), and it explains why Chaïm Perelman and Lucie Olbrechts-Tyteca state that hyperbolic shock is "fired with brutality" (290). The open violations of the rules of decorum and logic that hyperbole entails make its operations subversive, brutal, and fierce. When compared to the coadjuvant search for likeness in metaphor, or the establishment of the metonymical or synecdochical relationships between the whole and the part, or even the self-reflexive discordance of irony, the metalogic of hyperbole turns out to be particularly conflicted. The initial shock caused by the confrontation with the hyperbolic discordance is swiftly followed by the audience's realization, which (again, violently and abruptly) pierces through the impossible to give rise to a new understanding. The hearer realizes that the speaker using the trope does not actually imply the literal, exaggerated sense but tries to communicate something different—the meaning is reevaluated, reorganized, and refreshed.

At the same time, this crowning realization of truth is strongly dependent on the fitting communicative setting for the trope. The rhetorical notion of *kairos,* the apt context for delivery, is of vital importance for hyperbole—its communicative success relies heavily on how the members of the audience react to the excess with which they are being presented, and whether they can actually receive, digest, and ultimately embrace it. Since hyperbole concerns the disruption of conventions and norms, the speaker has to employ the rhetorical rule of *kairon gnothi* (know the opportunity) for the speech act of hyperbole to be felicitous—he or she has to know when to use it, how to use it, and with whom he or she can use it. Neal R. Norrick views hyperbole as a pragmatic category whose communicative success depends solely on the affective involvement of the hearers, on their willingness to cooperate with the hyperbolist in the production of the bloated simulacrum of reality. Ultimately, hyperbole necessitates a certain conformity of comprehension on the part of the audience if it is to be accepted rather than discarded as an instance of un-justified absurdity. The use of hyperbole is a balancing act, and, like a funam-bulist, the speaker has to maneuver nimbly between misunderstanding and crude overtness.

Of the most recent publications, Claudia Claridge's book (2011) is perhaps the most comprehensive linguistic study of hyperbole, insightfully drawing on both quantitative and qualitative approaches. It follows earlier studies such as Spitzbardt (1963), Loewenberg (1982), and Kreuz and Roberts (1995). In "There's Millions of Them" (2004), McCarthy and Carter compiled lists of lex-ical items that function as intensifiers and moderators of the hyperbolic. From the large-scale perspective, according to Claridge, the number of hyperbolic expressions employed in daily exchanges is rather moderate, with an average of one hyperbole per every thousand words in spoken conversational context (263). Used both for downtoning and emphasizing, hyperbole is most com-monly used for the expression of emotions and the projection of a playful image of the speaker, which also is accomplished through phatic insulting and ironic boasting within a small social group.

Claridge also stresses the use of hyperbole in the context of politeness strat-egies—both for face-threatening acts and for the redressive attainment of pos-itive politeness. McCarthy and Carter's study, in particular, comments on the communicative function of hyperbole in a conversational exchange. Since "hyperbole is a kind of 'structuring' of reality where there are competing reali-ties," it has great dialectic potential. In particular, "it can enable sharp focus on one account of reality and downplay rival accounts, and it brings the listeners into the perspective of the speaker in a powerful way" (152). Thus, hyperbole enables a number of interpersonal human effects, such as banter, empathy, sol-idarity, antipathy, informality, and intimacy, as well as serving different evalu-ative purposes. It also can serve as a pivotal means in sociopolitical dialectics, as I will illustrate in the context of southern literary idiom and the appropria-tion of verbal excess for the simulacrum of racist discourse.

Because of how complicated hyperbolic communication turns out to be, some commentators postulate that there is something ambivalent or even suspicious about it. Gérard Genette likens the hyperbolic move to "burglary," while, due to its surreptitious operations, its movements are never overt and simple (Johnson 3, after Johnson's translation from the French). Also, hyperbole's relationship with veracity is deeply problematic and paradoxical, primarily because the trope speaks truth through what could be viewed to be an open and insolent lie. Listeners are challenged to overcome the merger of opposites as well as the violation of truth, and having recovered from the brief state of surprise, they inevitably move from distortion to a new interpretation of phenomena. As Stanivukovic aptly argues, in hyperbolic discourse "a lie, expressed in linguistic terms, becomes truth on a hermeneutic level" (17).

The appreciation for hyperbole's potential as a heuristic tool has a long tradition. In his classical treatise on rhetoric, *De Beneficiis,* Seneca the Younger asserts that "the purpose of all exaggeration is to arrive at the truth by falseness" and that exaggeration "never hopes all its daring flights to be believed, but affirms what is incredible, that thereby it may convey what is credible" (7.23). The first part of this statement encapsulates the paradoxical nature of the hyperbolic, but it also stresses the particular directionality of the hyperbolic metalogic, the move from disconcerting falsity to new discovery. Because the ideas of falsity and truthfulness are fused together in hyperbole, the trope itself dramatizes the epistemological impossibility and may be viewed as a language game or an investigative method.

In her study on Renaissance figuration, Katrin Ettenhuber stresses this reflexive function of hyperbole: "By highlighting the limits of figuration and productively destabilizing the reader's view of linguistic norms and conventions, it encourages active reflection on different ways in which meaning is constructed and communicated" (210). Hyperbole thus performs yet another vital metatextual task with regard to "speaking about speaking." It not only points to the very making of language but also remains a pivotal rhetorical means of computation and understanding—and this duality remains essential to study of the southern literary idiom.

From the Hyperbolic toward the Grotesque

The hyperbolic and the grotesque are inextricable, and all the components of metahyperbole, such as the escalation of opposites, violent contrast, and the new understanding resulting from a shock, become fully epitomized in the contentious aesthetics of the grotesque. The journey of the grotesque, which started in the hidden frescoes of Nero's Domus Aurea, made its way through the drawings of Renaissance and baroque artists, and then through modernist literature to finally find a comfortable home in Dixie, is itself convoluted. A term that used to carry pejorative undertones and connote the outskirts of orthodoxy has, nowadays, not only shed these negative associations but has even taken on an air of propriety, or even respectability. It seems that, if a given text, movie, or a painting is dubbed "grotesque," it promises the kind of emotional engagement or shock that contemporary society craves so intensely.

In particular, popular recent TV series such as *True Blood, American Horror Story,* or *True Detective* seem to draw from the aesthetics of the grotesque, creating visions of disconcerting violence, uncanny scenery, and aberrant malformation that generate millions of dollars' worth of revenue. Unsurprisingly, most of these shows take place in the Deep South, or at least make conspicuous references to it. Because the grotesque aesthetic remains so vital for southern fiction, and because the term "grotesque" is recurrent in subsequent chapters of this book, this section seeks to explore the organic link between the hyperbolic and the grotesque and to show how the latter grows out of the former.

There are multiple dualities at the heart of the grotesque. Geoffrey Harpham argues that this aesthetic category "stand[s] at a margin of consciousness between the known and the unknown, the perceived and the unperceived, calling into question the adequacy of our ways of organizing the world" (3). While we can intuitively pronounce a given painting or a book "grotesque," pinpointing the key features of this aesthetics turns out to be a far more problematic. The early theorists univocally agree that the grotesque consists of a mixture of laughter and terror, and John Ruskin, the nineteenth-century English critic, distinguishes between the noble grotesque and the ignoble grotesque. The former would be associated with flawed human nature, the latter with lascivious frivolity.

This distinction is connected with another essential distinction within grotesque aesthetics—a divide into the horror mode and the comic mode. At the same time, that dichotomy is actually a merger, for there would be no grotesque if not for the paradoxical co-presence of these two ingredients. Depending on which of the two remains more salient and pervasive, we can consider different types or functions of the grotesque. In a nutshell, it may be that laughter renders the nightmare more bearable, but it is the nightmare that keeps laughter in check.

The division into the terror-oriented and the laughter-oriented grotesque is reflected in two distinct critical takes on its aesthetics. The first, delineated by Wolfgang Kayser, focuses on the etymology of the term—the Italian word "grotto," or hidden cave—and traces the history of its functioning, especially in German and French literature. For the German theorist, the grotesque signifies the ghostly, estranged, and demonic realm of the world that cannot be accounted for and that pressures and alienates our natural realm with its abysmal force. Essentially, to Kayser, the grotesque springs from the fear of life rather than the fear of death.

Mikhail Bakhtin differs from Kayser at the most fundamental level in *Rabelais and His World*. Bakhtin's scathing comments shift the point of view away from the German theorist's persistent negativity as he looks at the body as a positive element that remains in perpetual flux. Contrary to the classical concept that saw the corporeal as divisible, static, and coherent, Bakhtin saw it in a state of "becoming," testing the limits of identity and understanding. The body is ambivalent in this transformatory state, with all the bodily functions, like coitus or defecation, exposing its openness. Here, there is no Kayserian sense of pessimistic alienation in the grotesque but a more positive and ludic openness. Bakhtin puts a lot of emphasis on the folk tradition and the carnivalesque laughter that allows people to withstand the pressures of a stratified society ridden with class divisions and solemn rituals. Folk humor is grotesque because it seeks to bring all citizens to a common level, to remove the hierarchy, at least temporarily. At the same time, the grotesque transgresses accepted limitations and caricatures the inappropriate: "Exaggeration, hyperbolism, excessiveness are generally considered fundamental attributes of the grotesque style" (303).

What the two approaches have in common is the way in which they engage and deconstruct balanced norms, and to people who cultivate a classical aesthetic sensitivity and who value symmetry and decorum, the grotesque is unbearable. The confusion it brings primarily comes from its blatant disregard for the principle of mimesis. The grotesque does not seek to provide a faithful representation of the surrounding world, nor does it seek to represent shapes in their wholeness and proportion. Vitruvius, a venerable Roman architect and civil engineer, upon seeing the murals in Nero's palace, was shocked and confused. In *De architectura,* he writes of the grotesque fantasies painted therein: "Such things do not exist and cannot exist and never have existed" (7.5.4).

Vitruvius's criticism could be considered typical, as far as the reaction of the decorum-oriented critics are concerned. The hybridization of the grotesque forms and their drift from outside of the natural and the typical, toward the bizarre and the confused, constitutes an abuse to their sense of propriety. Like the hyperbolic, which violates logical decorum through excessive unruliness, the grotesque breaks the decorum of proportion and separation. Contrary to the classical idea of vertical organization of space, or the idea of roundness that connotes perfection, the grotesque destabilizes and subverts the notion of what should go up or down, or it deviates from a perfect completion and enclosure of circularity. As Harpham argues, "Though the grotesque is more comfortable in hell than in heaven, its true home is the space between, in which perfectly formed shapes metamorphose into demons" (8).

The mythical reality of the grotesque revolves around the idea of perpetual metamorphosis in which entities coalesce and permeate one another. The idea that things remain in flux, and that entities are essentially similar to one another, can hardly be reconciled with post-Aristotelian typology in which there is a distinctive label for everything, including the label maker. The hyperbolized body that is at the same time "open" and remains akin to other bodies may be considered dangerous and effectively transformed into a cultural taboo, as is often the case in the southern decorum.

In *Fiction and the Modern Grotesque,* Bernard McElroy claims that the grotesque can only exist within a grotesque reality. In a world that puts on a mask of stability and propriety but, underneath, conceals everything that is frightful, the grotesque can function undisturbed and can decompose decorum from the inside out—and this reflects the metafigurative process that is often put under scrutiny in my work here. This "grotesque world" is hardly a world one would willingly chose to dwell in, even if it constituted the "best possible world" in the Leibnitzian understanding of the term. In the segregated reality of Dixie, where the social fabric is framed by the oppressive "old order," as presented by Katherine Anne Porter, and protected by numerous mechanisms of language and physical violence, as portrayed by Harper Lee, grotesque "unruliness" becomes not only a means for the emancipation of an individual's voice but also an indispensable aesthetic paradigm. The hyperbolic grotesque allows the authors studied in this book to engage racial divides and prescriptive decorums of the body and to seek out the connections among various elements of the southern landscape that dissect the overbearing power of the myth over the region. In this sense, the excessive grotesque becomes an inalienable element of the southern literary idiom.

As a heuristic device, the grotesque also opens itself to different figurative interpretations. Harpham builds a connection between the metaphorical and the grotesque aesthetics, as they both "give a dominant impression of unity, though they are manifestly constructed of pieces" (178). The metametaphorical and psychological effects of the grotesque are visible in Harpham's idea of an "interval"—a brief moment when one is just a step away from recognizing the unruly multiplicity of forms in an object and has not developed yet a sense of the dominant principle that defines it, although one can clearly see that it is different from all that is homely. It is a moment of hesitation, revelation, and emotional surplus that ultimately remodels one's perception of things and offers a fresh insight into the world.

In general, however, it is not the metaphoric but the hyperbolic that constitutes the vehicle for the grotesque. In particular, to Bakhtin, the communicative force of hyperbole, as discussed in the introduction, constitutes an inalienable element of the appeal of the grotesque, which seems to rely unequivocally on the abnormality and asymmetry generated by unruly excess. While the hyperbolic mode fractures the elegance of logic and moderation, the grotesque infringes on the sense of what is proper and orthodox in an artistic representation. In fact, there is no grotesque without hyperbolic excess, although not every hyperbole is openly grotesque.

These two visions of the grotesque, the Kayserian and the Bakhtinian, translate into two aspects of hyperbole. The first one, dark and "demonic," alienates readers or onlookers through its uncontrollable discordance. The violent repulsion between the repressed and the conscious antagonizes one's preconceived sense of things, leading to alienation from a given artistic object. Interestingly, both Kayser and Derrida use the same epithet, "demonic," when discussing the grotesque and hyperbolic troping, respectively. Here, the deconstruction of meaning that takes place through the management of opposites reveals something uncontrollable, dangerous, and tainted. The result of this approach is an epistemological dismay.

On the other hand, the Bakhtinian take on the grotesque—as positive, ludic, and constructive—would be most visible when the hyperbolic mode is approached as a game, as a communicative pastime in which interlocutors willingly engage to render their exchange more enjoyable. Such a language game of excess may surprise, but here the undertone is comic rather than demonic. The excess generates laughter and allows the presentation of characters whose singular obsessions, exaggerated features, and preoccupations do not pose any threat to the reader or the onlooker. Teasing jokes are made and witty puns employed to form a phatic community. Such a hyperbolic game, played within the convention of the decorum of excess, does not seek to shock the reader, nor does it seek to deconstruct and subvert, just as the frivolous carnival used the grotesque to alleviate the tension of social constraints rather than seeking to start a revolution. The hyperbolic mode of wordplay, a playful pastime of *homo rhetoricus,* functions particularly well in the grotesque that bends toward the comic rather than toward the terrible.

At the same time, as Philip John Thomson points out, like the trope of hyperbole, the grotesque may serve as an "aggressive weapon" (58) toward the reader or the onlooker, due to its emotional impact. I will explore this later, especially in my discussion of how Flannery O'Connor engages the excessive. In terms of both the uncanny and comic rhetorical effects, the affinity between the metahyperbole and the grotesque is most directly visible through violent contradictions and unruly transitions. The metalogic of hyperbole, the conversion from a shock to a revelation, and the paradox of counterfactuality that transforms into a deeper understanding takes a path similar to the move of a grotesque "interval" that leads from the suspension of decorum to a new perception of phenomena and the principles that organize them. The mind of the reader or the onlooker has to recuperate after taking in the discordant and unruly input, and this dynamic, transitory state allows for an obscure epiphany, a revelation that is born out of shock and confusion.

The Hyperbolic South

Because excessive contrasts, clashes of opposites, or hurtful revelations are the sine qua non of artistic expression, and given that they constitute a universal creative engine that allows one to challenge the surrounding reality, one is left to ponder the reasons for their apparent distinctiveness in the culture of the American South. In other words, in what way is southern excess different from the principles of engagement visible in, say, John Steinbeck's *Of Mice and Men,* and why is this book dedicated to hyperbolic metalogic of the southern fiction and not to Western hyperbolic metalogic or the hyperbolic metalogic of New England? Finally, why is it that, in the context of the southern literature, hyperbole takes on such a distinctly sordid and grotesque form? Here, I seek to address such questions and, by comparing various takes on southern "speaking about speaking," to build a bridge between the hyperbolic metafiguration I have discussed and my analyses of fiction in the next chapters.

No discussion about the "southernness" of southern fiction can success-

fully proceed without such words as "contradiction," "paradox," or "opposition." These seem to be unavoidably recurrent in the host of publications on
the American South—where they are also customarily followed by a long enumeration of the phenomena within the American South that are fundamentally incongruent and yet, by some strange regional alchemy of mind, continue
to coexist. In the "nation's region," to use Leigh Anne Duck's famous phrase,
the laws of paradox roam unrivalled.

But it is neither the antithesis nor the paradox that can be argued to constitute the metafigurative underpinning of southern fiction. Both of these figures
are far less dynamic and antagonistic as hyperbole. In my discussion, I intend
to focus on those elements of "southernness" that generate the hyperbolic dynamics of antagonism and intensify its elements. Of course, since a significant
body of literature has been published on the subject of "southernness" in recent years, it is beyond the scope of my project to provide a comprehensive report on the full diversity of views employed in the debate; thus, this synopsis
inevitably features only a selection of studies and approaches that contextual-
ize the hyperbolic mode and the inimical relationships among its constituents.

Of all the metatropes used to contemplate "southernness," the metaphor of
a haunted space is probably the most prevalent. The narratives of the South
are fraught with hauntedness—be it Flannery O'Connor's "Christ-haunted"
South or Lillian Smith's "four ghosts." The trope stems from the interlocking
themes of southern fiction: past, guilt, memory, and the epistemological suspense between myths and reality. Most notably, the South is haunted by itself.
In their 1935 book *The South Looks at Its Past*, Benjamin Kendrick and Alex
Mathews Arnett understand southern restlessness as akin to the ancient belief
that "the spirit of a deceased wandered disconsolately until his body received
the religious ceremony of burial," and, in a similar fashion, for long decades, in
a ghostlike restiveness, the Old South "has stalked abroad to bedevil in some
sort the placidity of southern and, to a lesser extent, of American life" (103).

Understandably, the trope of hauntedness aligns well with southern gothic
aesthetics as well as with the pursuit of the South as "undead." The editors of
Undead Souths, Eric Gary Anderson, Taylor Hagood, and Daniel Cross Turner,
seek to study the tropes of undeadness and southern haunting in different historical and intercultural contexts, showing how figures of the undead remain
very much grounded and widely proliferated throughout the southern cultural landscape, both in narrative and in metanarrative terms. Moving out of
the simple correlation of the region (southern) with the genre (gothic), they

seek to pluralize regional and generic identifications. To them, the figures of southbound spectres "force us to reimagine an already imaginary South" and become "holograms of an otherwise inarticulate, often distressing past" (5).

Observably, there is much more to this trope than a mere ghost theme. In terms of "speaking about speaking," the persistently recurrent image of a ghost-ridden and restless space suspended between different modes of existence, real and unreal, present and past, live and dead, bears profound linguistic implications of cognitive instability and conflict. The authors discussed in this book grew up in this haunted world, and this is the kind of haunted shibboleths of storytelling with which they became permeated and which they often adopted in their writings, whether they wanted to or not.

In Michael Kreyling's *Inventing Southern Literature,* the rationale behind the creative process in the South is interpreted as the urge to rebuff, refute, and reject the past and to substitute the haunted history with a gentler myth. Such is the power of this compulsive *mythicizing* that, in the confrontation between southern fiction and the history of the South, it is the latter that has to step down. In the words of Kreyling, "it is not so much southern literature that changes in collision with history but history that is subtly changed in collision with southern literature" (ix). Existing beyond the unfolding history, growing industry, and developing technology, the South of the myth is perpetuated as a testimony to the coping mechanisms used in the thinking of the region and in remembering its past. Thus, this South turns out to be, to draw on the title of another Kreyling work, the South that wasn't there, whose longevity, sustained by the chronic fascination with "America's region" and fueled by movies, music, graphic novels, and computer games, has been evolving and enticing at an increasing pace over the years.

Right before the outbreak of the Civil War, in his poem "Longings for Home," Walt Whitman called upon the "magnet-South," the "glistening, perfumed South," stressing the region's amalgam of "good and evil." Whitman's evocation of Dixie magnetism is quoted by Jennifer Rae Greeson, who studies the extent to which the myths of the region are appropriated, fetishized, and turned into a decorum. In the words of Greeson, the South that occupies the American mind is not a "fixed or real place. It both exceeds and flattens place; it is a term of the imagination, a site of national fantasy" (1).

The word "fantasy" is instrumental for the hyperbolic metafiguration studied in this book, for the inception of the imaginary vision and its propagation necessitated impressive inventiveness and creativity—especially when this idealized vision, a "fantasy" of the South, was crafted and appropriated to serve as a cultural prototype. If the South indeed has the "ability to evoke America in extremis," as Peter Applebome argues, the egregious battles it fights rely on the fundamental ability to fashion extreme visions and systematically blow them out of proportion (11). The southern obsession with mythmaking required such an exaggerated prototype, in which the mythological image of, first, the Old South and, later, the New South played an instrumental role, providing momentum for the hyperbolic in the southern mind.

Tara McPherson stipulates that the study of the South is constrained by a certain "cultural schizophrenia" (3) in which the traumatizing legacy of slavery collides with the institutionalized nostalgia for the mythical space that was never there—the same space that was famously evoked when the Agrarians published their manifesto *I'll Take My Stand* in 1930, aiming to pull the South back from encroaching industrialization and plant it in the mythic, prelapsarian realm of old. This penchant for the whitewashing of a painful past, the hoisting up of the "burden of southern history" (to borrow the title of C. Vann Woodward's insightful book) and replacing it with a decorum-driven fantasy like Margaret Mitchell's best-selling *Gone with the Wind,* created the context for the clash of different visions of the South, for contrasting takes on its essence, and, consequently, for different modes of thinking (which seems to be of particular significance for this project).

In *The New South Creed,* Paul Gaston takes this role of myths in the South particularly seriously, stating that the southern myths are nothing like "polite euphemisms for falsehoods" but constitute potent "combinations of images and symbols that reflect a people's way of perceiving truth" (30). Thus, southern mythmaking becomes an instrumental mechanism whose central move is the advancement of a particular vision of truth, which has all the makings of a political ideology. The conceptual process that allows for the systematic functioning of the myth is viewed by Gaston as blending: "Organically related to a fundamental reality of life, [the myths] fuse the real and the imaginary into a blend that becomes a reality itself, a force in history" (30). Gaston implicitly stresses here the plastic force of the southern mind, which is capable of merging incompatible ideas to come up with the ephemeral "southern code."

This controlling decorum of southernness, which is generated through the merger of opposites and overcomes their natural repulsion, also manifests in the mass following it receives. Little wonder that Charles Reagan Wilson asserts that the myth of the Lost Cause effectively became the region's "civil religion." The vision of the whitewashed past, approached with reverence and respect, had its annual celebrations, groups of zealots like the Daughters of the Confederacy, awakening preachers, and the prescriptive "decalogue" regulating which takes on the region were permissible and which were prohibited. These code-driven modes of behavior and thinking formed one of the pillars of southern literature in the first decades of the twentieth century, and it is against this code, or in relation to it, that the southern authors discussed in this book engaged in their hyperbolic metafiguration.

This creed-like decorum of the southern myth provided its advocates with a generous set of rhetorical topoi, figures, and interlocking ideas that fueled the verbal repertoire of the South and allowed for the uniformity of regional thought and expression. In her study of trauma and memory in the South, Lisa Hinrichsen argues that southern literature "seems to engage in narrative fetishism in two aspects: first, in the nostalgic, pastoral visions of plantation harmony still anachronistically found in modern southern literature, and second, in [. . .] an unexamined, reflexive identification *as traumatized*" (12). Ostensibly, the South's "embattled rhetoric" (13), which is produced through these two drives, celebrates the loss. This sense of bereavement allowed the region to resist changes, on the one hand, and to retain its difference, while contributing to the sense of southern exceptionalism and the need to embed it into a narrative, on the other. In the ironic words of Jan Nordby Gretlund, "The South is a most fertile ground for fiction writers. Fiction has completely replaced moonshining as the favorite domestic activity" (138).

In such an environment, diverse narratives saturated with promulgated myths are inescapably intertextual. Building on Bakhtin's ideas of a dialogic narrative, Richard Gray, in *A Web of Words*, looks at southern literature precisely as a "web of words" in which different interlocking dialogues constitute an intertextual continuum of thought. Not unlike James C. Cobb, who claims that "the history of southern identity is not a story of continuity *versus* change but continuity *within* it" (7), Gray sees various southern texts as being knit together as a "speaking collective" (*Web of Words* ix). In this work, he is focusing on the "greater dialogue" in southern writings and on how texts communicate with one another "within and without." Gray also postulates, "To be in history means to be in conversation, with the dead as well as the living." Thus, he seeks to map the levels of voices and echoes that give the "text resonance and a reality that stretches beyond the immediate, a sense of being embedded in history" (x). Different levels of dialogue distinguished in Gray's work respond to various spaces of contrast in the southern literary idiom—such as, for instance, the topical clash between literature described as "southern" and literature from outside the South, especially from the North.

The process of this North–South divergence is discussed from a diachronic perspective by Cobb, who demonstrates how it escalated over the decades to the point of rupture. He traces the genesis of the southern identity back to the inception of a number of cultural scripts, like the pseudo-aristocratic cavalier topos—antithetical to the idea of the money-oriented, entrepreneurial Yankee Puritan. This particular bifurcation, popularized and fossilized for the purposes of the antebellum debate over slavery as well as for Civil War propaganda, contributed greatly to the inception of southern decorum and its cultural prerogatives. The image of the Old South, painted with a hyperbolized, whitewashed brush, provided a blueprint for the redemption of Dixie, for opposition to Reconstruction and devotion to the southern code.

All this obsessive fetishization of "southernness" has been challenged, especially since the early 1900s, with the mushrooming of more objective scholarship, which acknowledged, at least partially, the exploitive nature of the system in which sharecropping effectively substituted for slavery. Such studies as Broadus Mitchell's *The Rise of Cotton Mills in the South* (1921) sought to divorce the economic perspective from the antebellum romance, or at least to diminish the exonerating spirit of the latter. Although he was clearly enchanted with the industrial possibility of the New South, Mitchell did venture to criticize the Lost Cause and the hagiographic veneration it evoked. In 1930, discussing the "progressive future" of the South resulting from the industrial revolution (in a passage that could only evoke indignation and ire in any proponent of the antebellum Eden), Mitchell and coauthor George Sinclair Mitchell liken the Old South to an expired "fine gentleman" and ask, "Why embalm his remains and keep his few belongings like relics at the shrine of a saint? We paid him too much honor while he lived, and furthermore sad reminders are all about us in the South this long time afterward: poverty, race hatred, sterile fields, the childish and violent crowd gulled by the demagogue" (285–286). This passage is akin to the simile used by Kendrick and Arnett, which I quoted earlier—in both of them, the metaphorical South is a dead man walking, or rather an undead man still walking, an image that will be of relevance for my discussion of Faulkner's "A Rose for Emily."

As Cobb observed, "Mitchell's struggle with the inconsistencies and contradictions of the New South Creed reflected the increasingly critical scrutiny that it had begun to attract in the wake of World War I" (108). Nonetheless, despite similar deconstructive efforts and the metaphorical images of the South as dead, the mythologized decorum, with its powerful, prescriptive prototype, proved largely unshaken. The southern hyperbolic mind-set of that time emerged from within an open and agonizing conflict over the mimetic representation of the painful reality of racial inequality and the excessive, whitewashed image of the Old South plantation culture.

The protective and regulatory mechanisms guarding the southern code were opulent. As W. Fitzhugh Brundage describes it, "Organized white women tirelessly disseminated [the Lost Cause] history by writing and censoring textbooks, by promoting rituals of 'southern patriotism,' by scrutinizing the contents of museums and archives, and later by monitoring the activities of professional historians and archivists" (127). In academia, the tensions were strong enough to cost people their positions, especially when the United Daughters of the Confederacy assumed its role as a censor of historical publications, seeking to control the narrative, censor sentiments, and stigmatize those ready to undermine the validity of the Old South narrative. One of the victims of such tensions was Enoch M. Banks, who was forced to resign from his professorial position at the University of Florida midsemester in 1911, after he argued in one of his publications that slavery, rather than the issue of states' rights, was the true cause of the secession that led to the Civil War.

The journalistic attempts to unmask the fabrications within the southern myth were particularly focused on exposing how it embraced racial violence. In 1929, Walter White initiated a series of articles investigating lynching, which came out in *American Mercury,* edited at that time by H. L. Mencken, a prolific commentator on the South and a journalist who had famously covered the Scopes Trial in 1925. The series exposed the culture of racial violence in the South, the study of which was a genuinely life-threatening venture, as White experienced firsthand. The publication of White's famous article "I Investigate Lynching," in 1929, coincided with the publication of W. J. Cash's two journalistic pieces on Dixie racism, one of which presaged the book *The Mind of the South* (1949), an undisputed classic in the studies of southernness. Written with journalistic zest, Cash's study investigates the idiosyncrasies of the southern mind and how the "peculiar" history of the region generated the "fairly definite mental pattern associated with a fairly definite social pattern" (viii-ix).

Cash's view of the South was relentless in its depiction of the region as monolithically racist, intellectually stunted, emotionally confused, and unable to rationalize its present predicament. Southern society was, to him, divided along class lines and maintained through what he called the "proto-Dorian convention," which secured the position of economically challenged whites above the African American population, as long as the top of the social hierarchy, the white supremacist, was not threatened. In *The Mind of the South*, this economic consensus among different strata of the white population ensured the social status quo of the region. Through his criticism, Cash also attacked the Old South myth, exposed the societal divides, and accounted for the southern penchant for racial violence—even though Cash himself could not completely liberate himself from stereotypically biased conceptions of race.

Curiously, Bruce Clayton juxtaposes Perry Miller's *The New England Mind,* published just two years before Cash's book, with *The Mind of the South,* showing the fundamental methodological difference between the studies. While Miller's study of the New England Puritan mind is more tailored for the "probing of the thought of an era's intellectual elite who were assumed to be outlining and probing the assumptions of the people at large" (Clayton 117), Cash remains preoccupied with the study of the irrational patterns of thought exhibited by all groups of people, including those who have little impact on the shaping of "high" culture. Cash's interest lies in the visceral origins of myths that define the South as a culture of endemically conflicted "patterns of thought," and he seeks to expose the roots of the mind that can bend itself to accept the unacceptable. And although, as C. Vann Woodward argues astringently, Cash's study might as well have been entitled "The Mindlessness of the South" for its fatuous emphasis of the region as a nexus of contradiction and irrationality (*American Counterpoint* 264), the incubus of anxiety and incongruity unearthed by Cash explains a lot in terms of the region's propensity for metafigurative hyperbole.

Most importantly, Cash exposes the central ability of the southern mind to remain fundamentally selective in its reception of truth. Seeking to account for the awkward plasticity of the southern mind and its fundamental blindness, Pat Watters, a journalist from Atlanta, famously asked about the moral consequences of this southern propensity, two decades after the publication of Cash's book: "*How* were we able to achieve such insensitivity, such cruelty, with never a pang of conscience?" (30). To Watters, the answer was the compartmentalizing ability to bar from one's moral consciousness all stimuli that could aggravate decorum. Ostensibly, the southern mind has been capable of peeling away the signifier from the signified through what Watters calls "sympathetic magic." Assuming the voice of the regional community and speaking as "we," he explains that, by not mentioning the problematic issue, and by overpainting it with a mild narrative, "we were able to convince ourselves the thing did not exist" (30), despite all the deep-seated inconsistences. This creative imperative to internalize only those facts that fit the code and to relegate everything else into the mental sphere that Katharine Du Pre Lumpkin calls the "twilight zone" would be fundamental to hyperbolic metalogic.

The emphasis on this kind of a cognitive balancing act has been present in the literature of the subject for a long time. For instance, in *What We Talk About When We Talk About the South,* published three decades ago, Edward Lynn Ayers observes that, whether the South is portrayed as a "culture" or a "society" or even a "civilization," the fact that it stands as a binary opposite of the North becomes its "absolute characteristic" (65). Whatever is southern is thus inevitably juxtaposed against what is Northern and, through this divide, the southern "speaking about speaking" cannot steer clear of a litany of coexistent irreconcilabilities that ultimately bring about haunting restlessness.

This plasticity of the southern mind has also perplexed more contemporary commentators. In the opening chapter of her recent book *The New Mind of the South* (2013) (which, in spite of its promissory title, assumes a different angle than Cash's complex study), Tracy Thompson ponders the semantics of words such as "black" and "southern." Struggling with her family background and the biased narrative of her family history, she toys with the "intellectual Rubik's Cube" of southernness (3) and contemplates the selective strategies of the southern mind as "face-saving measures" (68). In particular, she reflects on how selective the memory of the community and her own family was in relation to the Civil War and racism, and on how, although the members of her family were persistently vocal about the destruction waged by Sherman's army throughout the South, there was no mention in their stories of the violence of commonplace lynchings. To Thompson, such constant whitewashing has ultimately generated a "mosaic of a thousand [. . .] contradictions, large and small," which fill up the southern mind. In consequence, if "F. Scott Fitzgerald was right—if the test of a first-rate intelligence is the ability to hold two opposed ideas in the mind at the same time and still retain the ability to function—then the South in [the years of Thompson's youth] was doing a phenomenal job raising the national IQ" (75). Thompson admits that when she was conducting the research for her book she had to adopt a similar mode of thinking, to rewire her brain to make it tolerant of contradictions and conflicts.

The hyperbole that famously puts on a grotesque face in the South is possible precisely because of the discordant divisions and code-driven conventions that govern the cultural context of the region. To Harpham, strong cultural dualities such as Schopenhauer's will and idea or Nietzsche's Apollo and Dionysius can be adopted in any society to provide clarity of reference and a seeming stability, but, at the same time, they may lead to formlessness, contradiction, and ambivalence. In effect, these "dualisms define the margin of ambivalence inhabited by the grotesque" and generate mounting cognitive tensions (68). Wherever there is a forced code and a prescriptive decorum of clear-cut axiological oppositions, the grotesque is bound to emerge. In a similar fashion, because of the dualistic decorum of race and regional allegiance framed by such binaries as white and black or North and South pressing on one another, southern culture, given Harpham's postulates, is inevitably doomed to having the grotesque as one of its central aesthetic forms of expression.

In *Dirt and Desire*, Patricia Yaeger problematizes the southern grotesque body as a testimony to how female writers in the entire region, throughout the twentieth century, sought to reclaim the carnal from a patriarchal and racist cultural environment. To Yaeger, in southern fiction, the body is turned into an excessive topos that absorbs the continuous impact of social and racial violence, so prevalent in a culture devoid of outlets. The southern panoply of distorted bodies, bodies in progress, and bodies in pain endows the somatic with the precarious power to meddle with the conflicted world and to bear testimony to its traumas. As a figure in southern fiction, the grotesque distorts the somatic harmony because it records the body's "social contamination" and a host of scarring disturbances that have impacted it. To Yaeger, the southern preoccupation with the grotesque thus becomes a "mimetic device," a witnessing transference of a "version of history from the other to one's own body" (235). This transplantation traumatizes the physicality and invariably blows it out of equilibrium, as the body cannot vent the mounting tensions and has to contain the witnessing in itself.

Interestingly, Yaeger's "somatic hyperbole" of the South, which emerges out of the conflicted world, is not a product of any epic traumas but of multiple minute distortions and daily paradoxes in the quotidian world of the South (236). Thus, by "re-creating a space of disorientation, the grotesque body enters southern texts with the iconic power to dazzle the reader's senses and to open her eyes to "the normality of the abnormal" (237). This opening of the eyes, the revelation in the zenith of Yaeger's "somatic hyperbole," is not dissimilar to the culminating moment of the hyperbolic process studied in this book.

In terms of "speaking about speaking," the South demonstrates its penchant for recalibrating and reinventing its identity and its oppositional mindset. And it is no longer necessarily Cash's white supremacist prerogative but *Southern Living* magazine that becomes the trendsetter and the guide to how one ought to live one's live with respect to the standards of southernness. The enduring perception of the South as America's Other—or Egerton's "southernization of America"—along with a growing commercial value, has transitioned into what Scott Romine dubs the "post-South." The mechanically reproduced fabrication of Dixie, with its commercialized motifs and simulations, which functions within a wider American perception and in the global imagination, is also to be seen through the popularity of mass entertainment. Martyn Bone's *Postsouthern Sense of Place* surveys the southern "sense of space" in a more commercial context. Bone's South is no longer a distinctive enclave protected from the ravages of time and history. Instead, it functions in both the national and the global environment, subject to the impact of capital. The more contemporary southern authors that Bone looks into, such as Richard Ford or Anne Rivers Siddons, have been operating in a palpably different metafigurative context than the writers investigated in the next chapters, but the question of whether the hyperbolic metalogic persists in the southern mind beyond the time frame discussed in this book seems an appropriate topic for a different study.

2

RITES OF PASSAGE

Katherine Anne Porter

For many years, Katherine Anne Porter's South Hill house near Saratoga Springs, New York, remained a recurring topic in her correspondence with Eudora Welty. Porter bought the residence in 1941, not long after the publication of *Pale Horse, Pale Rider,* and, curiously, it was the only mansion she ever owned. The purchase does not seem to have been the most fortunate investment. After the acquisition of the house, Porter could not move in for some time, as the old building required extensive renovations, and she later decided to get rid of it, mainly because its location proved too isolated and problematic during the wintertime (Givner 327).

Regardless of what became of South Hill, one can find an interesting, indirect literary comment in Welty's observations about the manner in which Porter restored the house. Welty stressed that the "planner [of the renovation] was profoundly a story writer," and in the skillful design of the house, Porter continued "putting the house together like a story in her head, restoring to it its history—a story that had as much to do with her past as it had to do with her future" (330). Welty notices a parallel between Porter's architectural design of the house and the artistic design of her fiction. Both involved a holistic, visionary overview and the understanding of how particular building blocks of the past and the present come together to constitute the whole. Yet, primarily, it is Porter's meticulousness and her sheer dedication to the artistic intent that Welty found impressive.

This artistic resolve to construct an emancipated narrative space became Porter's artistic trademark. In her comment on Porter's style, Kaye Gibbons likewise employs a paradoxical, spatial metaphor, stressing that Porter's language simultaneously pulls the reader vertically toward submerged meanings and horizontally backwards through time and memories (74). However elaborate, this narrative architecture is erected upon a number of fabricated and conflicted foundations. As Janis P. Stout stresses in her study of Porter's intellectual development, the writer's artistic endeavors are "structured not by a single meta-belief or truth-statement but by variance and tension" (270). I argue here that Porter's creative thought operates through hyperbolic design framed by the unstable variance of regional identity and the tensions of memory, which she employs to emancipate her voice from the dictates of southern decorum and to endow it with directionality and stability.

Confronted with the haunting grip of the "old order" and seeking to remonstrate against the complex network of norms and limitations inherent in her regional identity, Porter has to resort to the hyperbolic and its capacity to both challenge normative standards and generate new meanings. In her metanarrative design, she converges various events associated with family history and juxtaposes them against the ambivalent principles of regional decorum. By the constant pulling and pushing of the narrative, and by subjecting her protagonists to a series of excessive "rites of passage," Porter manages to construct an independent female voice that can carry through the notorious incongruences among her personal memory, the prescriptive culture of the Deep South, and the creative impulse to fabricate identity. In a way, then, the architectural unruliness of Porter's hyperbolic relies on the unruliness of her memory and its creative appropriation.

In *Katherine Anne Porter's Artistic Development,* Robert Brinkmeyer stresses the personal role of memory as Porter's artistic muse and principle of artistic engagement. Unlike the present moment, which is ephemeral, or the future, which is transient and precarious, the past was stable enough to work as a foundation for Porter's creative architecture. Reorganizing the past also allowed her to make up a new artistic tenacity, confronting the painful hollowness left by the absence of her mother. Porter herself overtly confessed that endless remembering is the very source of her fiction: "This constant exercise of memory seems to be the chief occupation of my mind, and all my experience seems to be simply memory, with continuity, marginal notes, constant revision and comparison of one thing with another" (*Collected Essays* 449). In a letter to Eudora Welty from 1935, Porter compares her creative process of remembrance to tapping her own spinal fluid and admits that she cannot explain how, through the "organic process of creation, the scattered and seemingly random events remembered through many years become fiction" (*Letters* 498). The sordid metaphor conveys both the intensity and the depth of Porter's creative reach, which pervades the very core of her mind and her body.

In her biography of Porter, Joan Givner points out that Porter's construction of family narrative in her fiction notoriously veers away from a family history: "She rarely invented anecdotes out of thin air, but rather created around actual circumstances a tissue of fantasies which embroidered and transformed them and gave them back to her in a form she could bear to contemplate" (20). Porter's artistic intent is visible in this imperative to mold her image, fabricate her family legacy, and then set them both in dialogue with the prescriptive gender models she became acquainted with during her youth—including, among others, the figure of her grandmother, who served as the inspiration for Sophia Jane Rhea in "The Old Order." This fictional, almost archetypal character became one of Porter's key tools in negotiating her troubled relation with the precarious old order of the South.

Because of these mimetic and linguistic tensions, Porter's hyperbolic metalogical thought manifests itself vividly in the Miranda cycle and its transitionality between diverse orders, predominantly between the powerful family narrative, which idealized superficial beauty and female fertility, and the oppressive cultural scripts, which curtailed women's creative and individual endeavors. Against the background of regulatory decorum, a female who sought to come up with her own voice of creative designation was a threatening excess, a misfit whose nascent identity would be considered grotesque because of its noncomformity to the normalistic policies of the region. Thus, the assemblage of identity Porter undertakes in the Miranda cycle requires the violent breaking of a model that had been implanted in her mind for years and toward which she felt an attraction, as is visible in her southern belle persona. In this paradoxical entanglement of tensions, artistic intent, and a sense of loyalty to her father, the hyperbolic mode of comprehension allowed Porter to find, in some of her stories, the space needed to develop the emancipative intensity of artistic intent that so appealed to Welty.

For Porter, each creative act of remembrance necessitated a complex process of negotiating meaning, of conjoining the language signifiers with the fleeting signified. Confronted with social pressures and permanent ambivalence about how the past ought to shape her life prerogatives, Porter had to develop the experimental conduit and narrative anchor of Miranda, an imaginary surrogate self who creatively pushes the limits of language. The stories that belong to the Miranda cycle, in which the protagonist comes of age and recounts her creator's real-life experiences, manifest a visible directionality of creative thought, a metafigurative quest for an emancipated identity, which emerges from the hyperbolic clash of memory and fiction. Poss proposes that the whole Miranda cycle portrays the evolution of a character, similar to a bildungsroman, and that the stories "manifest the typical structure of the genre which may be described as a secular version of the medieval notion of life as a pilgrimage" (21). Such an interpretation of the Miranda cycle is particularly inviting, given the series of ritualistic episodes that mark her passage through consecutive thresholds of understanding and maturation. And, at the end of this path looms the sacred prize of an independent, transformed voice that Porter could use to implement her artistic intent.

Thus, the Miranda cycle manifests Porter's drive to come up with a language of her own and a voice that would be genuinely representative, independent, and rich with meaning. Helen Levy believes that in the essence of the Miranda stories one can find precisely the "search for a language and a homeland true to the protagonists' female experience" (141). To support her point, Levy stresses the etymology of Miranda's name, which she links with *mirar,* the Spanish word for "to see." If a shifting vantage point and an evolving perception are the vital traits of Porter's surrogate narrator, the kind of seer Miranda turns out to be may indeed be able to internalize the tensions and to break away from the prescriptive narratives. As a result of this conceptual growth, the Miranda cycle constitutes a "unified set of tales sharing themes and metaphors seen through the eyes of one female observer," and, if "taken together, the Miranda stories constitute a type of modern spiritual autobiography" (132). Also, however, the Latin *mirandus* means "admirable," a word that inspired the name of Shakespeare's character in *The Tempest*. From this perspective, the admirable "brave new world" that Miranda sees in the course of her creative pilgrimage, the rites of the hyperbolic passage, is the realm beyond the old order patterns of thought.

The unruliness of the hyperbolic shock was needed to secure enough space to embark on this artistic pilgrimage. In the cultural model that was instilled in Porter during her childhood, the paths of the artist and the female remained divergent. Unlike her older sister, who enjoyed tending to her house, family, and garden, Porter tossed and turned between the models of femininity imposed on her and the gender models with which she felt natural. She had the congenial propensity for decorative beauty—which, as a southern woman of letters, she sought to demonstrate—but she simultaneously rejected the idea that female success can be defined only by childbearing and superficial, passive glamour. She had five husbands, and yet in her fiction she systematically demystified the notion of marriage as the only gateway for female fulfillment. These and many other gender paradoxes can be better understood when one considers that Porter's life spanned a period that brought tremendous changes to female gender roles. And her experiences in New York during the 1920s and Europe during the 1930s stood fundamentally at odds with the southern old order of her puritanical grandmother.

That theme of an emancipated voice struggling against the network of oppressive norms was also visible in Porter's early Mexican stories, which were inspired by her revolutionary experiences of 1920 and her engagement in the leftist political movement. The stories notoriously tackle the issues of feminine subjugation in a male world and the impossibility of breaking free from patriarchy. Porter's later, overtly autobiographical works are almost all situated in the Deep South and remain essential for the identity she assumed. Porter defined herself as an heir to this fabricated image of the South. As she famously declared in an interview with Barbara Davis, "I'm a Southerner by tradition and inheritance, and I have a very profound feeling for the South. And, of course, I belong to the guilt-ridden white-pillar crowd myself, but it just didn't rub off on me."

Porter stressed her accession to the lineage of the "white-pillar crowd" from the earliest stages of her literary career, when she drew a glamorous image of her grandmother's wedding in her essay "Portrait: Old South" or of her southern upbringing in an autobiographical piece, "Pull Dick—Pull Devil." Nonetheless, the profound image of the Old South she paints in her fiction is a sheer construct of imagination and a vision she actually never experienced firsthand. Porter spent most of her life in the southwest rather than in the Deep South ruled by the old order she so vividly portrays in her fiction. Her imaginary South is an amalgam of fleeting memories, burning ambitions, and creative constructs, a space she designs and contrives through the architecture of her inventiveness.

The Old Order Decorum

In Porter's short story, the eponymous "old order" springs from the matriarchal control the Grandmother maintains over her relatives and the country mansion. Once a year, Sophia Jane experienced a calling to visit the farm and forced her family to accompany her. The Grandmother dismisses her relatives' reluctance for the journey by emphatically proclaiming her need for a "breath of country air" (*Collected Stories* 321). Figuratively, breathing here becomes an antidote for Porter's notorious artistic sense of anxiety about the proximity of death. As a dynamic function of a living, healthy organism, breath signifies a continuous synergy with the environment and a healthy balance of the body. So the macrometaphor of respiratory rejuvenation stresses the life-giving, transformative power of the Grandmother, whose arrival on the farm is literally and figuratively accompanied by the advent of spring. Her matriarchal presence galvanizes all the people who had remained dormant prior to her arrival, resembling plants awaiting the vernal season, and her accession to the mansion is so impactful that it eclipses all other engagements and dependencies—the Grandmother becomes the sole focus of the narrative. The Grandmother's matriarchal power is manifested in the very byname of the character and her transformation from "Sophia Jane" into "the Grandmother." The moniker used in the story sets the perspective of the narrator, the young Miranda, but it also prioritizes the family bonds over the proper name, stressing her seniority in a familial network of the old order, as a linguistic point of reference.

From her first moment on the farm, the Grandmother energetically arranges the household to return to a state of propriety: "Within an hour someone would have driven away in the buckboard with an order for [. . .] so much carbolic acid and insect powder. [. . .] Every mattress cover was emptied of its corn husks and boiled [. . .], every hut was thickly whitewashed, bins and cupboards were scrubbed, every chair and bedstead was varnished, every filthy quilt was brought to light, boiled in a great iron washpot and stretched in the sun [. . .] The Negro women were put at making a fresh supply of shirts for the men and children, cotton dresses and aprons for themselves" (323). The passive voice in the long enumeration highlights the components of the old order, diminishing the relevance of the agents, the servants who are mere tools of the Grandmother's dominion. During the restoration of the old order on the farm, the family matron believed it was her role to "portion out activities, to urge or restrain where necessary, to teach morals, manners, and religion, to punish and reward her own household according to a fixed code" (328). The Grandmother viewed herself as authority incarnate, passing noncompromising judgments on everyone else's actions and decisions, molding the family to her prescribed ways. Her puritanical commands constituted the pillars of the etiquette by which the house was run and the basis for the architecture of the family decorum.

The Grandmother's old order is bound to a place, and it veers away from the capacity of the farm to maintain the agrarian ways. Symbolically, as a catalyst of spring that puts the wheels of life into motion, the Grandmother is reminiscent of Demeter, the classical female goddess of harvest and fertility, whose arrival marks the annual inflow of life, transforming the fertile land in a fundamental synergy. Riding energetically on her horse, Fiddler, and inspecting the mansion, the Grandmother develops an analogous, restorative affinity with her land, and her yearly advent provides a protective stability for the farm, ensuring that decorum is observed. Thus, the domestic labor the family matron initiates on the farm turns into an annual ritual of recovery and fertility, mirroring Porter's own creative process of unearthing memories and setting up the meta-architecture of the narrative.

In Porter's southern macrocosm, the Grandmother is not the only matriarchal custodian of the old order. Aunt Nannie, a former slave, has formed a strange kinship with the matron of the family, and the two elderly women are bound by an awkward appreciation of the past from which they originated. In the text, they are first described as watchful, contemplative beholders, overlooking the security of the farm while crafting embroidery, which encourages Helen Levy to compare them to the Fates, who spin the thread of the human lot in the Greek mythological world (155). During their vigil, Aunt Nannie and the Grandmother "talked about the past, really—always about the past. Even the future seemed like something gone and done with when they spoke of it. It did not seem an extension of the past, but a repetition of it" (Porter, *Collected Stories* 327). The two women believe in the inalienable nature of memory and conjecture that each change would take them back, full circle, to the old ways they had known. Their uroboric conception of time remains one of the constituents of the old order and its impenetrability, but, at the same time, it legitimizes their continued rule over the families.

In his essay *Epic and the Novel*, Bakhtin outlines his theory of the novel—and of the kind of relationship between past and present in which the past functions as the immutable ideal. Such an "epic time" of the narrative does not change, and unlike the future, which is unknown and blurry, it offers foundational stability and fixedness. To use Bakhtin's metaphor, the novel is like clay and can be molded, while the epic is like marble, a precious rock that does not undergo changes. When the two women spin their narrative of the past, they enter into the realm of tradition, erecting a wall that blocks them off from the present. The backwards fixation to which they religiously adhere, valorized and idealized, inevitably causes friction with any forward thought, and as long as they remain in the centers of their worlds, they may see to it that the wall of their epic past remains impenetrable.

In the two matrons' parallel lives under the auspices of the old order, there was one area of rivalry between them, a "grim and terrible race of procreation" (Porter, *Collected Stories* 334), in which Grandmother bore eleven children and Nannie thirteen. With a narcissistic admiration for their breeding capacity, the two women brought consecutive children into the world, thus asserting their principal place in the hierarchy of the old order as the archetypes of superfluous motherhood and fertility. By initiating the informal "race of procreation," Grandmother and Nannie proclaimed a vision of femininity in which maternity is the pathway to respect and significance. Their procreative alliance under the flag of the old order allowed them to assist each other in the rearing of each other's children, breast-feeding interchangeably when one of them was incapacitated. Observably, this surrogacy was still stigmatized by racial inequality, as Nannie felt internally obliged to favor the white child in breast-feeding, but the intimacy of this exchange continued to shock Grandmother's family. Although the transitory nurturing was abandoned at a certain point in the procreative marathon, the bizarre partnership they established through this exchange persisted—or at least the narrator leads us to believe this.

The final count of babies granted the laurel of victory to Nannie, but given that most of her children did not survive, the excessive contest can be viewed as a draw. Regardless of the outcome, however, this race of procreation remains a mad, hyperbolic chase in which the female body is subjugated to a singular, procreative drive and an incubatory purpose—the Grandmother removes all other drives and motivations from the sense of old order propriety. Childbearing is the sole marker of femininity for her, and whatever does not fit the paradigm of excessive procreation is approached with admonition or animosity.

Little wonder that, in her backwards sense of time, the Grandmother is particularly repelled by the "modern" woman, who is "beginning to run wild, asking for the vote, leaving her home and going out in the world to earn her own living" (333). Such actions are morally unacceptable for the Grandmother because of how they infringe upon the monolithic concept of procreative femininity. To the old matriarch, "modern" women are shamefully "unsexing" themselves (333), willingly depriving themselves of the capacity which, for Grandmother, constitutes the pinnacle of womanhood.

In Grandmother's world, her excessive and grotesque female drive for childbearing is juxtaposed with the notorious lack of potency visible in men. While the Grandmother was able to multiply the family successfully, her husband lacked the necessary resourcefulness to increase the family fortune, which he instead squandered on questionable investments. Thus, to her, men remain "selfish, careless, unloving creatures [who] lived and ended as they had begun." Likewise, the male life seemed to be filled with "manly indulgences, the sweet dark life of the knowledge of evil," as well as being "delicious," "free," "wonderful," "mysterious," and "terrible" (335).

The epithets used by Grandmother reveal a mimetic envy of men's uncontrolled, Bohemian world, whose alluring disorder abounded in outlets she did not have access to in her excessive, procreative femininity. In the dichotomous world of the Grandmother, the male story is much more artistic, dynamic, and wild but, at the same time, more sinister and sinful. By contrast, the Grandmother's womanhood generates no space for creative endeavors, and by pursuing art, the southern belle inevitably "unsexes" herself.

In "Old Mortality," just such an ominous, masculine narrative saturates Aunt Amy's contradictory drives to liberate herself from the old order and to remain at its mimetic center. Endowed with all the prototypical attributes of the southern beauty, such as fair skin, graceful movement, and dancing and riding skills, all of which would make her a perfect bride, Amy refused to marry or, by extension, to have children. At the same time, however, she enjoyed her status as an object of desire and had a rich love of adventure. Amy may have embodied the ideal for a magnolia-scented love tale, and she dazzled as the epitome of southern womanhood, but as the "ultimate portrait of a woman in suspension" (DeMouy 81), as a number of critics have observed, she is incarcerated in the narrative paradigms, and she spells her own undoing by pushing them to extremes. Thus, although Amy's character remains central to Miranda's family legend, the hagiographic reverence attached to her photos and memorabilia also reveals the violent power of the male narrative to control and subdue.

Amy is often described as "angelic" (Porter, *Collected Stories* 182), and her prospective beau bears the noticeably seraphic name of Gabriel. However, the story of their failed relationship is not a drama of celestial elevation but a narrative of a fall, permeated with death. Given all its twists and turns, Amy's tragic love tale seems to belong more to the realm of fiction than of reality, as Miranda notes: "The romance of Uncle Gabriel's long, unrewarded love for [Amy], her early death, was such a story as one found in old books" (178). Against the background of gender decorum, Amy's noncomformity and craving for attention turns her into an excessive figure of destructive rebellion, more resembling a fabricated character from a romantic novel than a person of flesh and bone. She constantly clashed violently with the decorum that spawned the prerogatives she enjoyed so much. At the same time, the complexity of her dilemma is simplified and enthralled by the male narrative, whose aesthetic principles are indiscriminately taken from masculine gothic fiction. When Harrison reads out the works of Edgar Allan Poe, he declares that Poe was "our greatest poet" (178), leaving no doubt that the possessive pronoun means "southern." Against the background of unrealistic romances, adopted straight from Poe's "Annabel Lee" or "For Annie," Amy's desperate struggle could only be ridiculed and relegated to the realm of fiction as a curiosity.

Aunt Amy's rebellion against decorum takes different forms. Aside from the notorious refusal to marry, she ignores Gabriel's compliments, which implicitly corner her into looking the way he fancies. When he compliments Amy on her looks and declares that he likes her hair long, she ostentatiously wears it bobbed. She also outrages her father by wearing a revealing Mardi Gras dress. The control of her body and clothes is a way for Amy to constitute herself and liberate herself from the male-dominated narrative. Lorraine DiCicco points out that, by paying so much attention to Amy's struggle with southern decorum, "Old Mortality" brings into focus the "pressures and anxieties suffered by adolescent females in Victorian America" (80). Amy refuses to have her body governed by the male narrative, and the awareness that she cannot liberate herself from the few privileges it bestows upon her takes on an increasingly desperate form. Over time, her body becomes subject to dramatic transformations—she is interchangeably excessively slim and overweight. DiCicco reads these changes as symptomatic of anorexia, medically associated chlorosis, and depression and an illustration of how the conflicted mind pushes the body into a state of volatile disharmony (90).

Amy's excessive mental and physical uncontrollability is not shunned by the patriarchy and matriarchy alone. To Cousin Eva, a suffrage activist, the extravagant conduct of Aunt Amy also seems inappropriately excessive: "She always got herself to be looked at. [. . .] She rode too hard and she danced too freely" (Porter, *Collected Stories* 215). During her conversations with Miranda, she manifests a condescending resentment toward Amy, mustering little support for a struggling relative pinned down by the oppressive weight of the patriarchal narrative. To Robert Brinkmeyer, Eva's ambivalence springs from the fact that she herself failed to achieve liberation from her family (*Katherine Anne Porter's Artistic Development* 170), and instead of cultivating feminist self-awareness and liberation, she remains bound by the family ideals of beauty and womanhood that she is unable to live up to. In Eva's view, Amy's rebellious drive led to nothing but "scandal" and "death" (Porter, *Collected Stories* 211).

This pessimistic judgment about the finale of Amy's struggle reveals the extent to which the old order is saturated with death, an element of decorum that Porter dissects in another story of the cycle, "The Fig Tree." There, Porter's contemplation of the beginning and the end of life, and their violent, obscure merger, deepens the edge of decorum and forces Miranda to reconceptualize her understanding of death. Initially, the two ultimate points of existence seem irreconcilable and disparate to her. Defined by their mutual exclusivity, life and death resemble the categories of a binary opposition, verifiable by sensory examination, in the same way that Miranda can tell the difference between different species of figs in the grove. If an animal that she finds on the farm fails to react to her presence and touch, if it does not produce sounds and remains motionless, she infers that she may pronounce it dead. Heather Fox points out that to Miranda, at this stage, death is a concrete state, defined exactly by the "lack of sensory response" (220).

The certainty with which she pronounces the beings around her dead or alive gives her a sense of stability, but it also forces the surrounding world into artificial, Aristotelian categories, monolithically defined by a set of prescriptive features. It is only in "The Grave" that, through a hyperbolic "rite of passage" (as we will discuss), Miranda fully realizes that the categories of life and death are not mutually exclusive and that they cannot be strictly demarcated. In the closing of that story, the effect of a hyperbolic epiphany is the emergence of a new understanding of her femininity, when the two divergent notions are merged in the context of childbearing.

In "The Fig Tree," the ritualistic episode teaches Miranda that the neat decorum of binary categories does not apply to her existential dilemma and that life and death have to be viewed as prototypical rather than exclusive concepts.

The lesson starts in the fig grove, where, under her favorite tree, Miranda finds a chicken that does not move. Its ominous stillness convinces her that the animal is dead, and she feels compelled to bury it. In a desperate drive to regulate the processes of death that she could not control when her mother passed away, and to alleviate the mounting tension, Miranda initiates a pseudo funeral.

Mary Titus stresses that Miranda's burial ritual is a preventive measure, intended to "protect the nurturing landscape of the fig grove from transformation into a place of terror and death" (124). However, as she prepares herself to bury the chick, she cannot complete the ritual, because the family is already leaving for the farm. When she puts the dead chick hastily into the ground, Miranda believes she can hear the wail "Weep weep weep" coming from the grave and suspects she buried the little bird alive (Porter, *Collected Stories* 356). Promptly, the lack of ritualistic closure and the sense of guilt become unbearable. The figurative clash of the incomplete ritual and the life-in-death it embroils with the dichotomous, sensory categories of life and death wreaks emotional havoc in Miranda, and she begins to panic and cry uncontrollably.

Ostensibly, Miranda's pressing sense of guilt for the premature burial of the chick reflects her repentant sense of responsibility for the death of her mother, fostered by Harrison's desperate ravings. But the emotional confusion also stems from the sense of epistemological failure of language to designate the fundamental categories of life and death, and the collapse of the system of meanings. Her excessive action, in which two extremes, life and death, are forcibly combined, violates the sense of decorum and leads her into a new understanding that she is not yet ready to internalize. Sobbing hysterically in the car, Miranda cannot explain the reason for her panic to her father and her grandmother because she knows that her anxieties about life and death are not compatible with the ideas that reside at the core of the old order. In trying to understand what has upset Miranda so much, her father asks, "Was it your doll?" (357), manifesting a fundamental lack of understanding of the complexity of her emotional dilemma. And when she lies to him, pretending that it is indeed a doll she is crying about, she both admits that she cannot communicate to her family the true reason for her distress and forces herself into a gender paradigm with which she is uncomfortable.

The consolation for Miranda's existential confusion comes from her eccentric Great-Aunt Eliza, who remains on the outskirts of the old order. She explains to her distressed niece that the haunting *weep weep* is nothing but the sound produced by tree frogs. This solution to Miranda's dilemma, delivered in a "most scientific voice" (361), does not romanticize death and life, and thus it constitutes a stark alternative to the family's hagiographic and poetic narratives of Amy's passing. It is a language that is not torn from within and does not carry the figurative baggage of death. Eliza also shares a scientific curiosity with Miranda: "When tree frogs shed their skins, they pull them off over their heads like little shirts, and they eat them" (361). This prefigures the ultimate hyperbolic epiphany from "The Grave," in which the removal of an animal skin becomes Miranda's ultimate rite of passage.

Later, Eliza bestows another fundamental scientific insight on Miranda when she allows Miranda to look through her telescope. The extension of the limited vision of the old order allows Miranda to behold "other worlds" that are informed neither by the matriarchal power of the Grandmother nor by the idealized patriarchal narrative. The revelation of the frontier beyond makes Miranda exclaim in amazement, "Oh, it's like another world!" (361), almost exactly like her Shakespearean namesake from *The Tempest*. The liberating awareness of the brave, new reality beyond the old order is the first step in the reassessment of her own identity and the regaining of her own voice. In the apocalyptic reality of the 1918 flu pandemic in "Pale Horse, Pale Rider," however, the grown-up Miranda will look at death very differently: "Death is death, said Miranda, and for the dead it has no attributes" (310). This self-contained definition through the rhetorical device of *ploce* is free of romantic idealization, but its paradoxical character also exhibits the failure of Miranda's language to designate effectively.

Hyperbolic Graves

When the speaker of one of Emily Dickinson's poems asserts authoritatively that "We do not play on Graves," she justifies her declaration in a Dickinsonian, enigmatic manner: "Because there isn't Room— / Besides—it isn't even—." In contrast, the eponymous graves in Porter's final story of *The Old Order* collection are encouragingly spacious, and they provide sufficient room for Miranda and Paul's playful exploration and their ritualistic rite of passage.

The association of Porter's story with Dickinson's poem is obviously far-fetched and of little immediate interpretative value. At the same time, however, the struggle with the most profound issues of life-in-death and death-in-life is integral to both texts. "The Grave" portrays a process of exploration in which Miranda passes over the threshold of hyperbolic epiphany in a complex process of learning about her carnal self, and, moving away from the normative decorum described earlier, she ultimately embraces the inevitable propinquity of human birth and demise.

The consecutive steps of Miranda's transformation in the story correspond to the stages of hyperbolic metafiguration, the excessive and violent breaking of the decorum of the "old order." First, Porter sets up the symbolic scenery in which the empty family graves are used by children as a playground, where they find tokens that connote their social prerogatives. Then, the southern decorum of femininity is evoked. Next, through a grotesque and bloody ritual in which the children flay a rabbit, the norm is pushed to the extreme and broken, while the intimate carnal interior of the killed prey is exposed, revealing the unborn young in the dead animal's uterus. This image triggers an immediate epiphanic shock in Miranda, as she puts the incongruities together. It also brings about a subsequent emotional aftershock, years later, described at the very end of the story.

The stage Porter preps for the excessive ritual is intensively rich with symbols. As Miranda and Paul, ages nine and twelve, stride into the family cemetery, they enter into an emblematic space of transition, which subsequently transforms their Edenic felicity into painful maturation. Driven by a "thrill of wonder," the siblings explore the old family graves, which were emptied when the bodies of their deceased relatives were moved to a different location. The garden is untamed and disharmonious, with "tangled rose bushes and ragged cedar trees" and "uncropped sweet-smelling wild grass" (Porter, *Collected Stories* 362). Its savage, prelapsarian nature encouraged Constance Rooke and Bruce Wallis to view "The Grave" as a recreation of the biblical myth of the fall of man. In their reading, the garden becomes the theater for the primal loss of innocence and the removal from the privilege of innocent purity. However, in this shoddy garden, it is the emptied graves that invite the children to explore.

As if to deepen the allure of the site, Porter puts considerable emphasis on the sensual experience of the site. When Miranda jumps into the hole that contained her grandfather's coffin, she takes a handful of soil and smells its "pleasantly sweet, corrupt smell, being mixed with cedar needles and small leaves" (Porter, *Collected Stories* 363). And the children explore the space that offers them such inspiring sensual stimulation—foreshadowing the ricochet epiphany that Miranda will experience years later. While, in a religious context, the emptiness of the grave could be construed as visual evidence of Christ's return and a hopeful promise for the ultimate resurrection of the flesh, here the emptiness of the grave redefines its very nature: "When the coffin was gone a grave was just a hole in the ground" (363). The family graves are no longer marked by the taboo of bodily decay or the sanctity of eternal life and instead become the space for trial and exploration.

The two emblematic spoils that Miranda and Paul uncover in two such holes in the ground, a wedding band and a silver dove, are ceremonially exchanged by the children in a playful sport of mimicry and desire. They are, respectively, "smitten" and "impressed" by each other's booty, yet, after the exchange, while Paul is compelled to elevate the find to the status of a rarity, stressing that the screw is one of a kind, his sister is devoid of covetousness and silent, content with the transaction's result. The dove, which for George Cheatham symbolizes the immortal soul and the Holy Spirit, is briskly demystified, and its symbolic capacity for an imaginative flight becomes thwarted once Paul discovers that the alleged treasure is a mere screw head from a coffin. At the same time, Miranda's ring takes on a powerful resonance as a symbol of femininity.

Notably, Mary Titus claims that, through the symbol of the dove, "Porter can wed the oppositions she found so troubling. For unlike the ring, which leads its wearer directly to traditional womanhood, the dove unites the female and the male, the fertile mother and the powerful word" (94). When the girl puts the ring on, she is transformed, and she internalizes the status of the female belle it entails as well as the promise of procreative potency and longevity, symbolized by the ring's circularity, both of which are highlighted by her family narrative's enduring captivation with beauty, betrothal, and bearing children.

The transformative power of the ring manifests itself in Miranda's immediate imperative to follow decorum. While Paul leads the way through the wild path, acting like a guide into the world of masculine prowess, his sister shows "no proper sense of hunting" and fires shots not to kill but to enjoy the sound and the feel of the gun (Porter, *Collected Stories* 364). For Miranda, the participation in the hunt is a bonding exercise and a diversion, whereas for Paul it is clearly a preparatory activity and a commencement of masculine rivalry. With the ring on her finger, she realizes that the clothes she wears, "dark blue overalls, a light blue shirt, a hired-man's straw hat, and thick brown sandals" are thoroughly unsuitable for a prospective belle, "for the year was 1903, and in the back country the law of female decorum had teeth in it" (364). Her trousers, although comfortable, suddenly begin infringing upon the rules of propriety and the nexus of prescriptive social decrees and undermine her status.

Like Atticus Finch in Harper Lee's *To Kill a Mockingbird,* who is scolded for Scout's rambunctiousness, which is linked to the lack of a model mother figure in the house, Miranda's father "had been criticized for letting his girls dress like boys and go careering around astride barebacked horses" (Porter, *Collected Stories* 364). The custodians of the rectitude of the old order whom Miranda had encountered earlier, "old women of the kind who smoked corn-cob pipes" for whom her late Grandmother was the respectable prototype of southern good manners and decency, had rebuked Miranda for not keeping up with the family traditions: "Ain't you ashamed of yoself, Missy? It's aginst the Scriptures to dress like that" (365).

The word "ashamed" is the rhetorical core of their admonition. The women try to pressure Miranda into guilt for the lack of compliance with the gender model, using the Bible as a source of authority. By an eristic extension, their *ad verecundiam* does not imply that the Scripture regulates the suitable dress code for young southern girls but that noncompliance with cultural scripts, even in their minute aspects, is morally damnable and tantamount to sinning. So too is shocking people—one of the prerogatives of evocative artistic activities, which, to Porter, seemed contradictory to decorum-driven prudence. Yet Miranda's wearing of overalls is not her sole act of noncompliance. Earlier, she had been given fur coats for her dolls. She does not care much for the toys, which are emblematic of feminine upbringing and old order domesticity, but she likes the act of covering them with the fur, of covering the artificial with the carnal, symbolically rebelling against the regulatory power of decorum.

All this mounting guilty regret, escalated by the wedding ring on her finger, triggers a strong impulse in Miranda to adhere to the old order. She feels compelled to align with decorum and embody the belle, in spite of the fact that this prototype is just an imaginary construct, that those who embodied it are dead, and that their graves have been symbolically emptied. So she feels the call to return home, take a cleansing bath, and put on talcum powder. Miranda also senses that she should "put on the thinnest, most becoming dress she owned, with a big sash, and sit in a wicker chair under the trees" (365). In other words, she should metamorphose into an image of fabricated, romanticized femininity found in the patriarchal narrative of "Old Mortality," in which objectifying beautification and passivity go hand in hand. However, as exemplified by the belles whose memory haunts the old order and whose images are canonized in family photographs, this oppressive model is a pathway to the grave.

With decorum burdening her with guilt, Miranda is just about to head back home, but then her brother shoots a rabbit and immediately begins skinning his prey. "The children knelt facing each other over the dead animal" and, as Paul begins to pull the skin off, the "flayed flesh emerged dark scarlet, sleek, firm" (366). The symmetrical positioning of the siblings' bodies, facing the dead animal from two sides, implies a ritualistic context, the commencement of a rite of passage that will subvert decorum and push the interconnectedness of life and death to the hyperbolic extreme.

As Gary M. Ciuba, in his Gerardian reading of Porter, observes, "If the gold ring conjures up lovely constructions of gender under the old order, the dead and pregnant rabbit embodies the link between mortality and sexuality deeply hidden in this culture" (76). Paul's penetrating knife, which reveals what is hidden deep within the carnal, under the coat of skin, initiates a ritual that will reveal to Miranda the mystery of the flesh. Full of admiration for her brother's skill with the knife, and driven by her natural curiosity, she is compelled to feel with her fingers the "long fine muscles with silvery flap strips binding them to the joints" (Porter, *Collected Stories* 366). Once again, just as when she scooped the soil from the grave, Miranda seeks to touch and smell the phenomena that she witnesses. She wants to sensually experience the items associated with death, in an attempt to understand, and she hungrily declares, "I want to *see*" (366).

However, the limits of her understanding are tested when Paul pushes his exploration of the flesh to the extreme and discovers that the rabbit was to have young. As Miranda's brother slits the flesh from the center ribs to the flanks, a "scarlet bag" with unborn baby rabbits is revealed (366). With a series of persistent cuts, Paul has to infiltrate one tissue at a time, and each laceration of his knife resembles passing through one of the numerous veils that cover the passage to the truth. In this violent manner, the unborn animals are disturbingly displayed to the outside when the inside of their mother's flesh is violently lacerated and exposed, covered in the shroud of the placenta, not unlike the way Miranda, in "The Fig Tree," sought to cover the dead animals with a wrap before placing them in their grave. The violent and relentless peek into what lurks beneath the surface—in this context, beneath the surface of skin—leads the siblings to a revelation of paramount significance, about the inseparable and paradoxical entanglement of birth and death.

The bloody ritual they perform is a ceremony of radical display. It is also grotesque, in the very etymological meaning of the term, unmasking the grotto of the flesh. With the slits of his knife, Paul makes his way through consecutive veils of the flesh, penetrating and exhibiting the innermost, intimate interior of the body. In this hyperbolic penetration, in which the body is literally stripped of its secrets, decorum breaks down and the taboos of the carnal are brought to light.

Thus, during her brother's liturgy, Miranda touches the tissues that normally are masked by the skin, and she incarnadines her curious hands in the blood of the animal, which is reminiscent not only of menstrual blood but also of the blood accompanying childbirth. While decorum dictates what clothes she should wear—in other words, what should be on the exterior side of the body—the flaying and the grim discovery underscores the divide between the inside and the outside and offers an excessive peek into the body's hidden functions. Paul's uncompromising knife leaves no vestige of secrecy, confidentiality, or restraint; instead, all the secrets are hyperbolically laid open. In this violation of decorum, the evisceration of the rabbit echoes Miranda's own splitting, in which she internalizes the realization that she is on a pathway to mature femininity and sexual potency, which, to her, will lead toward her death—as happened in the case of Miranda's mother, who passed away after childbirth. This extreme juxtaposition, in which Porter collides two opposites and fuses them together, is the essence of the hyperbolic violence of the story.

The discovery of a grotesque body within a body, so very different from the discovery of the ring in the family grave, breaks Miranda out of the comfort zone of decorum and shakes her to the core. As she begins to comprehend the implications that the grotesque discovery bears for her own physicality, the girl becomes "quietly and terribly agitated" (367). Miranda realizes that her body is to be a vessel for life, not unlike the "bloody heap" in front of her, and, given how her mother died in childbirth, she may end up lacerated and exposed in a bloody fashion, like the rabbit skinned by Paul. The procreative power promised by the ring may well be the harbinger of death. With the unmitigated and excessive peek into the carnal she has been offered, the blood on her hands becomes the baptismal epiphany of the extent to which birth and demise are inevitably connected.

Once the zenith of hyperbolic epiphany hits Miranda, she starts to tremble in terror. Although she has always suspected the truth that is being revealed to her, the sensual experience touches her particularly hard: "She understood a little of the secret, formless intuitions in her own mind and body, which had been clearing up, taking form, so gradually and so steadily she had not realized that she was learning what she had to know" (366–367). This sudden rise of her female consciousness is painful and traumatizing, and Miranda sets her limit when she refuses to accept the flayed skin of the animal from her brother. During their playful exploration earlier, she was willing to take Paul's booty and affirm the ring; now she declines the offering, which symbolizes the violation of the barriers of the body.

Seeing his sister's uncooperativeness, Paul realizes the impact his ritual has had on her, and he immediately conceals the young rabbits in their mother's body, wraps the skin around her, and buries the body in some bushes. What was violently revealed becomes once again hidden and the hyperbolic display of the interior is transformed into a taboo, as Paul warns his sister, "Now you listen to me, and don't ever forget. Don't you ever tell a living soul that you saw this. Don't tell a soul. Don't tell Dad because I'll get into trouble" (367).

Paul's litany of prohibitions, the stressful hammering of the imperative into his sister's head, implies the extent to which he believes he has overstepped the mark, showing her a vision that is neither appropriate nor safe for her. Seeing her reaction, Paul realizes that the bloody spectacle he presented his sister with seems to have impacted her more than he predicted; he understands that it was neither appropriate nor safe for her to be given the kind of encouragement he offered. If, as Miranda stressed, decorum dictates that shocking one's neighbors is against the Decalogue, then Paul's action amounts to a reprehensible sin. To conceal his wrongdoing, Paul asks her to literally forget the recent, formative experience—which is obviously impossible, precisely because of the extent to which what she witnessed impacted her. Since, by Paul's decree, the siblings cannot discuss the flaying with other people and cannot discuss it between themselves, the ritual becomes a haunting, forbidden memory she can neither internalize nor relegate—one that lingers in her subconscious like a painful thorn.

In his attempt to push the hyperbolic epiphany into oblivion, Paul sought to accomplish the impossible. On the surface, Miranda may comply with her brother's forceful request, but the vision of the eviscerated rabbit will remain hidden in her mind for years to come, waiting to resurface. The apex of the metahyperbole in which she fused the opposites changed her, and Miranda cannot unsee what she saw during their excursion.

The last scene of the story closes the metafigurative composition of "The

Old Order." Miranda is no longer subject to the "thrill of wonder" (362), but many years later, jaded, she roams through a "strange city of a strange country" (367). The redoubled epithet stresses her removal from the realm of her childhood. There, in this alien land, she sees and smells dried sugar candies at a street market, which suddenly reminds her of the "bloody heap" and the rite of passage she experienced with her brother. Here, Porter conspicuously uses the same adjectives she used to describe Miranda's smelling of the empty grave in the garden, and the sense of smell triggers an aftershock of her hyperbolic epiphany.

Reliving the haunting scene, now as a mature woman, she is "horrified" to realize how that childhood revelation and the subsequent maturing led her to the place she is in right now and to the level of independence she implicitly seems to be enjoying (367). It is the most mature version of Miranda that readers can see in any part of the cycle, the final product of the hyperbolic mode of comprehension. Her last vision, following the emotional tremor, also seems to anchor the source of her artistic inspiration in that revelatory experience. In an imaginative recollection, Miranda sees her brother turning the silver dove in his hands, a movement that symbolically harmonizes the discordant attributes of the two finds from the grave: the circularity of the feminine wedding ring and the creative, individualistic flight of the dove.

3

THE POLYPHONY OF THE PAST

William Faulkner

Beginning a chapter on hyperbolic figuration in William Faulkner's writings proved particularly challenging. My initial ambition was to try to avoid using the overquoted line from *Absalom, Absalom!*, uttered by the Canadian Shreve McCannon, who quizzes his Harvard roommate, Quentin Compson, about Dixie: "Tell me about the South. What's it like there? What do they do there? Why do they live there? Why do they live at all?" (142). The line is a notorious cliché, used routinely throughout not only Faulkner studies but also the bulk of southern studies. One can hardly question the usefulness or the appositeness of this quote, since it encapsulates a number of issues that remain perennial for the study of Faulkner, such as the idea of storytelling as a tool of regional exploration or the precarious albeit ambitious drive to find a justification for southern ways. Ultimately, however, ignoring the quote has proved impossible, simply because the entirety of Faulkner's fiction is hardly anything but "telling about the South," which is saturated with tensions and pressured by the figures of conflict.

This chapter looks at two aspects of Faulkner's hyperbolic storytelling, out of many abounding in his fiction. First, I focus on Faulkner's rhetoric and the polyphony of voices that fill up his fictional representation of the region. The interactions among these voices, adorned with individual systems of symbols, vocabularies, rhythms, and types of argumentation, are often antagonistic. Faulkner escalates these tensions on the metanarrative level to demonstrate southern paradoxes. And what inevitably crowns this escalation is a powerful and violent rupture, as these contrasting voices offer no space for a peaceful dialogue or harmonious resolution. For instance, in the short story "Dry September," readers witness an agonistic conflict that erupts in the public space of a barbershop as a group of men debates the facts of a crime that never happened. The language of factuality gives was to warped logic and selective judgment, and out of these antagonisms, a lynching party is formed and the violence of rhetoric turns into physical violence. This mechanism testifies to the extent to which Faulkner's southern chorus of voices in essence remains both hyperbolic and violent.

The hyperbolic in Faulkner can also be figurative. In Faulkner's widely anthologized "A Rose for Emily," it is the metafigurative clash between the undead past and the haunted present that can be construed as the vehicle of the hyperbolic. Here, the conceptual grids underpinning Faulkner's use of tropes allow him to dramatize the mental stasis of the region. I will look into how the metaphoric fabric of the text, on the micro as well as the macro level, unfolds against the background of artificial temporal inertia and the inevitable push of the flow of time. It is the increasing conflict between the two that, again, culminates in a vehement outburst and the emergence of the grotesque.

Both of these metahyperbolic elements of Faulkner's prose—the polyphonic and the figurative—are vital for the understanding how the writer strives to represent the South. Indeed, for the majority of readers worldwide, the name Faulkner remains synonymous with the literature of the region, and this makes him one of the most-researched figures in American letters. In fact, Patricia Yaeger talks of the huge "Faulkner industry" that has overshadowed southern studies, leaving relatively little space for more extensive study of, for instance, southern female authors (xv).

For almost a century, Faulkner has been analyzed from a host of perspectives, and at times has been simultaneously praised and chastised for one and the same thing. In the introduction to his literary biography of Faulkner, David Rampton points to some of the areas of contention, including Faulkner's concurrent perpetuation of "pejorative stereotypes of women," noted by Leslie Fiedler in 1960, and celebration of diverse womanhood, as argued by Linda Wagner; or the visible absence of God from his oeuvre, pointed out by the French writer Marcel Aymé, and the label of "Christian writer" that would sometimes be pinned upon him by such writers as Randall Starwart (Rampton 6). Also, as a consequence of a turn to African American studies, we have, in the words of Barbara Ladd, gained the "ability to historicize and amplify black voices" in Faulkner's works, in spite of the repeated accusations of racism leveled at him (134). Thus, it would seem that, in the words of Timothy P. Caron, "quite simply, we no longer have Faulkner but Faulkners; rather than a single author-function that can contain the various readings, analyses, and interpretations given to his work, we now have a plurality" (479).

If there is one element of this diversity that remains constant it is Faulkner's preoccupation with the region. The metafigurative image of a "pollen of ideas" ranks among the writer's exemplary ways of "speaking about speaking" of Dixie. In a 1932 interview, when asked about James Joyce's *Ulysses*, Faulkner shared his reflections on the Joycean writing method: "Sometimes I think there must be a sort of pollen of ideas floating in the air, which fertilizes similarly minds here and there which have not had direct contact" (*Lion in the Garden* 30). This affinity of ideas spread through the indiscernible minutiae of cultural and social regional mind-sets is visible in Faulkner's thinking about the region. It is as if each breath taken in Mississippi inescapably impregnated his mind with southernness, forming a bond with other southerners as well as a connection with the region, infecting his artistic design with thoughts and ideas idiosyncratic to the land and its mythologized, segregated, and hyperbolized identity. The effect of being surrounded by this "pollen of ideas," of inhaling it day in and day out, whether he wanted to or not, is the foundation of Faulkner's take on the "mind of the South" and the stimulation of his creative engine. At the same time, Walter Taylor stresses that Faulkner was ambivalent about the essential meaning of southernness and this was always reflected in his writing: "Faulkner's career [. . .] reveals an inner dynamic in which each work may be seen as part of a progressive effort to imagine what 'the South' might have been, or might have become, in both its benign and nightmarish aspects—and to imagine a series of protagonists who cope, or fail to cope, with it" (x).

Richard Gray's study of Faulkner's literary life, *The Life of William Faulkner,* adopts Bakhtin's idea of the polyphonic novel to study not only the dialogue among different voices of Yoknapatawpha County but also the tensions within them. To Gray, the diversity of these narrative voices creates a network of intertextual relations, drawing strongly on Faulkner's real life as a southerner. They employ their distinct vocabularies, idiomatic melodies, and sets of references. And this chorus of the South is driven by the simultaneous inclinations of connectedness, as the voices form phatic groups and communities, and of withdrawal, as they grow increasingly distinct from one another—thus providing the framework for the "social dynamics" of Faulkner's dialogic world and rich rhetoric.

Critics point to Faulkner's intricate fiction as a place of intersection for the "languages of resistance and opposition," moving from the hegemonic monolith of the dominant white discourse toward the dialogic and argumentative nature of the contemporary South (Hannon 9). Hence, Faulkner's multiplicity of languages and vocabularies is not a stable flow of memories evoked in contemplative tranquility. Rather, as with the social environment that surrounded Faulkner, there are constant sparks of tensions between different voices which, when placed together in a limited space, inevitably enter into an explosive reaction. It is this rich space between various voices of Faulkner's fiction that generates the hyperbolic. As these voices antagonize one another, escalate and collide, they become quintessential for the representation of the paradoxes of the region.

Faulkner described his own language as "complicated by an inherited regional and geographical [. . .] curse" (*Selected Letters* 215). The quote shows how Faulkner's figurative framework and semiotic power arises from the artist's lone communion with a region saturated with social tensions. As Gray observes in *The Life of William Faulkner,* the writer "had the privilege of being born at a moment when his society, his particular locality, offered him two peculiar advantages: a complex code, a dominant culture with its own elaborate blueprint or vocabulary for mediating experience—and a sense of rapture, sufficient critical distance from that code or culture to allow him to position and explore it" (15). Faulkner internalizes this code, fully aware of its fundamental importance for southern society, and plays with it, showing in his works how different individuals identify themselves with their regional environment through rituals of language, pushing it to the point of breakage, escalating tensions that result in a violent but essentially epiphanic rupture.

Through the creation of the imaginative space of Yoknapatawpha, Faulkner sought to negotiate the relationship he shared with the South. As he once said, "I am telling the same story over and over, which is myself and the world" (Blotner 213). For the most part, of course, this world was Lafayette County, Mississippi. This telling of the story of the South seemed to bear infinitely more significance for Faulkner than the elaboration on his private life. Throughout his life, he sought to become invisible as a person and to hide from the growing interest of the general public. Gray sees this tendency as partially theatrical and pretentious (*Web of Words* 2), arguing that Faulkner wanted to stay hidden because distance and concealment were the privileges of the aristocratic status to which he aspired. When, in 1930, he purchased Rowan Oak, a large, run-down mansion from the 1840s, and practiced horse riding, he seemed to evoke the myth of the Old South and to appropriate the prerogatives of a country squire lifestyle. In a way, he desired to vanish behind his texts and the quasi-aristocratic southern identity, leaving critics just enough material for the provocatively laconic synopsis of his life—"He made the books and died"—that he famously declared in a conversation with Malcolm Cowley, who urged him to share the details of his life for *The Portable Faulkner.*

Faulkner saw his writing as dedicated virtuosity, and he spent a substantial amount of time on rewriting his material and enhancing it to achieve the standard to which he aspired. This idealized vision of poetic equilibrium was fueled by the drive to explore the "passionate moment of the human condition distilled to its absolute essence" (*Selected Letters* 207)—the intent that later allowed him to dramatize the evolving social and political landscape of the South with a unique economy of artistic expression and an uncompromising intensity of language. And it is a truism to say that reading Faulkner takes a lot of time and patience. Over the years, he constructed a nexus of uncompromising narratives that compel readers to revisit the texts over and over again. In his novels, sentences pivot in a strange directions, sometimes spreading out over pages. Perspectives shift obscurely and the syntax is notoriously enigmatic, especially for nonnative speakers of English. Faulkner's readers are constantly encouraged to abandon their views about a stable narrative and to question the idea of objective perspectives on the past and, by extension, on the present. All of this makes the reading of Faulkner a creative act that relies on readers' activity and attention to navigate their way through the labyrinth of signifiers that make up the universe of the fictional Yoknapatawpha County. Such a narrative design also becomes a fitting metafigurative vehicle for the web of conflicts and tensions that scar Faulkner's world.

With a phenomenal outburst of artistic productivity in the early 1930s, the problems of human identity and integrity, confronted with the impenetrable forces of history and social change, came to the forefront of Faulkner's fiction. As Faulkner concluded in his Nobel Prize acceptance speech, the "poet's voice need not merely be the record of man; it can be one of the props, the pillars to help him endure and prevail" (*Essays* 120). This humanistic reflection on endurance, on human struggles against the world and the quest for identity, became the hallmark of Faulkner's artistic project. In this context, Philip M. Weinstein sees the Faulknerian protagonist as "the subject in process, the subject in contestation," who is thrown beyond the solid, undivided subjectivity into conflicting alignments. Little wonder that the mind of such a protagonist becomes the battleground for "interior disturbance" rather than a "locus of concerned action" (10), as seen, for instance, in the drama of Faulkner's classic short story "Barn Burning."

In Faulkner's Mississippi universe, the issues of race, of whiteness and non-whiteness, inevitably gravitate toward a figurative binarity. As Robert Penn Warren inquired at an early stage of Faulknerian criticism, "To what extent does Faulkner work in terms of polarities, oppositions, paradoxes, inversions of roles? How much does he employ a line of concealed (or open) dialectic progression as a principle for his fiction?" ("Cowley's Faulkner" 320). These questions are appropriated as introductory quotes by James Snead, whose study *Figures of Division* implicitly seeks to address them. Snead stresses that, in Faulkner's narratives, the figurative framework allows us to understand how the writer's thought processed the conceptual barriers of southern social divisions. Springing from a region "whose segregationist thinking furnishes us with an extreme case of social classification" (xii), Faulkner's fiction abounds in narrative ploys whose aim is to explore these divisions, to disturb the symbolic sense of chronology, and to subvert the divisive myths and racial semiotics of southern society. In other words, the enduring struggle of the characters of the Yoknapatawpha County always divulges how the world they populate is founded on the axiomatic oppositions of race, economic status, social prerogatives, gender, and tradition.

Thus, the collisions that are an immanent part of Faulkner's world are collisions not only of voices but also of the metanarrative temporal perspectives from which these voices spring. His characters are plagued by time, defined by their inability to break free from the figuration of past, the obsession with which keeps them metaphorically immobilized. In a frequently quoted passage from *Absalom, Absalom!,* Faulkner builds a metaphoric image of how the past affects the present:

Maybe nothing ever happens once and is finished. Maybe happen is never once but like ripples maybe on water after the pebble sinks, the ripples moving on, spreading, the pool attached by a narrow umbilical water-cord to the next pool which the first pool feeds, has fed, did feed, let this second pool contain a different temperature of water, a different molecularity of having seen, felt, remembered, reflect in a different tone the infinite unchanging sky, it doesn't matter: that pebble's watery echo whose fall it did not even see moves across its surface too at the original ripple-space, to the old ineradicable rhythm. (210)

Faulkner's historical experience is a process of painful repetition and replication and of a torturous struggle to break away from the trauma of the metaphoric pebble hitting the surface of water. Hence, what governs Faulkner's world is the metanarrative butterfly effect, a minor change in the course of the deterministic, nonlinear scheme of history that generates ineradicable, rhythmic "ripples" that influence the human condition for generations, extending way beyond the visible perspective of one individual.

Gray observes that the view of history presented in *Absalom, Absalom!* is a "version of Einstein's theory of relativity or Heisenberg's formulation of the indeterminacy principle" (*Life of William Faulkner* 206). This fundamental lack of narrative omnipotence is the trademark of not only *Absalom, Absalom!* but also the bulk of Faulkner's fiction. The beholder's position in relation to the events, to their alignment on the timeline in which notions of anteriority and precedence become blurred to the point of merger, is what allows Faulkner's fiction to deconstruct the idea of absolute temporality. This process is obviously expressed in the tropological fabric of his writings. The narrative of repetitions and recapitulations compels the reader to try to grasp meanings that constantly slip away. To follow up on the scientific analogies, one can say that, just as in quantum physics the very act of study of subatomic particles changes them, thwarting any attempt at objective determination, so too, in Faulkner's artistic paradigm, the act of looking at the past inevitably changes it.

The figurative subjectivity in historical narratives (discussed at the beginning of this book) is pushed to the next level by Faulkner. In his fiction, the perspective of the beholder entails an interpretative effort, affecting and modifying all the metasignifiers: the object of the study, the onlooker, and the process of perception. This speculative overture generates myriad contingent indeterminacies in which only instability remains stable and only the lack of guarantee can be guaranteed. Perhaps this is the reason why Faulkner studies so eagerly take up the metanarrative angle. All the hearsay, gossip, and urban legends retold in his fiction are the writer's metanarrative contraptions, carrying the story beyond the binary relation of history as the signified and the tale as the signifier. Instead, Faulkner perpetually juxtaposes different, colliding perspectives on one event in history to expose the lack of historical substance and the fundamentally dynamic relationship of the constituents of this process.

Thus, what is effectively featured in Faulkner's texts is history in the making. The past is reaffirmed and appropriated by the present moment, but the tales of old that are occasionally treated as pillars of stability cannot be trusted. The extensive network of diverse speculative speech acts, which crisscross and twist and in which the truth of a proposition becomes a matter of doubt, is a teasing lure for every reader who wants to bring an interpretative order to Faulkner's artistic ataxia. It is the discovery of the "the old ineradicable rhythm" of the past, and its tropology, that becomes the writer's artistic manner of engagement.

The Southern Agon

Faulkner's "Dry September" begins as a drama of language. Vague gossip about a dubious encounter between a local spinster, Minnie Cooper, and an African American, Will Mayes, spreads like a "fire in dry grass" (*Selected Short Stories* 60) and initiates tensions in the community that culminate in a ritualistic act of lynching. The background of sixty-two rainless days and an intense heat wave that drenches all characters in sweat contextualizes the story. The sweltering aura hovers over all elements of "Dry September," reminiscent of the manner in which, to some commentators, the hot climate has always been a factor shaping the mind of the South. For instance, in 1935, Clarence Cason published a collection of essays and articles entitled *90° in the Shade,* in which the eponymous overwhelming hot spell is blamed for crippling the southern ability to act dynamically and for the inception of a specific culture, visible in the house construction and cuisine of the South. The hot spell generates "the effect of creating a passivity which renders the inhabitants of the region much too willing to accept conditions as they are, be they right or wrong" (185). Cason also asserts that it is because of the climate of the South that its inhabitants like "pepper in their food, strong coffee, and the excitement of fights" (12). The nerves of the South are constantly irritated by the heat, leading to the stereotypical southern languor.

In a more famous passage, from *The Mind of the South,* W. J. Cash describes the haunting oppressiveness of the southern weather as a factor impacting the inhabitants of Dixie:

> There are days when the booming of the wind in the pines is like the audible rushing of time—when the sad knowledge of the grave stirs in the subconsciousness and bends the spirit to melancholy; days when the

questions that have no answers must insinuate themselves into the minds of the least analytical of men. And there are other days—in July and August—when the nerves wilt under the terrific impact of sun and humidity, and even the soundest grow a bit neurotic; days saturnine and bilious and full of heavy foreboding. (57)

Cash saturates the weather with meaning and presents it as one of the sources of the southern paradox—the oppressive heat and humidity are haunting people, irritating them and forcing them into a state of tired contemplativeness or continuing disturbance.

Interestingly, this prominent motif of temperature was much less conspicuous in the first draft of Faulkner's "Dry September." After the story was rejected by *American Mercury,* in 1930, Faulkner changed the original title from "Drought" and placed the depiction of the heat wave where it is now, before the portrayal of Minnie Cooper's descent into disreputability.[1] With these alterations, the dry spell of the South was moved to the forefront of the narrative.

Nonetheless, regardless of whether Faulkner subversively blames the lynching on the oppressive heat—as one of the lynchers says, "It's this durn weather [. . .] It's enough to make a man do anything" (*Selected Short Stories* 61)—or the sweat-inducing swelter functions as the prefiguration of hateful bloodshed, it is the vitriolic argument at the barbershop that truly initiates the violence of the story. In the debate, opposing modes of predication and irresolvable conceptions of truth are juxtaposed and escalated, culminating in the excess of brutality. Thus, in "Dry September," Faulkner's hyperbolic mode manifests itself in the agonistic debate within the southern polyphony over the guilt of Will Mayes.

The indeterminacy of the gossip and its ephemeral form are at odds with the demonstrative pronoun in the opening phrase "That Saturday evening." The transitory, shapeless rumor designated by such words as "something," "whatever," and a hesitant tricolon of metonyms—"attacked, insulted, frightened" (60)—merges figuratively with the air breathed by the men in the barbershop. The atmosphere permeated with contentious hearsay reminds one of Faulkner's "pollen of ideas." The very air becomes the vehicle for incendiary ideas that are organically fused with the fine particles and whose involuntary intake affects every exposed mind. In the barbershop, the ceiling fan stirs the oppressive air without refreshing it, "sending back upon [the gathered men], in recurrent surges of stale pomade and lotion, their own stale breath and odors" (60). Their breath, like their words, is caught in the uroboric paradox of circular repetitiveness, figuratively signaling the argumentative deadlock of the dispute that is soon to break out.

Faulkner's selection of the barbershop as the setting for "Dry September" carries strong implications for the linguistic drama of the story. It is a space in which the members of the community assemble, and its open character encourages clients to exchange opinions and confront one another. Thus, the space of the barbershop is essentially social, in the sense that it provides a framework for a clash of viewpoints and outlines the communal polyphony of voices. It also constitutes a space that undergoes a transformation during the story; as it becomes filled with language, and as the dispute over the alleged sexual assault goes around in circles—just as the sweltering air is bound in the vicious circles of loops driven by the ceiling fans—the small location accumulates more and more language tensions, ultimately becoming the theater of violence.

The notion of public space used for an argumentative duel witnessed by an assembly has its rhetorical roots in the classical tradition of agon. The concept of agonistic rivalry resurfaced in literary criticism three decades ago, after Harold Bloom appropriated it in his discussion of the anxiety of influence. Yet the actual rhetorical tradition of agon is less centered on a one-to-one poetic joust than on an open, public event in which differing voices engage in a public competition for the attention and accord of the listeners. Debra Hawhee stresses this difference in her distinction between *athlios* and agon, *athlios* being a dualistic rhetorical competition aimed at a prize, more in line with Bloom's thinking, while agon remains more of a "contestive encounter," a communal competition in which the gathering itself constitutes a pivotal element of the event (15–16). Winning the laurel of victory in the rhetorical athletics was every speaker's personal goal, but the communal exchange of views also performed a pivotal function as an institutional ritual of language that allowed it to furnish the public space. The disputations among diverse voices carrying novel views and the development of an engaging political debate might have been inimical at times, but that fueled the political life of the community.

With the public discussion in the barbershop in "Dry September," Faulkner creates an arena of a southern agon, in which divergent argumentative modes clash and argue about Will Mayes's guilt. Here, however, the undercurrents of language exposed by Faulkner are of a much more sinister nature than the ludic celebration of intellectual and linguistic prowess that the Epicurean orators enjoyed so much. For the participants in this southern agon, their patriarchal southern identity is at stake. To defend it, they escalate the verbal conflict with provocative, interrogative statements, and as the eristic tricks they employ take on more power and the brutal force of their arguments escalates, the racist discourse they employ eclipses all other voices.

The rhetorical agon opens in medias res, with the voice of disbelief and denial: "Except it wasn't Will Mayes" (Faulkner, *Selected Short Stories* 60). Here, the barber questions the validity of the inflammatory gossip. Right from the beginning, he sets himself in opposition to the nebulous accusations and, by extension, to the voice of all those who would be prone to subscribe to the racist scenario they entail. The arguments the barber deploys draw from his personal experience: "I know Will Mayes. [. . .] And I know Miss Minnie Cooper, too" (60). He essentially seeks to vouch for the innocence of the accused, and the issues of whom he knows and what he believes in become factors of validity. This strategy turns out to be precarious for the chief defender of Will Mayes because, by grounding his arguments in his private experience, the barber opens up his own credibility to a potential personal attack.

And so the belligerent reply of a hulking youth derails the exchange from the direction set by the barber. The youth sarcastically rebuffs the representative speech act of the barber ("Believe, hell!"), and immediately puts his words in the context of racial dichotomies: "Won't you take a white woman's word before a nigger's?" (60). In the alliterative description of the youth's clothes—a "sweat-stained silk shirt"—each monosyllabic word presages his impulsive and aggressive stance. In the exchange, his accosting antagonism manifests itself through a series of provocative questions. The language he uses there is framed in binary opposites, and for the hearers of the agon, the mere use of the words "white woman" and "nigger" in the same sentence unlocks a whole network of internalized associations that escalate the conflict.

Obviously, the youth's casus belli stems from the sense of violation of the axiological hierarchy of racial and gender relations. The preposition "before" in his question maps those relations onto a metaphoric space in which Will Mayes has (for him) an authoritatively determined figurative place, subordinate to the white woman. The arguments of the barber antagonize him so much because they seem to infringe upon this figurative arrangement of echelons, and thus they bear implications for his own racial status. The *erotesis*, the confrontational question he uses, takes control of the exchange by its dialogic power and seeks to capture his antagonist in the necessity of a reply. The interrogative form of the youth's utterance is hence openly provocative, seeking to corner the barber into either a heretical denial of the figurative racial hierarchy or a compliant affirmation.

The barber seeks to avoid the agonistic trap and returns to the fundamentals—he questions whether there is any case to be discussed in the first place: "I don't believe anybody did anything. I don't believe anything happened" (61). Yet the placid voice of the barber visibly lacks the bellicose facet of the youth's interrogative provocation. He seeks to establish a cornerstone dictum for the debate, avoiding the fallacy of *petitio principii,* or taking the unproven conclusion as a premise, and in this way he puts the very subject of the debate into question. What he does not seem to realize is that, once the rhetorical wheels of his revenge-seeking antagonists start turning, there is no going back. The exchange is no longer a debate over Mayes's guilt; instead, it becomes an ordeal of the racial identity and southern integrity of the people gathered in the barbershop. While the barber seeks to discuss the case in relation to his views on womanhood and to acquit Will Mayes, his antagonists persistently push the exchange onto a personal track and launch a truculent assault against the barber, making his racial affinity and southern identity the objects of the debate.

The client's response ("Then you are a hell of a white man") and the youth's other aggravating question ("Do you accuse a white woman of lying?") both articulate the same aggressive and expansive voice of the southern collective (61). The first eristic response, ad hominem, questions the racial and gender integrity of the barber, which, to the client, does not allow for any intermediary between the figurative axiomatic binaries. The youth's question, on the other hand, perpetuates his interrogative strategy, implying a connection between white skin and unconditional truthfulness. Again, he seeks to corner his antagonist into providing a defensive answer—a negative answer to the question he asks means the rhetorical triumph of the interrogator, while a positive one would fuel the conflict further and undermine the barber's position in the agon. The abusive label of "damn niggerlover" (61), which the youth throws at the barber at this point, is another way in which he seeks to dominate his rhetorical competitor. The barber's noncompliance with the youth's reasoning spurs the discourse into a state of overdrive as his persistent defense of Mayes only radicalizes the other members of the gathering.

The voice of the future lynch mob in the barbershop speaks in binary absolutes of race and gender, and with each dialogic turn their verbal antagonisms escalate. Hyperbolizing the figures and antagonizing the social polyphony, the client asks, "Do you claim that anything excuses a nigger attacking a white woman? Do you mean to tell me you are a white man and you'll stand for it? You better go back North where you came from. The South don't want your kind here." (62). This next topical binary used in the argument, that of a geographic and cultural antagonism between the North and the South, further escalates the figurative tensions of the exchange. The implication of the client's directive is that he usurps for himself the communicative role as spokesman of the South and, speaking as a metonymical voice of the community, he drives his antagonists beyond the Mason-Dixon line. The opposition between "the South" and the dismissive "your kind" conjoins the personal confrontation with the regional dichotomy.

McLendon's assertive statement joins the accusatory choir of the group, contesting the factual approach of the barber and his suggestion of a need to investigate what happened: "Happen? What the hell difference does it make? Are you going to let the black sons get away with it until one really does it?" (63). The interrogatives form the basis of this eristic strategy, as before, but McClendon's dismissive answer to the barber's approach stems from a different mode of predication, based not on facts and deductive reasoning but on internalized prejudices. To McLendon, the taboo has been broken and the crime has been committed; thus, the only way the tension can be lifted and the social order restored is through a ritual of scapegoating.

As the spiral of the agonistic conflict progresses, mere words cease to be enough for the elevated group and the demand for violent action surfaces. The moment those gathered stand up from their chairs, they signal the translation of the divisions in the language polyphony into the extralinguistic reality. Their behavior symbolically proclaims their readiness for action, and the drummer's words, "I'm with him," signal the final fragmentation of the gathered. The members of the lynch mob that is thus formed use a patriarchal excuse to justify the act of violence they are about to commit. The drummer continues, "I don't live here, but by God, if our mothers and wives and sisters—" (63), joining the patriarchal possessiveness and the regional affinity together to affirm his readiness to become part of the crowd.

As the group allegiances are proclaimed among the gathered men and enmity is strengthened, the next provocative question of the youth—"Who's with me?" (63)—ends the debate and calls the lynch party into existence. It also reveals the aggressive performativity of the youth's language and its expansive and acquisitive nature. The question is both an indirect call to action and a declaration of group allegiance, forming an antagonistic rift in the group, aggressively juxtaposing the "we" of the mob with the "them" of the potential defenders of Will Mayes. By contrast, the arguments of the barber lack the potency to withstand the mobilizing strength of the aggressive questions—from the very beginning of the agon, he has consistently been cornered in a defensive position. At this penultimate turn of the exchange, the barber's voice effectively ceases to exist. It is swallowed up (or engulfed, to follow up on the metaphor of wildfire from the beginning of the story) by the hyperbolically expanding voice of the lynchers.

The debate Faulkner places at the beginning of "Dry September" is locked in the hyperbolic impossibility of verbal resolution. The two sides of the dispute, the barber and his clients, speak divergent languages, framed in turn-taking sequence that, from the very beginning, is disentangling and falling back on itself. As the discourse becomes split into two antagonistic voices and the emotions escalate, Faulkner leaves his readers with little doubt about who has the upper hand in this agonistic confrontation. The language of the youth is impregnable against the barber's logical interludes, and with the force of the provocative questions, it expands and aggrandizes, appropriating the public space of the barbershop and inciting the people gathered there into the ritualistic act of violence.

The Undead Time

According to Edmond Volpe, "A Rose for Emily" is Faulkner's most frequently reprinted and studied short story (104). Over the ninety years that have passed since its publication, it has inspired a rich body of criticism, focused strongly on its complex narrative chronology and the attributes of its collective narrator.[2] My discussion of the story adopts a different angle, focusing on the tropological contrasts that Faulkner employs to demonstrate the southern paradox.

I begin by investigating the manner in which the corporate narrator conceptualizes the relationship between Miss Emily and the town in metaphoric terms and how the divide between them fuels the paradoxical tensions that are inherent in Jefferson. The micro- and macrometaphors of bodily decay and divided space make up the metafigurative fabric of the text, which, through the escalating tensions between the two participants in the drama—the normative collective of the town and the aberrant, reclusive woman—exhibits all the characteristics of hyperbolic design. My analysis seeks to demonstrate how those metaphorical images become entangled and ultimately culminate in the epiphanic apex, which takes place with the opening of the tomb-like mansion to the townspeople and the discovery of the decayed body of Homer Barron.

The central macrotrope of "A Rose for Emily" revolves around the metaphorical representation of Miss Emily's house as a mausoleum. In the famous opening sentence, the narrator likens Miss Emily herself to a "fallen monument" (Faulkner, *Selected Short Stories* 47), an essential element of the decorative, decrepit tomb that her mansion has become. It is not only the visibility of the house, which lifts its "stubborn and coquettish decay above the cotton wagons" and looms over the neighborhood, but also its tenacious resilience to the changes in the area that are emblematic of the temporal paradox of the Dixie that Faulkner takes as his subject. Miss Emily's house is a dead macrocosm, a world within a world, which remains both out of time and out of place. It is a figurative space in which the regular engagements of chronotope are warped and transgressed, leading to hyperbolic tensions.

The deadness of the house remains in a state of a synergy with its dead-like inhabitants. When Miss Emily passes away and her body is laid to rest in the "cedar-bemused cemetery among the ranked and anonymous graves of Union and Confederate soldiers who fell at the battle of Jefferson" (47), it is, figuratively, merely her whereabouts that undergo a change, for her ontological status as a lifeless person remains the same both before and after her demise. In terms of the metaphoric design of the story, she becomes dead and out of this world long before she actually dies, and the transportation of her body to the cemetery seems more like an act of exhumation and reburial. It is a movement from the sphere of temporal stasis to the final resting place in which she is symbolically placed alongside the departed of old—those who are metonymic of the bygone South and its paradoxical myths. Here, the collective narrator's choice of words—"Miss Emily had gone to join the representatives of those august names" (47)—clearly implies that it is the location she is thought to have belonged to in the first place, and by "joining" the dead, she has become incorporated into her mythical element.

As a consequence of this figurative scheme, Miss Emily's body takes on the metaphorical characteristics of a corpse. When the envoys of the Jefferson collective enter the dilapidated mansion to demand that she pay her taxes, the collective narrator talks of Miss Emily's small and spare "skeleton," as if her body were translucent, lacking in firm substance of the flesh. At the same time, her obese physique, supported by an ebony cane, is "bloated" and reminds one of a "body long submerged in motionless water" (49). The excess of swollen flesh and its simultaneously ghostlike pellucidity are reinforced by the image of the transparency of water. Figuratively, therefore, Miss Emily's body is depicted as an inflated corpse in a lake, a motionless floater, whose prolonged, posthumous exposure to water has triggered various processes of decay.

On the metanarrative level, her bloated, grotesque body enclosed in the tomb-like mansion is not only the prefiguration of the grisly discovery that the inhabitants of Jefferson make when they finally enter the protected space of household. Miss Emily's undead status, sustained by the figurative stasis of the house and its traditional longevity, also merges with how Faulkner conceptualizes the temporal ataxia of the region. This is not very far removed from some of the contemporaneous descriptions of the South mentioned in chapter 1, such as Benjamin Kendrick and Alex Mathews Arnett's *The South Looks at Its Past,* published in 1935, only five years after "A Rose for Emily." The macrofigure of the Old South as undead, whose haunting presence looms ever present in the American mind, seems to have had a particularly strong intertextual echo.

Miss Emily is not the only such undead southern figure in Faulkner's fiction. The metaphoric portrayal of Miss Emily's cadaverous physicality reminds one of another hallmark character in Faulkner's oeuvre, Reverend Hightower. In *Light in August,* the disgraced minister develops an obsession with his departed ancestor, becoming an apathetic witness to the quotidian life of Jefferson, before he is temporarily snatched out of his stasis by the arrival of Lena Grove. The figurative death becomes Hightower's way of life, and he hyperbolizes the past to the extent that he continues to live because of it as well as in it, unable to break from the monomania of the galloping cavalry ghost of his forefather. If movement is the visual emblem of being alive, then his notorious immobility and stationary pose, reminiscent of an "eastern idol" (90), are indicative of death. A parallel image is found in "A Rose for Emily," when the representatives of the Jefferson collective enter her mansion to spray lime in the cellar. The reclusive lady looks on as they do so, and as she carefully observes their desperate actions to drive away the stench of decay, Miss Emily becomes a motionless "idol," illuminated by the source of light located behind her "upright torso" (*Selected Short Stories* 51).

This act of observation from above without being observed is recurrent in both macrofigurative representations. In *Light in August,* the disgraced preacher's very name connotes a figurative tower from which, seated on high, he can remain the beholder of the reality of Jefferson, protected against the flow of time. Confined to his protective bubble, he does the beholding without much risk of being beheld. From his figurative "high tower," a house that is in effect hardly more than a sepulcher, Reverend Hightower continues to spy and observe, gazing motionlessly through the window. He invariably remains chained to the prison of time as events pass below him, failing to affect him or even attract his attention. Most importantly, when he gazes through the window, he does not see Jefferson in the present moment. Instead, his eyes assume the perspective of the inglorious past of the Civil War.

The defrocked minister's grotesque physique is as excessive and mis-shapen as his temporal detachment: "His skin is the color of flour sacking and his upper body in shape is like a loosely filled sack falling from his gaunt shoulders of its own weight, upon his lap" (Faulkner, *Light in August* 78–79). Faulkner consistently presents the preacher through the macrofigure of dis-integrating flesh, as if Hightower were a dead body that remains unburied, an emblematic element of the "undead South." Both Hightower's dilapidated apartment and his body are covered with the smell of decay. Hightower is "oblivious of the odor in which he lives—that smell of people who no longer live in life: that odor of overplump desiccation and stale linen as though a pre-cursor of the tomb" (317–318), and his body generates a similar foul fragrance: "When Hightower approaches, the smell of plump unwashed flesh and un-fresh clothing—that odor of unfastidious sedentation, of static overflesh not often enough bathed—is well nigh overpowering" (299).

These parallel macrofigurative strategies in "A Rose for Emily" and *Light in August* are similar in how they expose the paradox of the body arrested in the prison of southern temporal arrest. Its awkward suspension between life and death points to the ambivalent status of the South and the intertextual grid that Faulkner both observed and was a part of. This nebulous contrast is the carrier of the hyperbolic in the short story. Thus, the writer's use of tropes is central to the representation of the pathological power the past has over the collective consciousness of the region. It is not only the barrenness of the atro-phied remnants of the old order that defines them; it is also their firm grip on the South and the extent to which they "haunt" subsequent generations.

In "A Rose for Emily," Miss Emily's undead body is figuratively extirpated in yet another way. In conceptual terms, she ceases to be a person of flesh and bone for the people of Jefferson, becoming instead an abstract entity. In a famous tricolon, Faulkner limns her as "a tradition, a duty, and a care" in the eyes of the corporate narrator (*Selected Short Stories* 48). Her physicality ceases to be of any concern and she becomes incorporated into the space of southern myths. Miss Emily is valorized as a social institution, and the tricolon describes varying perception of her and different entanglements that the inhabitants of Jefferson have developed with her, such as respect and veneration—but not to her as a person. This depersonalization of Miss Emily by the southern collective is also the source of her drama. There is only one brief moment when she is "humanized." It is when she is abandoned by Homer Barron and deprived of the family fortune—in the words of the narrator, "left alone and a pauper" (52). Yet this expression of compassion is both superficial and ephemeral. Her needs and her despondency were never recognized, and ultimately she was driven to kill her beau, cornered by the social mechanisms of the southern code.

Miss Emily's drama remains inextricably bound to the bygone ideas of southern chivalry. Because her father drove away her suitors and left her nothing but the mansion, he considerably diminished her chances of finding a husband worthy of a daughter of the southern aristocracy. His patriarchal decision contextualizes her tragic story as a passive object to his decision-making, a mere image, a "tableau[, . . .] a slender figure in white" (51). Moreover, Homer Barron represents everything Miss Emily's father would have resented. Not only is he a northerner but also he is the ambassador of modernity, driving Miss Emily around in his tented, yellow-wheeled buggy. In synergy with the aura that surrounds him, which is antithetical to the code of values of the Old South, Miss Emily cuts her hair short during her romance with Barron. But later, as the chances for a happy ending for her life's drama fade away, her hair undergoes another transformation and turns gray—the metamorphosis of her looks becoming thus symbolic of the tensions between the present and the past. The shifting of these images corresponds to the tragic story of Miss Emily's life: the notorious hold of the past, her futile attempts to defy it, and, finally, her defeat and retraction into the temporal stasis.

Miss Emily's ambivalent presence is therefore an umbilical cord that joins the present with the past, a temporal bridge suspended between the Old South and the new generations. And in the figurative sense, the woman becomes metonymical of the regional myth. Although her body is relegated and her femininity is ignored, she becomes venerated with the hagiographic attention of a representative element evoking the complete vision of mythologized past.

Miss Emily thus becomes the metonym of the regional mythos, a ghostlike constituent that allows the panoramic images of old to be summoned. In this sense, she is recognized by the community as a necessary element for the construction of their identity, which is apparent when men show up at her funeral wearing their Confederate uniforms. The people of Jefferson need her as a reference point, whether she is dead or alive.

With the amalgamation of the categories of life and death in "A Rose for Emily," a different metafigurative divide is employed to organize the world of Jefferson. The bifurcation into the metaphoric inside and the outside functions as the demarcation line for the emblematic spaces of the story. The exterior of the house is susceptible to the flow of time and the transition of generations. Its evolution, visible in changing customs and laws, signifies the norm, against which the resistant, stubbornly atemporal space of the interior becomes a grotesque aberration and a source of hyperbolic tension.

The hidden inside, shaded from sunlight, social interaction, and institutional influence, is also a source of speculation in the community. Faulkner's collective narrator stresses that the forbidden space raised the "curiosity" of the female members of Jefferson (51). After Miss Emily's death, when the house is opened, its tomb-like interior is revealed to the curious public. Together with the macabre finding, it is a revelation that presents the death for what it is, and it restores the missing semantics to warped ideas.

Earlier, upon her father's demise, Miss Emily had declared to the visiting ladies that he was not dead, signaling the failure of language to describe her reality and her state of mind. This disconnectedness from the outsiders' system of signification, and her refusal to embrace what had been apparent to the patriarch of the family, epitomizes the fundamental, epistemological divide between them. Like the grotesque grotto of Nero's palace, the interior of the tomb-house, when finally revealed, shows the extent of the hyperbolic aberration and the magnitude of the disturbance of the norm. The unsealing of the mansion's doors is the concluding point of hyperbolic tension in the story, a moment of epiphany that discloses the decayed pathology at the core of what was considered "a tradition, a duty, and a care" of the community.

Because the figurative divide between the inside and outside spaces dramatizes the southern paradox and signals the coexistence of what can be construed of parallel temporal universes, communication between these figurative worlds is impossible. They are so distant that, when the inhabitants of these two chronotypes meet, their very language is doomed to fail. The signifiers cannot be attached to their designates because their systems of meaning operate in different contexts. Communication breaks down, obscured by the division of the macrofigurative spaces of the interior and the exterior.

When the townspeople try to introduce themselves, somewhat awkwardly, with "We are the city authorities, Miss Emily. Didn't you get a notice from the sheriff, signed by him?," she undercuts them: "Perhaps he considers himself the sheriff." And when they assert, "But there is nothing on the books to show [that she pays no taxes in Jefferson]," she replies, "See Colonel Sartoris," referring to someone who has been dead for a decade but who, within the limits of her temporal stasis, still functions as a valid point of reference (49). In Faulkner's polyphonic grid, the voices they use are contrastive and inevitably divergent. Moreover, the dogmatic statement that Miss Emily has "no taxes in Jefferson," which she uses as a shield against the communication from the metaphorical exterior, does not change throughout the conversation. She repeats it like a mantra, impregnable against anything her guests may say, as unchanging as the mansion and its host's ontological status.

Governed by evolving social protocols, successive generations undergo transitions while Miss Emily refuses to give in—she becomes an aberration to the norm set by the exterior space and the flow of time. In metafigurative terms, at the core of "A Rose for Emily" and pervading the chronological development of the events, Faulkner presents the forces that are responsible for the ejection of the household and its inhabitant from the flow of time. These excessive, oppositional drives are conditioned by the strength of the southern code. It is the warped excess of Miss Emily's drama that, when juxtaposed with the changing generations of the inhabitants of Jefferson and their normative system, inevitably generates escalating conflicts.

Ultimately, the envoys of the city council are "vanquished" (50) by the temporal stasis, unable to pierce the veil of collapsing signifiers. And language is all they have, whether verbal communication or written notes that remain unanswered. They notoriously shy away from taking any open action. At one point, the townspeople had been helpless when confronted by the revolting smell that surrounded the house, powerless to decide upon a course of action. The desperate question "Dammit. Will you accuse a lady to her face of smelling bad?," uttered by Judge Stevens, testifies to their helplessness (51). In particular, his "dammit" reveals frustration with one "member of the rising generation" who apparently does not understand that the decisive action he has suggested is against social decorum. The envoys of the town cannot undertake any action, because the entitlement of the code is stronger than the law of the land in the South and the figurative ghosts roam beyond the dictates of the authorities.

Obviously, Miss Emily is not the sole inhabitant of the tomb-like mansion. In all those conflicts, which are escalated and hyperbolized, Toby, Miss Emily's African American servant, is defined by his lack of prominence. Edmond L. Volpe stresses that, in the first manuscript and a carbon typescript version of the story, one can find two similar deathbed scenes between Miss Emily and Toby that did not find their way into the final version of the story (103–104). In those versions, Toby is offered the house, which he refuses, declaring that all he wants is to sit in the sun and watch the trains go by. Such an addition clearly would have disrupted the narrative harmony of the final text and dissipate the mystery surrounding the story's protagonist, so it is little wonder that Faulkner did not include it in the final version.

Considering Toby's name and its association with the phrase "to be," pointing to the future rather than to the past, as well as Toby's abandonment of the house and its temporal stasis after Miss Emily's death, T. J. Stafford, in his paper from 1969, argues for a more optimistic reading of the servant's role in the story. However, Toby's utter silence in the final version of the narrative, and his obscure background role in the unfolding events, remain consistent with the figurative patterns of "A Rose for Emily." Toby is voiceless not only in the symbolic sense but also in a literal manner. His voice "had grown harsh and rusty, as if from disuse" (Faulkner, *Selected Short Stories* 57), and becomes emblematic of his social detachment from the segregated society of Jefferson. Ultimately, his silence in the story translates into how he disappears, without any words of explanation or farewell, like a fleeting image or a ghost set free from the tomb-like house by the expiration of Miss Emily's temporal arrest.

All of these tensions between the figures of the interior and the exterior, as well as the metaphorical death and the flow of time, culminate in the scene of the opening of the house. Among critics, there seems to be an ongoing debate about what happened in the sealed room of Miss Emily's mansion. While some commentators (such as Elmo Howell or John Hagopian and Martin Dolch) argue that Miss Emily had not actually lain with her poisoned beau, others (such as Bride and Clements) see the apparent act of necrophilia as emblematic of Faulkner's ambivalence about the southern preoccupation with the past.

In either case, the collapse of the figurative barrier between the outside and the inside is tantamount to the alleviation of the temporal arrest, and it also is the apex of the hyperbolic in "A Rose for Emily." At this point, the representatives of southern decorum, as well as the readers of the story, are given an opportunity to peek into the hidden, grotesque space of the temporal stasis and to understand the regional anomaly. What the visitors from the figurative exterior ultimately discover when they enter the figurative interior is more than a possible indication of an act of necrophilia. Specifically, they find an amalgam of decay, misery, and stillness, which is indirectly projected upon them at that climactic moment of the hyperbolic and subjects them to the entire weight of the excessive tensions that the story has led to and in which it culminates.

4

BREAKING OUT OF HYPERBOLE

Lillian Smith and Katharine Du Pre Lumpkin

Of all the genres of southern fiction, it is perhaps social autobiography that most vividly encapsulates the hyperbolic tensions that haunt the region. It is yet another way for the southern "rage to explain," as Fred Hobson puts it, to manifest itself. Beginning in the 1940s, southerners brought forth myriad texts that report on their authors' lifelong, embattled struggle to negotiate their relationship with southern culture and to try to liberate themselves from the grip of their racist background. Apart from the two books discussed in this chapter—Lillian Smith's *Killers of the Dream* (1949) and Katharine Du Pre Lumpkin's *The Making of a Southerner* (1946)—this group of texts also includes Ben Robertson's *Red Hills and Cotton* (1941), Willie Morris's *North Towards Home* (1967), and Larry L. King's *Confessions of a White Racist* (1971). All of these books provide a dramatic account of their authors' rebellion against their cultural background and, ultimately, their attempt to break away from a nexus of southern ideas about the segregation of races.

The significance of such texts for the comprehension of the functioning of the southern mind can hardly be overstated. They curate southern culture and politics and provide a critical, albeit subjective, understanding of the regulatory mechanisms of the South's quotidian world. In a study tellingly entitled *But Now I See,* Fred Hobson compares these southern social autobiographies to conversion narratives and highlights their resemblance to the writings of the "born again" New England Puritans. In Hobson's view, these southern authors, having renounced the principles of segregated society, undergo a "conversion" that compels them to reject racism, much as the colonial-era participants in the First Great Awakening, inspired by revival sermons, sought to reject their sinfulness. In consequence, the memoirs can be construed as chronicles of moral revelation as the authors remodel themselves according to a new set of principles and valorize a new moral outlook.

The conjunction "but" in the title of Hobson's study implies the figurative blindness that preceded the restoration of sight and stresses the magnitude of the mental shift explored in these narratives. This liberation, for almost all of these authors, necessitates a painful and complicated process in which they recreate themselves, make themselves anew, severing the bonds with their past mind-set. And in order to engage in this intricate self-liberation, they need a new platform of references, a new code of behavior, and a new set of cognitive paradigms.

Hence, in social autobiographies there is both a violent act of self-purging and an equally violent yet ultimately more constructive act of creation. What makes social autobiographies particularly interesting is that they recount, step by step, the linguistic means the authors employ to separate themselves from their cultural heritage—they are "searching," testing the borders of the "inside" and "outside" of the culture. Surely, the overall purpose of each differs with each text. Sometimes texts serve as a gateway to redemption of past sins, sometimes they are used by their authors to argue white victimhood, and sometimes they are simply vehicles of sentimental reminiscing. But they always involve an internal struggle, not unlike the one Huckleberry Finn experienced just before he declares, "All right then, I'll go to hell," and chooses his relationship with Jim over the dictates of the racist culture.

The indictment of the southern mind interred in these writings has profound linguistic implications, for the act of personal recreation the authors undertake becomes an act of metalanguage. In his comment on an apartheid exhibition that opened in Paris in 1983, Jacques Derrida stated, "There is no racism without a language," adding "The point is not that acts of racial violence are only words but rather that they have to have a word" ("Racism's Last Word" 292). The formation of a divisive system requires a special type of communication that adopts sets of metaphors, references, rhetoric, and ploys that not only serve the maintenance of the oppression (in the words of the French philosopher, such a language "institutes, declares, writes, inscribes, prescribes") but also dissociate the discourse from humanism, dividing it from within. This language of oppression, driven by a certain vision of the world, maintains itself by perpetuating this very vision—and if it is to be rooted out effectively, one who would escape the system must undertake a "self-inflicted lobotomy."

In the texts under scrutiny, the author's hippocampus, the area of the brain where all the memories, cultural paradigms, and impressions are stored, needs to be brutally invaded by a new "I" that seeks to dissociate itself from its past oppressions and from words, phrases, and references in which the author has been immersed during her upbringing. In metafigurative terms, a novel, disaffective mode of comprehension is evoked.

In this agonizing process, the hyperbolic mode becomes a viable means of disassociation. By blowing things out of proportion, by conjoining opposites to demonstrate how bloated they actually are, and by violating cultural decorum, the emerging new self of the author can distance itself from its cultural roots and form the space needed to hoist itself up from its original cultural position. The unruliness of hyperbolic metafiguration allows for cultural decorum to be challenged and broken, and ultimately secures the space for the author to reform herself. What distinguishes Smith's and Lumpkin's use of the hyperbolic is the way in which they engage the trope's potential to generate new meanings in order to reorganize the patterns of thinking that have been fossilized in their brain synapses during childhood. They seek to reclaim their idiosyncratic voice from the oppressive southern culture and to reorganize their manner of thinking and feeling. In the words of Scott Romine, "Through autobiography the self seeks to 'reauthenticate itself' in the absence of 'culturally prescribed roles'" ("Framing Southern Rhetoric" 96).

The phrases Smith and Lumpkin use in their autobiographies, "intellectual deafness" (Smith) and "twilight zone" (Lumpkin), signify the haunted plasticity of the southern mind, which enables it to hold two opposing ideas at the same time and to override the painful truth with selective thinking. Figuratively, both the deafness and the twilight become emblematic of the regional knack for the purposeful forgetting of facts and events that do not fit into the cultivated myth. Thus, on the metanarrative level, Smith and Lumpkin use their writings to explore the hyperbolic "unruliness," to reorganize the cultural semiotics of their vision of the South, and to discover that there are indeed other Souths beyond the one prescribed to them. At the same time, this "reauthentication" is uncanny, as it engenders a double of the author, a new linguistic self that emerges from the tension of the transition and speaks metonymies, scrutinizing the relationships between the whole and its constituents rather than the holistic (and stereotypical) racist metaphors of the old order. It is between these voices—the old one, which forms the decorum, and the new, emerging one, which disrupts the former—that the hyperbolic emerges as piv-otal metanarrative tool of expression.

In both texts, the reader is provided with the description of the childhood worlds of the authors, and considerable attention is paid to the families' efforts to suppress any element of reality that did not fit into the myth the Smiths and the Lumpkins lived by. The "intellectual deafness" and the "twilight zone" were meticulously formed throughout the authors' childhood years, instill-ing in them the network of social scripts and the southern decorum of racial propriety and teaching them the southern art of mnemonic omission. In both cases, it is a disturbing episode—the ousting of a girl named Jamie, in the case of Smith, and the beating of a black cook, in the case of Lumpkin—that pushes the mounting tensions between what is seen and what is taught to the met-anarrative point of breakage. These flashpoints, both violent, whether phys-ically or mentally, are the catalysts of the hyperbolic in *Killers of the Dream* (Smith) and *The Making of a Southerner* (Lumpkin), causing a powerful shock to their identities and allowing them to "reauthenticate" themselves.

Hence, in these two texts, the autobiographical voices are inevitably both subjects and objects of the narrative, and they aim to theorize their white vic-timhood and to dramatize the white struggle against the past mind-set. Point-ing out the "whiteness" of these writers' narrative perspective, Lisa Hinrichsen sees the texts as manifestations of "white psyches entangled by unconscious forms of denial and disavowal that obscure historical and personal complicity in perpetuating legacies of inequality" (94). In her view, the language of pain and moribund victimhood instrumental to these writings is an appropriation that allows authors such as Lumpkin, Smith, or Morris to claim trauma as a stigma of political belonging, and she shows how they struggle to discuss race in the South from their relatively privileged positions.

In consequence, "their texts paradoxically come to illustrate the elasticity of white ideology and solidify their own racial privilege" (99). For all their gargantuan efforts to disassociate themselves from the solely white modes of comprehension they seek to repudiate and extirpate in these very texts, deep inside, the results are fraught with ambivalence. To Hinrichsen, then, the so-cial autobiographies are dissimilar to Hobson's "conversion," which implies the possibility of a complete reform of the mind and the soul, a "new birth." On the contrary, they bear testimony to the impossibility of a thorough change and to the depth of penetration of the mind by the southern idiom. To fall back on the analogy of lobotomy, for Hinrichsen, no targeted brain operation can be successful because the disease has metastasized throughout the entire body.

Cutting the Umbilical Cord

In his foreword to Lillian Smith's *Strange Fruit,* Fred Hobson portrays Smith as the "most courageous, outspoken, and uncompromising white southern liberal of her generation" (vii). This tribute to Smith's absolute determination succinctly expresses her uncompromising views on racial issues in the South. As a native of Florida, Smith was raised to embrace the privileges conferred upon the white population by the Jim Crow system. According to James C. Cobb, Smith's "solidly middle-class origins made [her] seem an unlikely crusader against the status quo" (193), yet she quickly grew to detest the system and became one of the most avid supporters of racial integration.

She also made it her life's goal to pass her integrative views on to others. When she took over her father's Laurel Falls Girls Camp, in 1925, in Georgia, she transformed it into an innovative educational institution that provided viable space for the discussion of social issues and the propagation of a progressive outlook. Simply put, the camp was a laboratory for new ideas. Apparently, Smith much preferred debates about human sexuality, religion, and race to instructions on how to plant berries. At the camp, she also met Paula Snelling, her lifelong companion and coeditor of a literary magazine, *Pseudopodia,* which was subsequently transformed into *North Georgia Review.*

Smith herself used to say that her personality was split between "Mary" and "Martha"—with Mary dedicated to artistic activities and Martha bent on the conscientious mission to make social change.[1] While Lillian-Mary labored on the writing of consecutive books, *Killers of the Dream* (1949) and *The Journey* (1954), Lillian-Martha delivered talks, wrote letters, and aided civil rights activists. Although, as I suggested earlier, this cooperation was at times fairly bumpy, Smith's support for Martin Luther King Jr. was complete and unflagging. And there was reciprocity. When King was famously arrested by the Georgia police in 1960, and later released after a phone call intervention from the soon-to-be president, John F. Kennedy, he was actually driving Smith to her cancer therapy. King also mentioned Smith in his "Letter from Birmingham Jail," listing her among the mouthpieces of racial equality, who were small in number but "big in quality."

Loveland's verdict on Smith's writings can be considered harsh, for it stresses Smith's significance primarily as a social activist and public persona. So, indeed, Smith might have had a point about her writings being underrated. There is something edgy about them, and in some ways they are so enchantingly uncompromising that they appeal to the reader on a fundamental level. Or perhaps it is her insight and the unabashed emphasis on the interrelatedness of the "ghosts" that haunt the South and the determination to unearth the connections among the issues of race, sexuality, and religion that coalesce into a grotesque network of unrest. Whatever the case, surely more academic attention ought to be dedicated to her texts, and the recent publication of Margaret Gladney and Lisa Hodgens's *A Lillian Smith Reader,* which provides an overview of her versatile body of writings—including, apart from fiction, essays, articles, and lectures—seems to be not just a fitting way to commemorate the fiftieth anniversary of her passing but also a necessity.

Among Smith's writings, *Killers of the Dream* gives the most relentless critique of the fundamental assumptions of the southern culture of the first decades of the twentieth century, ranging from white supremacy, through oppressive patriarchy, to restrictive religiousness. By exploring these issues, Smith sought to expose and foil southerners' uncompromising struggle to maintain segregation. The primary objective of her works was to demolish the walls that divide people, races, and genders by exposing the hypocritical and twisted foundations of these figurative barriers. Smith's battle against racism, then, was in fact part of a larger crusade, one directed against needless separation of any kind, especially any divide that separates the mind from the body or that disjoins what ought to be felt from what is actually felt. The overriding theme of her work is a struggle against fragmentation and a proliferation of physical and mental wholeness. And a vital element of the war that Smith wages concerns language, especially the way it crosses with cultural and psychological issues of the Jim Crow South and the way its mechanisms can become vehicles for repressive or progressive thought.

The ghostly images and motifs of haunting return persistently throughout *Killers of the Dream*. The very first simile in the very first paragraph evokes an eerie, southern gothic–like imagery: "like a ghost haunting an old graveyard or whispers after the household sleeps—fleeting mystery, vague menace to which each responded in his own way" (25). Such an opening prepares the reader for a journey into the narrator's past, one that unearths recollections that are terrifying and cathartic at the same time. Rather quickly, the reader is warned that the therapy needed to cure oneself of southern racial prejudice is highly invasive and that the side effects are unavoidable. And in the case of *Killers of the Dream,* they were widespread—the book was taken by a number of southerners as offensive, and the author herself as belligerent. Smith's bitter critique was viewed as a betrayal of her culture, and the criticism she received hindered her development as a writer. To Smith, however, the book was a self-exploration and the negotiation of her new code of values. As she says in the introduction, "I was in dialogue with myself as I wrote, as well as with my hometown and my childhood and history and the future, and the past" (13).

The apparitional images continue to "haunt" the subsequent passages of the book, giving expression to the escalating friction between the new emerging "I" of the narrator and her repressed, painful childhood past. Their presence in the text becomes an iconic representation of the author's struggle to cleanse herself of the influence the region has on her mind—an attempt that can hardly be successful unless it includes meddling with the private corners of the narrator's mind. The ghosts Smith evokes are irredeemable, tenacious, and harrowing, but they are not her individual stigmata. As she stresses, the "haunted childhood belongs to every southerner of my age" (25). The "hauntedness" she experiences permeates the whole generation and the whole culture, and the unrest visible in her language mirrors the racial violence of the region and the formative impact of the idea of segregation on her conscience. Through a series of recollections, Smith explores the deformed principles of her childhood, reflecting on such actions as shouting racial insults at black children or pushing them off the sidewalk. With shame and shock, she concludes that such practices were not seen as "sins" at the time, nor were they in any way morally dubious.

The autoreflexive study of her own childhood mind-set and the conscience that failed to see abuse for what it was, driven by the hyperbole of racist disproportion, becomes a way of exploring what Smith later describes as "intellectual deafness." There is one figurative image that particularly encapsulates the change in the relation between her and southern culture. Smith views herself as attached to the South by a metaphorical "umbilical cord" (26). This macrofigurative image is particularly telling, if one considers all its implications.

As an offspring of the South, the narrator was nurtured by the cord that fed her with what was instrumental to her survival and growth. Without this intake, she would have withered away. But what was supposed to be constructive and natural did not turn out to be so, for the southern nourishment was contaminated, disturbingly intimate, and served in a manner that the child could not refuse—to the extent that the child did not realize that it was being fed. The powerlessness of the body against the intake, and the leash-like control of the umbilical cord that smuggled the excessive notions of race into the bodily system of a child at its most pure and vulnerable moment, is viewed by Smith, at the moment of writing, as nothing short of abuse. This abusiveness becomes perversion, as the presence of the sinful in the blissful is revealed as grotesque. But the uncanny connection between the figurative bodies of mother and fetus, the excessive dependence and the merger of their corporality, reminds one of the Bakhtinian grotesque. There is no boundary between the metaphorical bodies, and since they are one, it is impossible to tell exactly where one ends and the other starts. In such a dualistic system, the transitory power of the umbilical cord becomes the vehicle of ultimate control.

It is no surprise, then, that ending this disturbing dependence requires a surgical operation, and thus Smith talks of cutting the umbilical cord. In a way, the whole book is exactly that: a metanarrative act of termination. The oppression of the racist force-feeding is terminated by the metaphoric laceration in which the intimate linkage between her and the culture she grew up in is severed. This painful operation of estrangement signifies a marked change in terms of the figurative metalogic. Romine observes that Smith's self-construction as a "survivor" of the racist culture bears the signs of a shift between the metafigurative modes of cognition—not unlike those that Hayden White delineates—and he seeks to demonstrate how "in telling about the South, Smith relies on her self-construction as a southern outsider, a construction that, in creating a dialogic tension between narrative persona and the 'South,' enacts a de-centering of traditional southern rhetorical tropes" (Romine, "Framing Southern Rhetoric" 107).

If the two bodies connected by an umbilical cord can be viewed in terms of a merger, akin to metaphoric fusion, whereby the narrator was instructed to view the world through the racist tropology (such as the association of African Americans with subjugation and a lower position in the metaphorical space of the society), then the severing of the cord is a revolution in thinking, a violent collapse of the previous mind-set, caused by the hyperbolic act of pushing things to the point of breakage. It is a rapid jump away from the metaphors of racism. In the words of the narrator, a "metamorphosis takes place: *something happens within*: a new chaos, and then slowly, a new being" (*Killers of the Dream* 14).

The cutting of the umbilical cord also splits the narrator's personality in two. As she writes in the foreword to the book, among a series of questions she wrestled with while working on *Killers of the Dream* was "and who am I? besides my name, what else? and who is this other Self that watches me? does it go to sleep when I do?" (12). The other "self" that observes her and haunts her is the offshoot of the southern culture, a sign of guilt and repression. The new persona has a different perspective on southern practices and can use a different moral scale to judge people and their behavior without the hyperbole of race. But the emergence of the new "I" also means the regaining of the narrator's truly own voice. She discovers that when she can think in a new way, she can also speak in a new way—although the reclaiming of her voice is a gradual process that reveals to her a new mode of comprehension. What makes Smith's use of the hyperbolic mode unique is exactly that she employs it constructively to reclaim her language—and by reclaiming her language, she reclaims herself.

To Smith, southern culture is fundamentally oppressive. In the words of the narrator, it "bind[s] the curiosity of childhood as the Chinese once bound their little girls' feet" (150). In terms of the metalogic, it created what could be viewed as the southern decorum of racial excess, which contextualized cultural hyperbole and taboos, and this racist culture's oppressiveness was observably contagious. The way Smith sees it, as far as the education in the southern way of life goes, once you became adept in the "code," and once you dedicated yourself to the propositions that governed life in Dixie, you inadvertently became the carrier of the mental violence that was exercised upon you.

What is then so hyperbolic in the southern world that Smith is presenting to her readers? To answer that question, it would be much easier to list the things that are *not* hyperbolic. To Smith, the process of becoming the southerner means absorbing a number of conflicting ideas and learning to disregard their incongruous character in view of the excessive emphasis on the issues of race. In other words, the notion of the blackness or whiteness of skin becomes such a vital foundation for southern culture that all other concepts, including logical reasoning, individuality, or even compassion for another human being, are disregarded. As she recalls, "The mother who taught me what I know of tenderness and love and compassion taught me also the bleak rituals of keeping Negroes in their 'place.' The father who rebuked me for an air of superiority toward schoolmates from the mill and rounded out his rebuke by gravely reminding me that 'all men are brothers,' trained me in the steel-rigid decorums I must demand of every colored male" (27). The twisting and turning of whatever would be natural and intuitive, the divisions of the figurative space, and the complete subjugation of all aspects of life to the one factor of skin color become the prerogative.

Of all the inconsistencies, the most hurtful for the narrator was the change of heart required of her in her attitude toward the family's black nurse. The narrator found it particularly hard to accept that the "mammy" who had looked after her throughout her childhood, and who showed her a great deal of mother-like dedication, "was not worthy of the passionate love" of a grateful child, and must be given a "half-smiled-at affection similar to that which one feels for one's dog" (29). Smith was reprimanded and told that her intuitive emotional reciprocity of kindness was erroneous and misplaced, simply because of the nurse's skin color. In this way, the Jim Crow culture encouraged her to reject the natural impulses of her mind as well as her body and to repress what seemed instinctive. The tension between the implications of her skin color, on the one hand, blown up beyond all proportion and overshadowing everything else, and what seemed balanced and legitimate, on the other hand, generated a hyperbolic "shock" and a sense of confusion. Her emotionality was stigmatized by southern paradoxes and stretched out to match the dictates of the racist culture, which, as she stresses, victimized her.

Along with the issue of race, religion also seems to have been pushed to the extreme in Smith's family. As she recalls, "God was not someone we met on Sunday but a permanent member of our household" (32). The children were obliged to read the Bible in its entirety each year and to memorize relevant passages, while their father occupied the position of a patriarchal custodian of the family's religiousness. The narrator recalls how her father, who was a mill owner, once heard an alarm call during a prayer. He continued praying, ignoring the fire siren, disregarding the fact that his business was in jeopardy, and it was only after he had finished his worship that he ran out of the house to save his mill.

Her father's uncompromising dedication to religion merged with equally uncompromising ideas about racial hierarchy and segregation, as if, in order to support the structure of Jim Crow, two pillars were needed—one for social propriety, providing scripts of how to behave, and another for moral authority, providing a pseudo moral compass. One excess coalesced with the other, and each enhanced the authority of the other and pushed the limits of southern decorum further and further. Ultimately, because of this conjunction, "God became the mighty protagonist of ambivalence" (85)—as the years passed, the moral dubiousness of segregation took its toll on Smith's faith.

Whenever Smith mentions her deepening immersion in southern culture, she persistently uses words and figurative phrases associated with rigid schooling. What she was taught at home were "lessons," while the rules that regulated their home activities were viewed as "commandments." In Smith's account, too, the passive voice and the modality of obligation are ostensibly recurrent. The narrator describes the full curriculum of southern education: "We learned the intricate system of taboos, of renunciations and compensations, of manners, voice modulations, words, feelings, along with our prayers, our toilet habits and games" (27–28). Both she and her peers were the subjects of training that taught them to ignore the paradoxes of daily life in the South and to regard southern racial excess as something ordinary.

To Smith, one of the most cunning and perverse elements of the system consisted of the fact that it was the very institution of the family that enabled the acquisition of new acolytes. "Wrapped together, [the lessons] were taught us by our mother's voice, memorized with her love, patted into our lives as she rocked us to sleep or fed us" (84). Smith stresses that these "lessons" were injected into her and her peers through a very intimate relationship between a child and a parent and that the relationship that should normally connote innocence was effectively abused to perpetuate the abuse.

Moreover, any educational system has its regulatory mechanisms, and this one was not short on the means of castigation. A pure, petrifying remorse was the punishment for violating the unwritten rules of southern culture or the family's ways. This sense of guilt pervaded the body so strongly that, as Smith recalls, it triggered physical reactions, like an acute nausea, whenever the mind marshaled the body to undertake an action violating the southern code, such as dining with African Americans. It is as if the "lessons" were taught so persistently and so successfully that their excessive ideas of disparity became part of the very structure of southerners' brains. Rebelling against them, resetting the mind-set, required a herculean force, and the sense of uncontrollable physical discomfort was an offshoot of the struggle.

The outcome of all these pressures, tensions, and repressions governing the society was its "hauntedness," visible especially in Smith's narrative of the three ghosts. By giving in to the hyperboles of race and ignoring everything else, the minds of southerners fell into "intellectual deafness," which allowed them to cope with the irreconcilable antiphony of seemingly contradictory ideas: "white supremacy and democracy, brotherhood and segregation, love and lynching" (115). Smith's family's mode of comprehension did not recognize antithesis for what it was, nor did it see anything contradictory in various quotidian paradoxes of their daily life. The three ghosts, which Smith describes extensively, constitute a direct consequence of the suppression of the natural need for logical congruence and of the instinctive needs of the body.

The first ghost was conjured up by the taboo of interracial sex, a part of the "race-sex-sin spiral" (121). In Smith's depiction, the repressed desire of white males drove them to engage in relations with African American women whom their racist culture compelled them to despise—and "succumbing to desire, they mated with these dark women whom they had dehumanized in their minds, and fathered by them children who, according to their race philosophy, were 'without souls'—a strange exotic new kind of creature, whom they made slaves of and sometimes sold" (120). The fear and guilt that such men experienced from engaging in interracial sex led to excessive protectiveness of their female partners, whom they suspected of the same "forbidden" desires that they themselves indulged.

In her description, Smith juggles the terms with strong Freudian connotations and stresses that repressed desire and lingering unfulfillment become the triggers for patriarchal violence. But the desire Smith discusses is also deeply mimetic, insofar as the African American women paradoxically possessed a lively sense of freedom from the oppressiveness of southern culture that the white, patriarchal men both longed for and detested. These conflicting emotions, and the increasing tensions, pushed the men beyond the border of taboo and placed the burden of the hyperbolized guilt upon their shoulders.

Obviously, this is not the first time Smith tapped into this subject. Her debut novel, *Strange Fruit* (1944), was a tragic story of an illicit interracial relationship between a white man and an African American woman in the post–World War I reality. The book generated a fair amount of controversy and was banned in Boston for its allegedly indecent language and erotic innuendoes. In the words of one of its reviewers, described in Tillman's "*Strange Fruit* in Retrospect," it was an "uncoated story of frustration" and, as it tapped into one of the most sensitive taboos of southern culture, the story exposed the fragility of southern cultural constructs and the extent of the system's grip over the southern mind (288). For all the controversies, however, the ultimate success of *Strange Fruit* was confirmed when the novel was translated into fifteen languages and transformed into a 1945 Broadway play. By dressing the ghost in Freudian clothing in *Killers of the Dream*, Smith delves into the subconscious, suggesting the ultimate uncontrollability of the human body and its instinctive impulses and implying that the whole restrictive system of southern culture was failing exactly because, by restraining and curbing, it pushed racial hyperbole into a state of overdrive.

The second ghost is almost literally conceived by the first. It is the "South's rejected children," born out of interracial relations. There is something deeply grotesque and saddening in the way Smith portrays such children, doomed to live in the permanent social "outskirts" of repudiation. The merger of cultural impiety with their objective innocence shocks and exposes the incongruities of racist culture, especially as Smith organizes the narrative in such a way as to bring out the clashing opposites in the most vivid manner: "Little ghosts playing and laughing and weeping on the edge of the southern memory can be a haunting thing" (*Killers of the Dream* 125). The children are voiceless, devoid of means to establish themselves as human beings worthy of equal treatment or to defend themselves against the accusations that are there but are never openly issued, the allegation of breaking a taboo, which they had no part in.

Finally, the third ghost represents the dubious relationship between white children and their African American nurses, who often acted as wet nurses. In the context of the restrictive culture of the segregated society, interracial wet nursing, although widely practiced, becomes in itself an obscure excess. It taps into a wide spectrum of sensitive areas in the southern mind, but in spite of its awkwardness and the challenge it posed to the social divides in the segregated South, it was tolerated. The anxiety it evoked stemmed not only from the occupation of the same space (under the Jim Crow system, African American nurses were permitted in segregated areas) but also from the visceral dependence of the white infant upon the nourishment of the nonwhite body that was the subject of contestation. This awkwardness was mixed with the ease with which the "mammy" was able to nourish the baby. Again, the psychoanalyst in Smith goes on a rampage of observation, pointing out all of the awkward emotions experienced by the child as it is gradually submerged in the racist culture.

In the case of all three of the ghosts that haunt the South, the issue of race is pivotal. Without it, and without the excessive attention attached to it and the complicated code of conduct it involved, there would be no space to create so many diverse levels of sexual, social, and behavioral tension. The lingering power of the three ghosts is perhaps the most pervasive aftermath of the hyperbolic shock. Smith was speaking out of her own experience, but her observations take on the shape of the generation's voice. Also, as a heuristic method, the concept of the "three ghosts" may seem problematic, due to its Freudian and poetic character, but it nonetheless has a potency that can inspire other fruitful insights.[2]

At the beginning of the book, Smith evokes the episode that perhaps most vividly revealed to her the paradoxical constructs of racial prejudice and triggered the violent, hyperbolic explosion of the mounting contrasts. Smith recalls that the event long remained hidden in her memory, and it was only after some years that she realized its significance for the "opening doors" of her mind, as she puts it. This is yet another macrotrope through which Smith examines her own body and its figurative strength, which allows her to renegotiate her language. To Hinrichsen, Smith's use of open and closed corporeal imagery "points to the body as a site upon which white communal southern identity perpetuated itself" (113), and it is through various tropes of walls, closed doors, and enclosed spaces that the segregated mind of the South sought to achieve rigidity and conformity.

The metaphors Smith uses at this point are less violent than "cutting the umbilical cord," but the notion of crossing a threshold and moving between spaces is in itself vital for the episode that triggered the hyperbolic shock. A white girl was spotted in a dilapidated shack in a black neighborhood, and a group of white clubwomen, suspecting that she probably had been kidnapped, decided to intervene and ask the town marshal to take her to the white community where, they thought, she belonged. It is hardly surprising that they miss the ironic relativism of what they are doing—that is, abducting a child without any prior background checks, after having accused others of kidnapping. The girl, Janie, was taken to Smiths' home to live with them and to occupy the same space as young Lillian, where they played together, dined together, and shared household space, meals, and toys. However, the family soon discovered that the girl was in fact "colored," and she was made to leave the home and move back into the segregated area. What is most dramatic is the mother's attempt to explain the situation to her child and to answer the narrator's pivotal question: "Why is she leaving?"

> "Because," Mother said gently, "Janie is a little colored girl."
> "But she's white!"
> "We were mistaken. She is colored."
> "But she looks—"
> "She is colored. Please, don't argue."
> "What does it mean?" [. . .]

"It means," Mother said slowly, "that she has to live in Colored Town with colored people."

"But why? She lived here three weeks and she doesn't belong to them, she told me so."

"She is a little colored girl."

Finally, the narrator declares hopelessly, "I don't understand," which is echoed by her younger sister: "I don't understand either." In response, their mother says, "You're too young to understand. And don't ask me again, ever again, about this!" (36–37).

This conversation needs to be quoted in its entirety if the true drama of the event is to be understood. The exchange is like a grotesque ping-pong match and represents a fundamental failure of communication. As such, the episode unmasks the faulty logic of the southern system of segregation, in which the steel-rigid categories that regulate the principles of daily life cannot actually contain or effectively describe reality, leaving the parental guardians of the system at a loss for words and arguments when confronted with natural curiosity of a child who demands an explanation. The child has not been yet subjugated by the metaphors of southern segregationist rhetoric, has not yet appropriated the figurative framework of the racial divide, and has not fully embraced the extensive connotative package of the words "black" and "white," and thus she inquires, demanding to know the rationale behind the decision. The parents are unable to respond, for the language they would use in the reply is so disjunctive that their children would not be able to take the answer in. Their answer—"No because no"—constitutes a logical paradox and is a white flag to explication. The parents fail as spokespeople of the South because the explanation of Jim Crow can only be done in Jim Crow language, with the employment of appropriate figures that can only be understood by someone who has internalized the hyperbolized mind-set and is immune to the shock of the southern paradox.

If the excessive nature of their answer is to be comprehended, the mind—in the words of Smith—has to already be "split" in two, it has to operate on the level of acceptance of excessive disjunction to fully grasp why a child who is "white" actually "isn't" white. The split of the mind that Smith evokes reminds one of how Derrida characterized the divides inherent in a language of racism, quoted earlier. In this sense, to counter these divides, the mind of the South inevitably has to be metafiguratively hyperbolic.

The semantics of the word "white" thus has little to do with skin color and physicality—it belongs more to the semiotics of ghosts. Janie's physicality resists categorization and thus causes a disturbance in the boxed world of cultural imagery. It does not conform. The artificiality of this normative division becomes fully exposed upon the revelation of her racial background, and is even made ridiculous in the eyes of the advocates of the system. The narrator's father laughs loudly, having learned that the girl they took in is in fact "colored." At this point, the hyperbole breaches the border of ridicule and causes the father's amusement at the sheer absurdity of the situation, at them having been misguided, and at how feeble and subjective their categories of recognition turn out to be. The situation exposes the fabrication of the community's mind-set, and even a custodian of the segregated status quo notices the irony of the situation. What makes him laugh, however, also augurs Janie's tragedy.

The ousted girl is taken from one district to another, and from one family to another. Accompanied by Janie's powerless cries, her transportation represents the shifting between racial categories, which are not just abstract concepts of the southern society but also physical areas of the town through which her "unfitting" body is ferried. And it is being moved as an object rather than a subject—a fragment of reality that has to be forced out to a place specified by the paradoxical southern decorum.

As a simultaneously white and nonwhite "body," Jamie undermines the normative, hyperbolic principles of the Smiths' household and challenges the norm. Thus, the shock of her eviction and the paradoxical conversation sets off the hyperbolic by pushing the contrasting categories to the point of breakage. On the metanarrative level, the fundamental conflicts driving the thinking and the language of Smith's childhood South become exposed. Little wonder that Janie becomes a taboo topic that must never again be mentioned. And what Smith does after the girl's banishment is to "kill" her memory—Janie is forgotten as an image that disrupts the seemingly consistent jigsaw puzzle of the southern mind-set.

While inspecting her past and the metamorphosis she underwent, Smith makes use of a variety of different genres and shifts among different vocal perspectives. In the book, one can find a parable, an account of an allegorical play, or reflections characteristic of an academic sociological study. In her search for a renewal of identity, Smith also tries on different speaking personas—such as when she recreates the voice of her confused young self, in the scene discussed above, repeatedly asking the perennial question *Why?* In the narrative, her mature self is constantly judging the damage done to her by the restrictive system of the South and allowing the contrasts to be highlighted. But Smith can also put on the hateful mask of white supremacy and evoke the voice of the "invisible authority": "Your skin is your glory and the source of your strength and pride. It is white. [. . .] Remember this: your white skin proves that you are better than all other people on this earth" (87).

The transitions among these voices are often done neatly, but at the same time, the consecutive roles the narrator assumes make more and more mental space for her to complete the transition from the object subjected to cultural imperatives to a conscious subject with her own voice. In the case of the persona just quoted, Smith purposefully highlights the figures of the system, stripping them of all their innuendoes and presences to expose the naked bones of the white supremacists' logic. Rhetorically, the voice of white supremacy is shocking in its unabashed appraisal of the privilege bestowed upon her by her white skin—it presents the monolith of decorous language against which the anxious question "But why?," asked by the childhood narrator, becomes an act of confused desperation.

Beyond all these intertextual strategies, Jamie pervades in the narrator's memory as a ghost, and she resurfaces decades later, allowing for an acute critical judgment of the artificial reality of southern prejudice—not unlike Miranda in Katherine Anne Porter's "The Grave," discussed in chapter 2, who experiences a flashback of her childhood trauma as a grown-up. Thus, it takes years for the shock and violence to be transformed into a new understanding, for the new meaning to be generated out of the excessive breakage. But immediately after the episode, after Jamie is rendered taboo and cast out, the narrator confesses to having forgotten her. The girl herself has no voice; she is mute in the figurative turmoil that she involuntarily evokes in the minds of the participants of this drama. She cannot voice her preference to stay with the family in the "colored" district of the town or to remain with the Smiths in the "white" district. Her powerless returning to the point from which she left is in itself symbolic, for it closes a vicious circle, emblematic of the helplessness her situation. Effectively, therefore, she is bound to remain like a ghost, haunting the author's memory.

As the startling episode with Jamie pushes the southern paradoxes to the state of overdrive, it allows for the hyperbolic metalogic to come to fruition. Through most of *Killers of the Dream*, Smith illustrates the violence behind the "intellectual deafness" and the suppression of the conflict between southern racial decorum and the natural impulses of both the body and the mind. All these antagonisms, whose linguistic, psychological, and cultural aspects she delves into, culminate in the violent confusion accompanying Jamie's removal from her family house. And it is through this shock and the state of emotional overdrive that the metahyperbolic move becomes complete and leads the narrator to a fuller understanding of the South.

Thus, the drama of *Killers of the Dream* comes forth as a drama of language—of voicelessness, on the one hand, and of revocalization, on the other hand. Here, the emergence of the new linguistic "self" is the ultimate outcome of the hyperbolic. And, for readers, it forms a metanarrative process that allows for the full understanding of the traumatizing racial prerogatives of Dixie.

The Twilight Zone

In *The Making of a Southerner,* Katharine Du Pre Lumpkin casts a glance at the history of the South through the history of her family, which is of respectable Georgian stock with a rich plantation past, and recounts how she was brought up in an atmosphere permeated with nostalgia and the glorification of southern ways. The diachronic perspective assumed in her memoir allows her to trace the evolution of the southern mind-set and to understand the roots of its racial prerogatives. What becomes visible in such a representation is the unfolding process of excessive cultural internalization and the formation of a selective approach to history, verging on blatant fabrication.

The grotesque character of her father, William, a Civil War veteran, who epitomized the South and who went through all the stages of the "making of a southerner," helps us to understand the indiscriminate mind of Dixie, which, according to Lumpkin, "lived evasions and manufactured realizations" (214) and was characterized by a specific, selective mind-set. As an ardent follower of the Old South myth, Katharine's father wanted to pass that mythologized proclivity on to his children, and likewise intended them to undergo the process of the making of a southerner. The title of the book itself is overt in its emphasis on the very process of generating another citizen of the Dixie and on the mental "state of becoming."

Curiously, William's influence impacted not only Katharine but also her two sisters, Grace and Elizabeth, who tarried with the ghosts of the South throughout their whole lives, each of them in her own way. Grace turned to writing and produced a number of proletarian novels that dramatized the reality of the Great Depression, of which *To Take My Bread* (1932) is perhaps best known. Unlike her two sisters, Elizabeth did not wander from the principles of her upbringing, and throughout her life she remained a devotee to the cult of the Lost Cause and a notable speaker at the Confederate veterans reunions.

What Lumpkin explores through her memoir is not the emergence of a new voice, as is the case with Lillian Smith, but an attempt to look beyond the mythologized family narrative. The hyperbolic in *The Making of a Southerner* is the outcome of the mounting tension between the narrative of the Lost Cause and the facts of everyday life in Dixie at the beginning of the twentieth century. Lumpkin's voice falls short of a full emancipation from the mythological catechism, and for all her efforts, it remains entangled in the conflicted network of prescriptive habits and practices that "made" her a southerner. Nonetheless, the outcome of the hyperbolic mode in her book is a partial discovery of other Souths beyond the one she was immersed in, and of the ability to question ideas that were set down in family tradition as axiomatic. Thus, my discussion here will focus on the rhetorical mechanisms that allowed for the formation of the "tropological space" of the mythological South and on the metahyperbolic revision the narrator of *The Making of a Southerner* is forced to exercise in order to go beyond the myth.

The opening pages of the book feature an account of the plantation life of the past and its prescribed ways. Here, Lumpkin presents the foundations of what later becomes the family decorum. She elaborates on how the family house was run and on the way her patriarchal grandfather managed his thirty-seven slaves. In her story, the African Americans were notoriously dehumanized by the metaphors of commerce used to describe them as a commodity and by having labels with prices put on them. Her grandfather ruled the slaves with an iron fist and was careful to prevent any context in which they could express their grievances. At this point in her narrative, Lumpkin does not really judge the daily practices of plantation life, even when presenting her readers with its murky brutality. She seems almost nostalgic about the strength and authority of her grandfather, whitewashing and justifying his actions, to the extent that, in the words of Lisa Hinrichsen, her readers may find themselves "seduce[d] into the position of mastery" (106).

Through the machinations of the southern mind, both the slave market and the horror of human bondage are relegated to the "twilight zone" of

Lumpkin's childhood memory (*Making of a Southerner* 15). This limbo-like sector of her mind is the realm of murky ambivalence and anxious taboos, not much different from the space occupied by Smith's four ghosts of the South and ruled by intellectual deafness. Here in the twilight zone, unilluminated and morally dubious contradictions and paradoxes can lie unchallenged, and thus this figurative space nurtures what was described in previous chapters as the fundamental ambivalence of the southern mind. Only the violent power of the hyperbolic shock may allow one to move beyond the parameters of the twilight zone safeguarded by the sense of regional belonging, family loyalty, and sheer force of habit.

This mental dismissal in the opening parts of the narrative is reinforced by the symbolism of what later became of the former slave market in Charleston. In the very place where humans were trafficked, the narrator later finds a candy shop and a museum of slavery. The grotesque nature of the transformation of the former slave market into a biased historical exhibit, the whitewashing of the theater of suffering, is revealed when the custodian ensures the narrator that the museum shows nothing grisly or disturbing and boasts that it has only "pleasant things" on display (15).

Claudia Claridge, in her comments on the rhetorical aspects of hyperbole, stresses that it "can help to evoke an extraordinary environment and an atmosphere that sets the world described or created apart in some ways from other worlds" (253). This ability is the figurative genesis of the Old South of the Lost Cause that Lumpkin presents. She demonstrates how, through the use of hyperbolic troping, the territory of the Old South becomes a tropological space of hyperbole, yet another twilight zone, but this time not individual but communal. The term "tropological space" is adopted here from Michel Foucault's study on figuration (126) and is used to signify an artistic space of logical appropriation that is summoned into existence by the collective imagination. This fictive, supra-individual possible world can become a mythological space of hyperbolic repression and excessive exaggeration.

In his study of metaphorical figuration, Paul Ricoeur postulates that, in poetry, "speculative thought [. . .] bases its work upon the dynamism of metaphorical utterance, which it constitutes according to its own sphere of meaning. [. . .] The splitting of reference and redescription of reality submitted to the imaginative variations of fiction strike us as specific figures of distanciation, when they are reflected and rearticulated by speculative discourse" (*Rule of Metaphor* 370–371). The grotesquely paradoxical "pleasant" museum of slavery, saturated in the Lost Cause mythology, is such a tropological space, in which the painful is hidden to preclude the space for any speculative or unruly thought that is heretical to the collectively embraced social belief.

It was a brutal beating of an African American cook that forced Lumpkin's mind out of the twilight zone. The episode is one of the catalysts of the hyperbolic in the narrative, and it revealed to her the extent to which the gentle nature of the southern myth is a mere illusion. In the account, what comes to the forefront is the unabashed violence manifested by the "master of the house" (there is hardly any doubt, of course, that it was her father, William, who committed the act), who, irritated by the cook's "impudence," hit her repeatedly with a stick. The anaphoric sentences that the narrator of *The Making of a Southerner* uses to describe the event stress how the witnessing of the violent act provided her with an insight to something she should not have seen: "I could see her writhing under the blows of a descending stick [. . .] I could see her face distorted with fear and agony and his with stern rage. I could see her twisting and turning as she tried to free herself from his grasp. I could hear her screams" (132).

Terror-stricken, she saw the beating as a disturbance of the household's stability and the proportions of the body, proving how thin is the line between cordial, everyday reality and disruptive, disharmonious violence. The shock of the violent outburst has a revelatory function, as Darlene O'Dell explains: "In Lumpkin's childhood eyes, William Lumpkin is no longer father; he is the white master"; consequently, the narrator herself becomes a "child inheriting traditions," and in order to cope with the treacherous nature of the collective white memory, she has to learn how to forget, to initiate the twilight zone amnesia (65).

The shocking revelation of the brutality hidden so close under the sugarcoated surface of everyday life was too much for the narrator to bear. The hyperbolic clash turned out to be so powerful that it caused physiological symptoms—which is also the case for the grown-up Jean Louise in *Go Set a Watchman,* who comes to understand Atticus Finch's racist views. Lumpkin saw her father's potency for brutality fully manifest and, unable to come to terms with what she witnessed, she covered her ears and crept away on "trembling legs." Later, the episode makes her much more observant of the issues of race and comes to delineate for her the crux of whiteness. Since the difference between being or not being a victim and having or not having one's body "twisted" in an act of violence boiled down to one's skin color, it was a sheer instinctive impulse to pay constant attention to the social regulatory mechanisms of racial identity. But what the episode also did was to initiate the revisionist process that allows her to break out of the hyperbole of the Lost Cause.

Having been "uprooted" from Georgia with his family, Katharine's father looked at the post-Reconstruction South with an unhealthy amalgam of concern, indignation, and disappointment. Everywhere he saw "scal-wags" and "nigger-lovers" preying "like harpies on prostate country" (Lumpkin 87). He was particularly disturbed by the changing interracial relations and the changing status of African Americans. Sporadic episodes signaled a gradual shift, as when a white teacher in Greensboro held an umbrella over an African American woman, causing a social uproar. William responded to the crumbling of the "old order" by turning his eyes back to the past vision of the plantation reality and by engaging himself in the activities of the Ku Klux Klan. And his desperate detachment, as well a persistent refusal to embrace the surrounding reality, creates the foundation of the Lost Cause cult in the Lumpkin family.

The Lost Cause was a congruent social and political agenda.[3] First introduced in Edward A. Pollard's *The Lost Cause,* published as early as 1866, the fantasy of the Lost Cause was promptly popularized by such writers as Thomas Nelson Page, whose *Red Rock* (1898) absolved the participants of any lynching from guilt and responsibility—all within the paradigm of the myth. Politically, it stemmed from the nurtured and crafted public memory of the Confederacy, which shielded the wartime efforts of ex-Confederate veterans from criticism and put their deeds in a more positive and constructive context. It represented the South as morally and culturally superior to the North, plantation life as glamorous, the bitter and ignominious defeat in the Civil War as an actual triumph of a superior civilization, and the institution of slavery as benign or even benevolent. The goals behind the formation of the mythology were diverse. It was crafted to elevate morale and to justify the past decision to secede from the Union, to make sense of the humiliating defeat and the devastation of the southern landscape by General Sherman's "bummers," and to reassure southerners that their motherland would "rise again."

Obviously, the implications of the myth reached far beyond the memoirs of veterans and the galvanizing speeches delivered at their reunions. Through books, articles, and political rallies, the Lost Cause enjoyed a broad cultural circulation and came to impact the management of public space and the functioning of many cultural institutions. The erection of commemorative monuments, like the war memorial at Stone Mountain in Georgia, the presence of Confederate flags waved at all public occasions, and the echoing "Dixie" at public festivities—all of that had a strong foundation in the Lost Cause, drew inspiration from the myth, but at the same time perpetuated it. And with the writings of such historians as Ulrich B. Phillips, the idea gained an aura of scholarly credibility. In *The Making of a Southerner*, Lumpkin explores the social-political context of the myth and deconstructs it at the same time, proving that, in the words of Jacquelyn Dowd Hall, in the South "disfranchisement, segregation, and the battle for memory went hand in hand" (448).

The Lost Cause martyrology secured the perimeter for white supremacy, but at the price of closing the southern mind against an overwhelming abundance of pressing facts. This one-sidedness was hyperbolic in nature, governed by the excessive emphasis on the myth of the South and its martyrology. The hyperbole of the Lost Cause was amalgamative, consisting of numerous components. In his pioneering study of the subject, published more than four decades ago, Rollin Osterweis enumerates the most vital, romanticized constituents of the myth, like the chivalric planter; the magnolia-scented southern belle; the good, gray Confederate veteran; and, last but not least, the obliging old Uncle Remus (ix). Each element of this kaleidoscopic vision was exaggerated in its own way, having one feature, such as chivalry or obedience, blown out of proportion.

In some ways, the excessive emphasis worked here in a manner not dissimilar to the mode of satire, except that, when one was locked in the protective cocoon of the myth, one did not see the constituents of the Lost Cause as excessive and potentially bordering on ridiculous. In fact, one did not seem to see anything else. In the nostalgic vision of the South, the planter was stripped of all his faults and shortcomings and coated in nobility reminiscent of a medieval knight. Slaves were grotesquely joyful and obedient, with an implausibly distorted hierarchy of values, placing dedication to the master over their own freedom. All these hyperbolical, one-sided "types" of the Lost Cause were interlocking and increased one another's appeal.

The conundrum behind the Lost Cause relied on the tensions it generated between the imaginary, one-sided vision of the South and the complex reality of everyday life. The prosaic world of the larger part of the struggling population little resembled the fabricated, polarized vision of nostalgic plantation reality. Thus, living in the narrative of the Lost Cause required a highly selective approach to reality, admitting from the surroundings only those stimuli that matched the imposed vision, and systematically avoiding acknowledgment of all potentially incongruent and thus corrosive elements. The mind of the Lost Cause devotee was particularly attuned and trained to internalize only the elements that fit the decorum of the myth.

Catechized in the gospel of the Old South, the family in *The Making of a Southerner* internalized the monolithic and unchangeable view of the southern past as an article of faith. The individual cases that proved the general excessive image wrong were dismissed exactly because they proved the axiomatic image wrong. The narrator provides one example: no matter how many honest African Americans there were, in the language of the white supremacy, "as a race" they remained thieves (135). The mental process captured by Lumpkin in the text consists precisely of an attempt (whether ultimately successful or not) to shed this selective mind-set and to acknowledge reality with all its complexities and variations.

Language was the adhesive for the construction of the myth, and the narrator recollects that the Lost Cause brought with it a new vocabulary to describe the evocation of the ideological decorum. Appomattox was always a "disaster" to the South, never a "defeat." All the southern endeavors were aimed at keeping "blacks in their place"—a phrase that returns in *The Making of a Southerner* like mantra whenever the narrator assumes the voice of white supremacy. Just as in Lillian Smith's *Killers of the Dream,* the quotation marks stress that it is an appropriation from the language of white supremacy, which the narrator seeks to renounce. In addition, the grammar of that voice mirrors the binary logic of opposition, of thinking in terms of either/or. The exclusive conjunctions emphasis that the South was at the crossroads of either "white supremacy" or "black domination" (128). And whenever the surrounding reality could not be forced into these dichotomous categories of grammar and logic, when the facts of life poured through the mythologized scenario of the Lost Cause like water through a sieve, tensions and violence erupted.

The ghost of the Lost Cause kept haunting William Lumpkin's life as he jettisoned the changing reality for the sake of a perpetual evocation of the past, inadvertently turning himself into a grotesque. Having anchored himself in the sentiment, he increased the contrast between the nostalgia for the old life and the world around him. The unrealistic and preposterous attempts at the reanimation of plantation life drove him to the purchase of a farm—an estate his family had no clue how to run after his sudden death. Little does the narrator mourn her father's parting, focusing more on how his attachment trapped them in a financial gridlock from which they could not liberate themselves, and how the emancipation from his influence opened her mind to alternative thoughts. What came next was the acknowledgment of the fact that there were aspects of the South that went beyond the Lost Cause mythology.

Looking beyond the Lost Cause was also hard for the narrator because the South claimed it held the copyright on its vocabulary. As W. Scott Poole argues, the Lost Cause "provided white southerners with much more than a prop for flagging self-esteem"—it had a grammar of its own, which served as a vehicle for the patriarchal and racial southern conservative ethos (598). As the emblem of southern culture, this charged language was not only indispensable but also inalienable to the southern mind, and as such, it could not be employed by anyone from outside the mythologized narrative.

When studying in New England, for example, the narrator of Lumpkin's book felt offended by northerners' attempt at its mimicry, even for the sake of a seemingly innocent phatic exchange. "They aped our Southern ways, took over our terminology bodily, saying 'darkey,' and even 'nigger.' To my scorn, some said 'coon,' a term we never used" (202). The vocabulary of the South belonged to the South, and could not be successfully appropriated by anyone from the outside. The use of the plural pronoun here testifies to the collective ownership of this vocabulary as an element of cultural heritage and to the desire to protect the southern way from any foreign appropriation.

In the course of the narrator's life, it is mainly under the pressure of "incongruences" that the protective cocoon of the Lost Cause begins to disintegrate. When her northern acquaintances provide her with facts about the plight of African Americans in the South, for instance, she feels the protective power of the romanticized myth dissolve under the pressure of their data-driven arguments, despite all the eristic training she had received as a child, when her father commissioned her to partake in mock debates defending the "old order." Rhetorical pathos, an appeal to emotions, was giving way to Logos, an appeal to reason. Breaking with the hyperbolized image of plantation life meant acknowledging the existence of an alternative to the "old dogma, that but one way was Southern, and hence there could be but one kind of Southerner" (235). The only way for her was to open herself to different "Souths," as the myths kept gradually crumbling down.

At Sand Hill, where the Lumpkin family moved in William's last attempt to reanimate plantation life, it came as a surprise to her that the African American workers were in fact somber figures who labored in silence and not Uncle Remuses singing merry songs and fulfilling their duties with joyful dedication.

At Sand Hill, she also learned about the conditions in the poor rural South and about the millions of southerners who had never owned slaves, proving that there were indeed aspects of Dixie that did not center on plantation life, and that overwhelmingly large numbers of the population cared more about their present financial predicaments than about the evocation of the plantation ways. Such episodes gradually revealed the excessive, monolithic myth for what it was and exposed the excessive one-sidedness of the decorum it propagated.

The final stage of the narrator's process of the "unmaking of a southerner" takes place when she reclaims her critical reasoning and independent voice to such an extent that she is able to reexamine the family history and household anecdotes. For instance, in the Lumpkin family narrative, Jerry, her grandfather's foreman, was given everyone's condescending approval for his memory skills; having been read passages from the Bible, he would memorize them quickly and recite them with impressive ease. This patronizing applause from the family members made for an eagerly repeated anecdote.

Having established herself as a new southerner, and having learned to look beyond the set narratives, the narrator embarks on a revisionist mission and reinterprets this anecdote, realizing that, most probably, Jerry's illiteracy was just a sham and that he simply read the passages he had allegedly memorized in the blink of an eye. She stipulates that he deemed it necessary to conceal his skill, playing the game of subordination and fitting into the Lost Cause stereotype of a childlike grown-up devoid of any skills that could threaten his superiors. Through this realization, the narrator is able to pierce the veil of the mythologized plantation narrative, and she learns how to subvert and reinterpret the facts of the past, which had been handed down in family tradition as axioms.

Thus, she starts to give the family myths a reality check and, having established their excessive and fabricated nature, she moves on to deconstruct them, struggling to cleanse her voice of the deeply embedded grammar of the Lost Cause—though not always succeeding. In the words of Lisa Hinrichsen, Lumpkin's "prose reveals her affective indebtedness to her disavowed inheritance" (101). Having managed to push aside the veil of southernness, she nonetheless remained bound to its nostalgic magnetism. To borrow Smith's metaphor, Lumpkin could not entirely sever the umbilical cord.

In *Reconstructing Dixie*, Tara McPherson places Lumpkin's book in the context of Margaret Mitchell's *Gone with the Wind*. Separated by a mere decade, both texts concern the same hyperbolic and mythologized take on the southern past. Lumpkin's narrative is much more ingenious in her treatment of the Lost Cause and the use of what McPherson calls "strategic southernness," the reworking of southern truths through their initial acceptance. In effect, "Lumpkin doesn't freeze the origin of southernness behind the white columns of Tara, but neither does she give up on the region" (243–244). Such a heuristic method makes her approach much less radical than Lillian Smith's in *Killers of a Dream,* and although both autobiographies drive the nail deep into the southern mind-set, their struggles with southern ghosts and myths are driven by different rhetorical weapons.

Thus, in her book, Lumpkin crafts a narrative in which the South does not function merely as the realm of nostalgic dreams, nor is it just a lugubrious theater of horror and abuse. *The Making of a Southerner* is about the constructive regaining of the present moment and the ultimate conjoining of both personal memory and a family history. At the same time, there is little violent resentment, of which one can find many traces in Smith's autobiography. Lumpkin grows out of the southern hyperboles as one grows out of tattered old garments, and she does not seem to try to sever her "umbilical cord" with a linguistic scalpel. In this sense, one can sense in her a systematic sociological researcher. Moreover, racial inequality and partisan social economics concern her much more than the topic of repressed sexuality, a fact that is immediately visible when one sets the two books alongside one another.

At the same time, Lumpkin's dramatization positions her emerging "I" of the narrative against the opposition of the "we" that is a mythical construct and that partly dies with her father. Her goal is to deconstruct the hyperbole of a fabricated, nostalgic realm, to demystify the excessive principles that govern the southern perception of the past and to point out other Souths beyond the myth.

Both of these authors, in spite of their relatively advantaged status in the haunted world they describe, portray the mental scars and emotional injuries as inalienable to a regional belonging and as endemically characteristic of having been brought up in Dixie. The rhetoric of both books limns a palimpsest of past pain and moribund victimhood. And, whether it is a repressive "ghost" or an oppressive "myth," they both manage to cast off southern decorum by breaking it with the violent strength of hyperbolic metalogic.

5
HYPERBOLIC DISSOLUTION
Tennessee Williams

In his foreword to Carson McCullers's second novel, *Reflections in a Golden Eye*, Tennessee Williams discusses the gothic tradition of the American South. He stipulates that there is "something in the blood and culture" of the region that has triggered both an "emotional" interest in the "morbid" side of human nature and a sense of "dreadfulness in modern experience" (*New Selected Essays* 48–49). A number of Williams's early texts flirt with this kind of aesthetic and evince the hyperbolic metalogic that is put under scrutiny in this book; this is also true of their "plastic" dramatic design. Williams's interest in "morbid," repressed desires, mixed with a semiautobiographical framework, allowed him to render the wounded and broken world interred in his texts particularly haunting. By debunking prescriptive social conventions and scandalizing cultural opposites, the playwright manages to come up with rules of artistic engagement that mesmerize, shock, and puzzle.

In this chapter, I seek to study the hyperbolic metalogic in Williams's four early plays by exploring how different southern belles, trademark characters of his drama, collapse under hyperbolic tensions and how their forced evictions to mental institutions come to represent the destructive effect of excess. Williams's hyperbolic is thus a detrimental force—it testifies to the ruinous effect of the repressive decorum and completely consumes his female characters. Since, through its violent metalogic, the playwright recreates the drama of what happened to his sister, Rose, this chapter opens with a discussion of Rose as a haunting motif in his oeuvre. Next, departing from Williams's problematic relationship with Rose and her struggle with mental illness, I will look into the metaphoric disparity between John Buchanan and Alma Winemiller in *Summer and Smoke* to show how the playwright designs the metafigurative framework of his drama, preparing the way for the hyperbolic clash. Finally,

I will discuss three cases of female characters who are removed to institutions due to their advancing mental disarray: Bertha from *Hello from Bertha*, Miss Collins from *Portrait of a Madonna*, and, the most famous of them all, Blanche DuBois from *A Streetcar Named Desire*.

One can hardly dissever Williams's embattled fiction from his embattled life. The playwright himself was well aware of that synergy, and in his *Memoirs* he asked his readers provocatively, "Shall I attempt to entertain you, now, with my theatre or my life, assuming that there is much difference between them?" (108). The tale of Williams's life has been told a number of times, and there are hardly any stones left unturned there, especially after the publication of Lyle Leverich's landmark *Tom: The Unknown Tennessee Williams*, complemented recently by John Lahr's *Tennessee Williams: Mad Pilgrimage of the Flesh*. Also, a number of adjacent, focalized studies, like John Bak's biography of Williams as an artist, *Tennessee Williams: A Literary Life*, uncover the diverse minutiae of the playwright's life. The overall image that emerges from all these publications is of a deeply wounded mind. He grew up in a household scarred by the mismatched marriage of his parents, in which the puritanical inclinations of Edwina Williams to chastise her children and the upfront belligerence of the hard-drinking and womanizing Cornelius Williams generated vitriolic frictions. Such a tense environment strongly affected both the future playwright and his sister, Rose, and each of the siblings suffered the repercussions of their upbringing in a different way.

Williams worked laboriously, if not obsessively, for professional success as a writer, revamping the American dramatic scene. A substantial part of his triumph may be attributed to his theatrical design, which he called "plastic" drama. Through the plastic formula, a creative use of nonverbal means of expression like lights or music, the playwright sought to replace the worn-out forms and practices of realistic theater with a "memory play," a mixture of expressionism, a neo-Romantic story, and symbolism inherited from Joris-Karl Huysmans and Villiers de l'Isle-Adam. The aim behind the formula, as Williams himself declared, was to "release the essential spirit of something," which required "a stripping down, a reduction to abstracts" (*New Selected Essays* 26). This plasticity was akin to the ambition of visual artists contemporary to Williams who sought to use nonrepresentational painting to turn their art toward the fundamentals of expression.

Moreover, the compendiary dramatic form used by Williams contributed to his success. In his early plays, the neo-Romantic, autobiographical scenario is framed in a lyric form resembling a short story, inspired more by Anton Chekhov than by the complex narrative formulas of the realistic drama derived from Henrik Ibsen or Seán O'Casey. This compactness allowed Williams to make better use of his unparalleled flair for dialogue, in which he combined sharp wit with the natural rhythms of southern speech, which he molds to escalate the tensions of his "fugitive" world.

The thematic frame of Williams's drama and fiction rests upon a recurring scenario of a destructive encounter between a faded belle and a virulent male—a conflict ostensibly reminiscent of the tragic spectacle he witnessed in his childhood home. The clash between the two often takes place against the background of the haunting drifter figure, whose lack of presence generates acute pain and the sense of unfulfillment. William repeats this scenario with a manic compulsivity, developing it in different contexts and exploring its expressive potential. Almost always, his southern belles' excessively old-fashioned manners and charm suggest a wishful longing for the antebellum life, which is dismantled by the masculine figure and proven to be a haunted fabrication. The playwright thus figuratively associates the female with a forlorn past and decay, while the masculine in his drama is allied with the invigorating present moment and presages a future fulfillment. The conflict between the painful present and the idealized past proliferates the clash between the tropes of animalistic promiscuity and repressed fastidiousness, and between carnal and the spiritual needs.

Caught in such a network of tensions, Amanda Wingfield from *The Glass Menagerie* constitutes the epitome of the Williamesque southern belle. The claustrophobic world of her apartment remains suspended between a world that has long since faded, a mythological space of prelapsarian happiness, and the present moment that is malignantly inconsumable. Amanda desperately seeks to mold her "here and now," to make it adhere to the imaginative past, and the dinner party she organizes for the gentleman caller is an exaggerated enactment of a script she has appropriated from a cavalier yesteryear. However, as she tries to reconcile the irreconcilable, her actions become disturbingly exorbitant.

In terms of theatrical conventions, the dinner party she organizes is reminiscent of a play within a play. When Amanda makes her entrance to greet Jim, skipping around the living room in an anachronistic dress of yellowed voile with blue silk, and starts a coquettish conversation, her excessive, theatrical mask conforms to the illusory conventions of a neo-Romantic pastoral romance. This enactment is not benign. It constitutes a "trap," as she overtly admits to Laura, to catch a beau for her daughter, but, at the same time, it pushes social convention to a desperate extreme. The harder she tries, the more she fails, and her grotesquely exaggerated endeavors spell the undoing of the entire family when the idealized dream collides with reality.

In Williams's world, there is no peaceful or constructive resolution to such excessive conflicts. The scenario of the belle's desperate encounter with brutal reality is enacted within the megahyperbole. The opposites push in conflicting directions, crossing the boundaries of decorum, and when they ultimately are forced to meet, their run-in turns out to be particularly violent. The moment the concrete and carnal collides with the illusory and feeble, they implode. The result of these disquieting confrontations is the shocking realization of human hopelessness, followed by the initiation of a slow, painful process of decay, which ultimately leads to the dissolution of the southern belle, who is doomed to be abandoned or evicted.

The arrangement of opposites plays an instrumental role in Williams's hyperbolic script, and his plays are always deeply saturated with contrasting binaries springing from the figurative juxtapositions of the flesh and the spirit. A number of critics have pointed out this tendency. Signi Falk argues that by setting these two elements together, Williams sought to confront the Victorian decorum of repression and obsessive propriety in the South (70–71). In the context of a restrictive culture bent on upholding propriety, carnal passion and intercourse remained, for Williams, "the only valid expression for life," and what followed is that the "opposite of passion is death" (76). Likewise, Alice Griffin's discussion of *Summer and Smoke* (81–103) focuses on how Alma awakens to her body against the background of the antagonistic coupling of the spirit and the flesh. More recently, Robert Siegel's study of Williams's "metaphysics" moves away from the dichotomous take on duality and suggests that body and soul in the playwright's world should not be viewed as an exclusive duo but as two sides of a "running dialogue" (111), which are not as segregated as they would seem.

Williams's theatrical conventions changed over the years, gradually moving away from the poetic and plastic productions for which he had gained an unrivaled reputation. The beginning of the 1960s brought a turnaround in his playwriting, and *The Night of the Iguana*, which premiered on Broadway in 1961, seems to be a caesura, marking the moment when Williams's writing transitioned to the theater of excess and the grotesque. This is also the beginning of Williams's "stoned age." Struggling with "blue devils" and creative blockages, Williams replaced strong coffee with increasing amounts of barbiturates and liquor, especially after the untimely death of his longtime partner, Frank Merlo, in 1963. His escalating addictions and mounting depression eventually forced his brother, Darkin, to put him in an asylum in 1969. The confinement, for which Williams never forgave Darkin, hardly helped him, and the whole decade that followed was stamped by the deterioration of Williams's public image as well as failed attempts to regain his old spark. Each new play he authored was considered a shameful blemish on the formerly illustrious career of an artist who had once competed with Eugene O'Neill for the laurel of America's foremost playwright.

In her recent study of Williams's drama, Annette Saddik postulates that these late plays are exemplary of a "theatre of excess," which seeks to achieve liberation through exaggeration, chaos, and laughter: "Williams' excesses serve to highlight the ambiguities and inconsistencies of living in and experiencing the world—the excesses that leak out of closed systems of meaning, that seep through the cracks of the rational, the stable, the complete, and point toward the essence of the real" (6). In his plays from the 1970s, Williams pushes the contrasts to such an extreme that the reader has only one available reaction to the overwhelming excess: to laugh. But it is not the kind of laughter associated with positive, constructive mirth; instead, it is a substitute for lamentation. Saddik takes this equivocal chuckle as quintessential of the ambivalence of Williams's late oeuvre. And if, in this transitory turbulence, there was one thing that Williams was not ambivalent about, it was his obsession with what happened to Rose.

On the very first page of his biography of Williams, Leverich points out that, throughout his life, the playwright "had two overriding devotions: his career as a writer and his sister, Rose" (1). Actually, there was hardly any distinction between these two commitments. Williams's oeuvre remains notoriously haunted by the memory of his sister, and the memory of his sister also served as a creative engine for his fiction. In the words of John Bak, she was both his muse and his "security blanket" (3). Williams's coalescing devotions not only took the most apparent form, as in the short story *Portrait of a Girl in Glass,* which later metamorphosed into *The Glass Menagerie,* but also figured in the themes of harrowing loss and in detached female characters, often southern belles, who, in desperate circumstances, are forcibly placed in a mental asylum or some sort of ominous hospital institution.

This theme remains central to how Williams portrays the culmination of the mounting anxieties and the violent resolution of the dualistic hyperbolic tensions with which his writings are so strongly saturated. In Williams's drama, especially in his early texts, which are most organically connected with the southern social landscape, the hyperbolic clash of contrasts leads to a violent confrontation that always consumes his despondent characters. At the end of Williams's hyperbolic shock, there is no constructive epiphany but only the dissolution of identity.

The study of Williams's obsession with his sister's progressing mental disease is particularly helpful for understanding the tensions to which the southern belles are subjected in his fiction. Some of the first serious symptoms of Rose's condition came in the form of physical distress, not long after her prospect of a relationship with a junior executive at the International Shoe Company came to naught. Williams's sister complained about abdominal pains, and when no one could determine the actual source of her discomfort (and as a reasonable alternative to an exploratory surgery), it was suggested that the pain might have a psychosomatic cause. This was not unheard of in Williams's family, as Edwina Williams came from a line stricken with hereditary mental problems. A mixture of afflicted genes and the mother's puritanical mentality may have acted as a catalyst for her daughter's malady.

Later on, Rose went through a number of breakdowns, and while, initially, her dementia praecox would subside after a few days of unrest and she would return to her quiet, regular self, her sanity was continually hanging by a thread. Gradually, as more and more obscure eccentricities appeared in her demeanor, including delusional conversations with the dead or keeping a bucket of water in front of her bedroom at night, she became so withdrawn that she had to be confined to Saint Vincent's Sanitarium, and then to the state asylum in Farmington, Missouri, in 1937.

The hospital was not new—it had started taking patients in 1903, when the new moniker "state asylum" replaced the previous overtly pejorative "asylum for the insane." According to Asylum Projects, the patient population at the Farmington institution was steadily growing at that time, reaching its peak in the mid-1950s with more than 1,800 convalescents. The hospital was far from congenial. The medical personnel induced high fevers in paretic patients by injecting them with malaria germs, and not long after Rose was admitted, the state asylum introduced both lobotomy treatments and electroshock therapies. Over three years, almost two hundred lobotomy operations were carried out as a means of helping patients with severe mental complications. Rose would rank among the patients subjected to such radical treatments. She received more than sixty electroconvulsive shock treatments as well as one of the first prefrontal lobotomies performed in America.

Prior to Rose's institutionalization, Williams had been drifting away from his sister for some time, and he later regretted that this estrangement had prevented him from noticing the symptoms of the dementia early enough to seek an effective remedy. To help himself process the guilt, Williams wrote two poems permeated with a sense of remorse and irreparable loss (*Notebooks* 82, note 137). In "Valediction," the speaker states, "She went with morning on her lips / down an inscrutable dark way," leaving those who "witnessed her eclipse" at a loss for words. The murky corridor that consumes the fading female figure stands in contrast to the memory of the departing sister, "who was always light of wit," while the speaker's timid speculations about what his sister could have thought and said stress her absence and show how she keeps haunting his memory.

Likewise, "Elegy for Rose" is permeated with the sense of tormenting loss, and the title itself suggests that the text can be construed as nothing short of a lamentation for the dead. With more elaborate imagery than "Valediction," the second poem identifies Rose with a "metal forged by love" that is so "volatile" and "fiery thin" that it may disintegrate, even in a gust of wind. With her substance lost, only Rose's "ghost" endures. This lingering spectral "shadow" constitutes a "rapture never quite / possessed again," a festering, painful wound that cannot be healed, regardless of how the speaker may try to alleviate the ache and "recapture" her "ghost" through writing, by weaving a "web of a song."

Visiting Rose in the hospital was painful for Williams. As he recalls, "Visited Rose at sanitarium—horrible, horrible! Her talk was so obscene—she laughed and spoke continual obscenities" (*Notebooks* 177). She frequently exhibited such excessive, sexual outbursts. While Williams managed to confront his sexual identity through his writing and his promiscuous lifestyle, Rose was given no such outlet and, under the influence of Edwina, had been forced to subdue her desires. The illness revealed all that was repressed. Yet, after being subjected to a prefrontal lobotomy in 1943, Rose lost all her vigor, and it became obvious that she had to be institutionalized for life.

The consent for the invasive procedure had been given by her parents. Williams, unaware of the plans for the operation, was away and did not participate in making the burdensome decision. In his memoirs, he dated the lobotomy six years before it actually happened—during 1937, when Rose was first hospitalized and when he himself was preparing to leave for Iowa to finish his undergraduate studies. Bak observes that "it was probably more convenient to ease a guilty conscience if he remembered having already left the family— and Rose—*after* the lobotomy was performed" (71). Later, with the inflow of money from the success of his plays on Broadway, Williams was able to provide Rose with private care, and he moved her to another institution, the Institute of Living in New England, and later to Stony Lodge in Ossining, New York. The fear that he might suffer a similar fate, along with the guilt-ridden memory of Rose, would haunt Williams for the rest of his life, just as the image of Laura haunted Williams's fictional alter ego, Tom, in *The Glass Menagerie.*

In Williams's drama, the sense of helplessness and loss at the thought of Rose's incarceration is accompanied by the sense of an overwhelming finality. In his *Memoirs,* the playwright recalls how he was once scolded by his sister for deriding the mentally incapacitated. "You must never make fun of insanity," Rose told him. "It's worse than death" (76). These words, recalled by Williams, could have been a mere common conversational emphasis, but they also could have yielded a more profound insight. In Rose's view, the loss of the capacity to think rationally truly constituted a fate worse than death, and Williams seems to embrace a similar idea in his works. In the playwright's conflicted world, insanity and forceful institutionalization continually translate into a state of nonliving that evokes the estrangement of death but lacks its finality. The amaranthine mental pain experienced by the alienated southern belles in his texts cannot be remedied, and as it escalates to the point of a hyperbolic embroilment, it consumes them completely.

The mental asylum, in the form of an obscure "strange place" or an ominous hospital, becomes for Williams a symbol denoting personal disintegration, alienation, and tragic unfulfillment. Also, as a motif, it is quintessential for the representation of tensions in his fiction and the representation of the tragic finale of the hyperbolic in his dramas. As the misaligned, faded, and writhing belles cling to their nostalgic obsessions and pose a threat to the fastidious decorum, they have to be extirpated and evicted by the ominous envoys of "normal" society. Because they cannot be reasoned with or counterpoised, they remain at the metafigurative collision point of the contrasting forces that govern Williams's world, and they become undone by the excessive pressure of these forces.

The hyperbolic conflict visible in the dramas studied here has its source in the belles' excessive fragility and in a desperate hunger for carnal and spiritual fulfillment that cannot be satisfied. Their insatiable longing and wounded desolation escalate to the point of breakage, at which point the broken-down belles are treated as pariahs and are ruthlessly expelled from the rational world. Their expulsion effectively spells for them a fate worse than death, since they are left to suffer, buried alive in a menacing space, an institution from which they cannot return and in which their fading will reach its nadir.

The swan song of Williams's fading belles, who are so tragically locked up between worlds and struggle to withstand the pressure of excess, is almost always nostalgic. The belles' desperate attempts to bid farewell to the world on their own terms, whether by writing a love letter to the departed, playing an old record on a gramophone, or taking the arm of a man they believe to be a kind gentleman-stranger, are poignant but useless. Hard as they try to retain their selfhood in this way, their forceful removal, emblematic of the violent nature of a hyperbolic clash, strips them of their subjectivity, and the visiting doctors or nurses effectively handle them as objects. In this climactic moment of their removal, Williams shows the uncontrollable power of excess, which he sees as the force undoing his sister and which he appropriates to abrogate his fictional fading belles.

Fire and Air

In *Summer and Smoke,* Williams's artistic design revolves typically around a broken heart and an unfulfilled carnal desire. Through a thwarted romance between Alma Winemiller and John Buchanan, set in Glorious Hill, Mississippi, the playwright clashes two divergent elements, the spirit and the flesh, and contemplates their fundamental incongruence. While *Portrait of a Madonna, Hello from Bertha,* or *A Streetcar Named Desire* portray the final act of hyperbolic dissolution of the self, in *Summer and Smoke,* Williams sets out to study the circumstances that lead to such a dramatic downfall. Thus, although Alma is not forcefully institutionalized at the end of the play, the drama presents her "tortures of the damned" (*Notebooks* 238) and augurs a path that inevitably leads to a hyperbolic dissolution of his other fading belles.

In the drama, two ill-matched lovers cannot bring their relationship to any kind of fruition. John Buchanan, the son of a doctor and a "Promethean figure" (*Theatre* 2: 132), indulges in carnal pleasures, while Alma, a timid southern damsel and the daughter of a preacher, embraces his courtship but rejects him when he proposes sex. In *Memoirs,* Williams views Alma as representative of a certain type: "[She] may very well be the best female portrait I have drawn in a play. She simply seemed to exist somewhere in my being and it was no effort to put her on paper" (109). As the play progresses, the tables of passion and repression turn for the two characters. Alma sheds her inaccessibility and declares that "the girl who said 'no'—she doesn't exist anymore, she died last summer" (*Theatre* 2: 243). Now it is John who assumes the stance of righteousness and rebuffs her open advances.

Throughout the play, John and Alma remain bound in this asynchronous cavort, taking turns at mutual attraction and rejection. Their stances are never harmonized, and the game they play is never the same. Consequently, as they respectively sway from one end of the spectrum to the other, they become estranged beyond remedy, and it is this estrangement that augurs the fall of Alma, who is doomed to become yet another withering southern lady in Williams's fugitive world. This turnaround at the center of the play is accompanied by a figurative reversal. The tropes of solidity and airiness, as well as of fire and cold, are captured in the figurative containers of Alma's and John's bodies. Thus, in *Summer and Smoke,* the figuration performs a fundamental metadramatic function.[1]

Williams could hardly be more explicit about the dualistic imagery of the play. In language terms, it rests almost exclusively upon the metaphors of airiness and material solidity, and these obviously connote the contrasting mindsets of Alma and John. The antagonistic micro- and macrofigures build up the disparate metalogic of hyperbole embedded in the entire text. The symbolic confrontation of the two elements commences as early as in the prologue of the play, when the two adolescent characters hold a flirtatious conversation by a water fountain adorned with a sculpture of an angel. The statue towering over their encounter is the quintessence of the paradoxical tensions that plague them later in the play. The celestial, beautiful, and evanescent being is obscurely encased in the cold and crude matter of stone, and the wings, which should elevate and ascend, instead remain motionless and heavy, foretelling Alma's foiled attempt to soar free and her ultimate fall.

The faded inscription at the base of the monument cannot be made out, and when Alma tells John to read it, she has to ask him to touch the bleached letters. Through this direct touch, a sensual experience he will not be allowed to partake of with Alma, John deciphers the word "Eternity," whose sound gives Alma cold shivers. This conventional turn falls within another macrofigurative domain of the play, the contrastive metaphors of temperature, which are scattered throughout the text. Alma will have notoriously cold hands, and she will often experience shivers, always internally craving John's carnal heat but never able to revel in it.

As the pair contemplates the central figure of the stone angel, Alma elaborates on how she understands eternity. "It's something that goes on and on when life and death and time and everything else is all through with," she says, offering John an emotionless vision of a void, of ethereal infinitude that transcends the carnal heat of passion of which he is the avatar. She also suggests here a direct bridge between this airy and exquisite concept and herself, stressing, "My name is Alma and Alma is Spanish for soul." It is hardly surprising that this definition incites John's opposition. He retorts by recalling the image of his dying mother, provocatively highlighting all the sordid details of her sickness: "Her face was all ugly and yellow and—terrible—bad-smelling!" (*Theatre* 2: 129–130). His carnal rhetoric, stressing the body and its functions, remains fundamentally at odds with Alma's quixotic observations, which are permeated with airy religiousness, to an extent that his words leave her flabbergasted. Likewise, his subsequent, successful attempt to kiss her and let her hair loose renders her "bewildered," and she seeks comfort in the cold embrace of the angelic statue.

This initial figurative clash escalates with time, as John and Alma, instead of moving toward each other in a romantic concurrence, gradually push away from each other. Alma performs as a singer and takes on a Philomeic nickname, "The Nightingale of the Delta," connotative of lightness and fragility. Delicate sound becomes her medium, and she is artistically associated with a voice transmitted through the very air that she embraces as her defining element. Williams also makes this figurative point clear in stage directions, stressing that "In Alma's voice and manner there is delicacy and elegance, a kind of 'airiness,' which is really natural to her as it is [. . .] to many Southern girls" (2: 139). While elegant and proper conversations remain Alma's preoccupation, John studies to be a doctor and makes significant discoveries in bacteriology. In contrast to Alma, reading the anatomy chart and peeking into what is hidden inside the human body becomes, for him, the defining preoccupation.

Alma is both impressed and enthralled by his perspective on life and its complexities, which is that of someone who "deal[s] with these mysteries under the microscope lens" (2: 142). However, the allure she feels does not allow her to recognize and comprehend the "demonic unrest" that consumes him. John is pushed to seek physical pleasures, driven by the "excess of his power [that] has not yet found a channel" (2: 132). Williams metaphorically presents John's inordinate preoccupation with the physical and the sensual as a shapeless, smokelike, accumulative energy that fills up the figurative container of his body and presses against it from the inside. The "excess" he experiences pushes him into increasingly erratic behavior, such as indulging in alcohol and engaging in casual relationships. By following this carnal calling, John breaks the rules of propriety, the decorum to which Alma adheres as a southern belle and a minister's daughter. She tries to encourage in him the behavior she would expect of a proper southern caller, and she meaningfully gives him a handkerchief to keep his face clean. Such a gift, however, cannot contain the fiery "devil" he holds inside. Alleviating the fractious tension and "indulging his senses" (2: 167) is the only way he can avoid the dissolution of the self and save himself from turning into a decayed grotesque.

Alma, on the other hand, chooses timid repression. When John mockingly diagnoses her as having a "doppelgänger" (2: 144), he makes a pivotal, ironic point about her repressed self. The macrofigurative metaphorical fire of carnal passion she has inside her is deeply concealed behind her cool appearance of a southern lady and her sense of duty to her father's Episcopal church. As she declares, "I have to be more selective than most girls about the—society I keep" (2: 153). Since her mother behaves like a callow, spoiled child, loudly demanding ice cream and mocking Alma's romantic life, Alma has to assume the social duties not only of a minister's daughter but also, effectively, of his wife. Unlike John, she has no channel to vent her energy, and she allows it to accumulate in the figurative container of her body.

When Alma reads aloud the poem "Love's Secret," by William Blake, during a reading group meeting, she unwittingly confirms John's diagnosis. The speaker in the poem manages to express her feelings to her beau, but this confession only leads to misery: "No sooner had he gone from me / Than a stranger passing by, / Silently, invisibly, / Took him with a sigh!" (2: 175). In Alma's case, the "stranger" who snatches the speaker's lover could be her doppelgänger, the hidden self of carnal passion, which has been repressed but which waits to take control of her body and to ignite her buoyant, ethereal camouflage of a "water lily" (2: 186), as she describes herself. The tensions between her two selves, and the ultimate symbolic victory of the body over the soul, only throws her further out of balance, as she herself admits to being consumed by a figurative internal fire and confesses to the death of her other, proper self, who rejected John's proposal of sex.

When Alma declares that the girl who shuns physical intimacy is no longer there, "suffocated in smoke from something on fire inside her" (2: 243), she employs the figurative language of solidity and the image of a body as a container, which earlier characterized John. The smoke that asphyxiated her previous, spiritual self came out of a fire that had been set up by John, the "Promethean figure" of the play (2: 132). This epithet, used by Williams in stage directions to describe John, refers to the mythological benefactor of mankind who stole fire from Mount Olympus and gave it to humans, against the will of Zeus, and was sentenced to suffer for his transgression, and it evokes the ideas both of carnal givenness and of carnal punishment.

The matter of flesh and the antimatter of the mind, in their excessive forms, cannot be blocked together, and their implosion poses a threat to the stability and safety of the self. As John confesses to Alma, "I am more afraid of your soul than you're afraid of my body" (2: 222). The figure of chiasmus he uses here binds the two characters, as well as the notions of the soul and the body, in a paradoxical arrangement, symbolically showing their exclusivity and setting the framework for the hyperbolic clash. On the metafigurative level, the chiastic structure itself is reminiscent of how Alma and John interchangeably become attracted to each other and reject each other, and of the constant incompatibility of their shifting views on the relationship between the body and the soul.

At the end of the play, Alma realizes how they have changed, and she recognizes that John has grown to see more in the interior of the human body than is suggested by his anatomy chart. As he explains, the diagram "shows that we're not a package of rose leaves, that every interior inch of us is taken up with something ugly and functional and no room seems to be left for anything else in there" (2: 244). The metaphoric vessel of the human body, for him, turns out to include also an "immaterial something," an ethereal and airy spirit that is essential for the elevation of the human body from the status of an "ugly machine." With a terrified reply—"You talk as if my body had ceased to exist for you" (2: 247)—Alma realizes that he is now blind to her liberated body and her liberated self, which she has just discovered. The unrepressed self and the body that is open, unconstrained, and sordid is no longer of interest to John, who chooses to engage in a stable and perdurable relationship with Nellie, Alma's former music student. The Nightingale of the Delta's lack of internal balance and overinflated spirituality deprive her of happiness. The only thing left for her is to follow John's initial path of "indulging the senses," by sleeping with random men and drinking excessively.

The two diametrically opposed transformations of *Summer and Smoke*— the metamorphosis of gambling and whoring Jack into a respectable doctor and a gentleman and the conversion of ladylike, proper Alma into a girl who "says yes" to traveling salesmen—demonstrate the volatility of human nature and the unassailable strength of repressed desires. In addition, the time frame of the two parts of the play, "A Summer" and "A Winter," revolves around the macrometaphors of contrasting temperature—during the hot spell, Alma's inner fire remains mysteriously dormant, whereas the cold season awakens it. Likewise, the festivities featured in both seasons, and in both parts of the play, reinforce the figurative imagery of desire. First comes Independence Day, when Jack and Alma meet again as adults against the background of a "pyrotechnical display" (2: 146), and then comes Christmas, when hope for their permanent union is thwarted and the exchange of gifts effectively translates into their parting.

Through all these figurative binaries and transitions, Williams demonstrates that the carnal and the spiritual may become entangled but that they do not merge. And this is exactly the reason why Jack and Alma fail in carrying out their romance. In *Summer and Smoke,* the new understanding that arises from the clash of binary opposites is that of Alma's inevitable misery, of the essential lack of congruence and disharmony. The end of the play, foretelling Alma's dissolution, is the reclamation of the body and the carnal that Alma suppressed, spelling her own inevitable unhappiness.

Dissolving Belles

Published in 1953, *Hello from Bertha* ranks among Williams's early Midwest plays. Like *Portrait of a Madonna*, the short drama, nascent as it may be in terms of plot, exemplifies the same figurative metalogic of hyperbole as Williams's mature endeavors, and his signature motifs of forlorn longing for love and a dramatic clash of opposites, coupled with a harrowing sense of hopelessness, find a full voice here. David Radavich observes that, in his Midwest plays, Williams sets his drama in an environment that is different from that of the Deep South. The playwright presents the Midwestern home as "neither hierarchical nor troubled by ancestral ghosts, but nestled firmly in its environment," but even so, he manages to infect it with typically southern tensions and to graft upon it the malaise of unrest that Williams would associate with New Orleans.

Hello from Bertha revolves around a dramatic wait for the inevitable. In a brothel in the "valley," the red-light district of Saint Louis, Bertha, a large, blonde prostitute, is lying in a bed, overcome with inertia, illness, and depression, presumably sensing her impending death. She hardly fits the idea of a southern belle in social terms, but the anxious air of decline surrounding her is exactly the same as that of Blanche and Miss Collins. The room in which she resides is permeated with Williams's typical sense of dilapidation, symptomatic of his use of contrastive excess. As the playwright points out in stage directions, "The wall-paper is grotesquely brilliant—covered with vivid magnified roses—and is torn and peeling in some places" (*27 Wagons* 183). The flamboyant wallpaper withers away, exactly as the seams of a stable world give way to the contrasting tensions Williams so eagerly brings forth in his plays to illustrate the painful discordance of the human condition. To dramatize this in this short play (as he did similarly in *Portrait of a Madonna* and *A Streetcar Named Desire*), the character of an unbalanced woman is pushed to the point of rupture, dissolving under the unbearable pressure of hyperbolic excess, and this dissolution takes place on a few simultaneous levels: the physical, the mental, the linguistic, and the social.

Unlike other plays discussed in this chapter, *Hello from Bertha* does not feature a southern belle. Instead, Bertha is a female hustler[2] who is haunted by her erroneous life choices and lost hopes. Her prostrate figure, lying on the bed, unable to move or to make a decision, is afflicted by an unknown ailment and mounting despair. The question Goldie, the manager of the brothel, directs at Bertha at the very beginning of the play—"Bertha, what are you going to do?" (183)—is akin to the question that plagues Amanda in *The Glass Menagerie:* "So what are we going to do the rest of our lives? Stay home and watch the parades go by?" (15). It is a question that reveals a fundamental fear of what the future holds, mixed with the premonition of an inevitable catastrophe. In fact, it is not a genuine inquiry about a plan for the future but more of a statement about the *lack* of a plan and the hopelessness of the present predicament. Like Blanche and Miss Collins, Bertha has no future.

Goldie tries to remain "sensible," and her goal is to keep her business going. As she explains to Bertha, the "girls" need the room Bertha is staying in for their clients. Having allowed Bertha to remain bedridden in the apartment for two weeks, waiting patiently for her to come around, Goldie finally decides to intervene. In response to Goldie's inquiries and words of encouragement, Bertha groans and tosses around in the bed like a wounded animal trapped in a snare, unable to liberate itself from pain. She deflects answers, repeats her obscure, laconic retorts, and zones in and out as if in a malignant fever. Her mournful inertia is overwhelming and excessive and it adumbrates no recovery, no meliorism, and no control. Bertha also rejects Goldie's offer to summon a doctor or a priest. The doctor could potentially cure her body and the priest could provide consolation for her soul, but Bertha does not want either. The source of her excessive, feverish malignancy is so deeply rooted that she senses she is beyond remedy.

Bertha is haunted by the memory of her bygone love, Charlie, a hardware seller from Memphis, with whom she had a fiery affair in the "back room" of his shop. This remembrance is both the source of her turbulent ailment and her sole remaining anchor to reality. Bertha keeps slapping the bed, and her voice turns into a "sobbing mumble" whenever she mutters "Sweet Charlie" (27 Wagons 185). As with a number of other male characters in Williams's oeuvre, Charlie's notorious lack of presence takes away all prospect of hope, and it is the memory of him that is most arduous for Bertha, as she exclaims in desperation, "I love you so much it makes my guts ache to look at your blessed face in the picture!" (190).

Williams strips Bertha of everything—she is penniless, sick, and deprived of any kind of leverage. Her only resource, her body, which she was selling away, can no longer support her. Bertha's physical inertia is another way in which the dissolution of her identity takes place—her body becomes barren and useless. Deprived of this last asset, she can only try to fool herself into thinking that there is a flicker of hope in her predicament. As she says to Lena, a fellow prostitute, "I may be a little down on my luck right now but—that's all! That's all, ain't it, Lena? I ain't old. I still got my looks. Ain't I?" (191). The insistent questions are particularly despondent, insofar as she knows that these words of encouragement and reassurance are devoid of truth. Her language is as powerless as her body. And when she shouts out hysterically, it is more than just a tantrum. This is an outburst of desperation, an excessive spasm prophesying the apex of the hyperbolic and her imminent departure.

When Bertha tries to look for her last money, Goldie reminds her that she spent it all on a bottle of gin before she became bedridden. Bertha drinks to forget, just like Blanche DuBois, but the malaise that plagues her at this point cannot be alleviated by alcohol. In the last sections of the play, she falls into a hysteria, calling Goldie names and accusing her of the theft of her last money. Desperate, she is unable to respond to Goldie's reason, and she hurls threats she cannot fulfill: "I've got friends in this town. Big shots! Lawyers, politicians!" (190). Through her powerless exhortations, it becomes evident that she has utterly no one to turn to, that her death is to be a lonely one, preceded by the dissolution of her mind. Her physical immobility, social seclusion, and lack of power, both verbal and physical, create a hyperbolized image of life that is more akin to death.

Ultimately, Goldie calls for an ambulance and tells Bertha that they will put her up in a "nice, clean ward" (192). Dying Bertha is to be removed from the brothel as an unfitting element that, on the one hand, cannot be put to any use and, on the other, causes erratic commotion. As an excessive, awkward pariah, out of place, she has to be evicted. And, like Miss Collins, as her last act of will, Bertha plans to leave a letter to her old beau, who has long since passed beyond her reach and who chose another woman over her. In her last muttered words, the dying prostitute dictates the text of the letter to Lena, who only pretends to set it down. This good-bye letter is a symbolic testament to her life: it is never actually written down, let alone delivered to the addressee. In the letter, Bertha declares that she is sane, calls for Charlie to come over and bail her out, "for old times' sake," and signs the message "Your old sweetheart, Bertha" (193). Initially, she wants to add a postscript asking Charlie about his wife, but then she changes her mind and vehemently tells Lena to scratch these last words out. This self-correction is her final act of will, a passing tribute to how she wants to retain her dignity and keep the communication between them about them only.

The wait for the removal to hospital adds a sense of irredeemable finality to Bertha's decay. The pending eviction means that she is being treated like an object rather than a subject and that there is no active agency on her part anymore. Bertha's ultimate powerlessness and lack of influence become evident even to her, insofar as she has no choice but to submit to others making decisions about her ultimate fate. This lack of decisive potency on her part is yet another level of her dissolution—not only is her ability to move lost but so is her will to self-constitute. Bertha's language reveals this realization, expressed in her desperate fury at Goldie for relegating her and for bringing up her inevitable death. The dying prostitute is full of anger at the brothel manager because "she comes in here talking soft about callin' a priest an' havin' me stuck in the charity ward" (192), but, more importantly, she is desperate about the extent of her own dissolution. She tries to protest against being discarded but lacks the potency to rebel against her condition in any physical way. Her threats are thus feeble, meaningless, and a testament to her helplessness rather than to any true capability to resist.

As we will see with Miss Collins from *Portrait of a Madonna*, the inert Bertha becomes detached from the world around her, hopelessly fixated upon a single element of her past, the memory of Charlie, which at some point in her life represented a hope for happiness. This nostalgic fixation, the mental malady, and the inertia of the body are one, but the name of Bertha's illness is never identified in the play—and the exact medical label is actually irrelevant, like the crime in Franz Kafka's *The Trial*, which is never revealed. What matters here is the very grotesque perturbation of abnormality in the seemingly normal world, the "plastic" hyperbole of desperation, which leads to a moribund dissolution of identity. What Williams aims at is an understanding of the utmost mental angst, of a complete and hopeless collapse and disintegration through excess.

Given the malaise that afflicts its main protagonist, as well as her ultimate fate, Williams's early one-act drama *Portrait of a Madonna* seems like a compact trial run for *A Streetcar Named Desire*. Both texts feature a morbidly unhappy, faded southern belle who is removed from a cramped, asphyxiating space and locked up in a mental asylum. There is, however, a deeper affinity between the two dramas than the obvious similarities in the story line. *Portrait of a Madonna* is permeated with an air of irremediable desperation—and, in this sense, Miss Collins falls into the same category of Williams's theater as Blanche DuBois. Williams's engagement of the hyperbolic mode is likewise similar. In both texts, he juxtaposes different elements to maximize tensions and then pushes them to the extreme, intensifying the southern belles' harrowing alienation, which ultimately spells their undoing. And in both cases, their ultimate removal to an institution is symbolic of their helplessness and lack of potency.

The plot of *Portrait of a Madonna* manifests Williams's mastery of a compact dramatic form, akin to the form of a short story. His craft is visible in his ability to generate feelings of sorrow and desperate finality without a lengthy representation of what preceded Miss Collins's break from the world. In the case of *Portrait of a Madonna*, the short drama is just a final episode of a long tragedy in which the colliding, excessive opposites have been eating away at Miss Collins mercilessly for twenty years, depriving her of sanity and gradually pushing her toward a phantasmal folly. What Williams presents his readers with is, therefore, an outcome of a hyperbolic process: a disintegrated human being who breaks down and collapses, having been pressed by external forces.

Portrait of a Madonna is claustrophobically dense, and it testifies to the violent power of the hyperbolic astriction that preceded the climactic moment of Miss Collins's drama. An uprooted, senile southern lady, gradually withering away in an apartment up North, deprived of all social and cultural paradigms that provided her with a sense of stability, and notoriously mesmerized by past traumas and a long-lost love, she remains at fundamental odds with the reality that surrounds her. All the elements that make her up—her outdated manners, her attire (with a notable pink ribbon), and her obsolete mind-set—are strategically intensified by Williams to set her in contrast to the space and the people around her, turning her into a walking grotesque.

Miss Collins's behavior matches her looks. As an upright belle, she remains incurably passive, waiting for the kindness of strangers and claiming that southern ladies were "never brought up to manage financial affairs" (Williams, *27 Wagons* 91). Succumbing to the idea of propriety, she has cultivated the prerogative of repressing all her desires and of following the dictates of the church. She cannot interact with the world around her, and her only chance to feel like an object of someone else's kind thoughts or desires is to make up stories about being visited and ravished by the man who has broken her heart. Williams designs her, thus, as a grotesquely unfitting element in a world that does not care for her misery, and as a mental wreck so traumatized that she can no longer uphold herself.

As the consecutive layers of Miss Collins's psyche are exfoliated, a scarred, excessive interior is revealed that turns out to be degenerate and detached beyond repair. The southern lady has to be put into a mental hospital, removed from the normal life with which she remains at odds. The collapse of Miss Collins's mind becomes fully visible through the juxtaposition with decorum, with the normal and the mundane, represented by the porter and the elevator boy, who, together with readers and spectators, become witnesses to how unstable Miss Collins has become. On the outside, her grotesqueness may be apparent in her awkward, worn-out clothes or in her manners, but essentially it is the result of her inability to establish a connection with the world around her.

In Williams's world, time is never a healer; it is always a silent, slow destroyer. And for Miss Collins, the flow of time involves a particularly disintegrative decay. She is obsessively anchored in a different reality in which she can still hope for a happy ending to her life story. The image of the belle persona she desperately tries to assume (of which the flagrant handkerchief, just like in *Summer and Smoke,* is an emblem) indicates her craving for fulfillment—exactly the kind of completion that never comes in Williams's suffocating and conflicted world. The illusory nature of her hopes, and the cultural and religious role she would like to be expected to assume, collide violently with her confined, barren life. This decay is intensified with time and pushed toward the climactic moment of her ultimate disintegration.

Miss Collins cannot shake off the shame of people taking "malicious delight" (98) in her misery. The antithetical phrase echoes throughout the whole play, signaling Miss Collins's anxiety about humiliation and having the feeble nature of her persona publicly demolished. Originating from a bygone world of southern propriety, Miss Collins seeks to command the respect entailed by her faded position and her background as a lady. She stresses that she is a minister's daughter and asserts that she was a paragon of rectitude—the one who "made the dress for the Virgin and Mother" for the church pageant (89). It is no surprise that, over the years, her southern pride has achieved the status of urban legend among her neighbors: "She's proud as peacock's tail in spite of 'er awful appearance" (91), says the porter at the beginning of the text.

The faded belle clings to her supposedly inherited respectability and veneration as one of the last remaining anchors of sanity. Thus, what is most haunting for her is the constant reliving of the traumatic experiences of having her woe shamefully exposed, of having been caught without her umbrella in full daylight, "penetrated" by the eyes of the woman to whom she lost her mating rivalry and whom Richard has chosen over her (99). Since, just like Blanche DuBois, sunshine unmasks her misery, Miss Collins remains a creature of shadows and of dim memories. She lives *by* the ghosts of the past and she lives *for* the ghosts of the past. She is haunted, and she ultimately metamorphoses into a ghost herself.

The two direct witnesses of Miss Collins's ultimate downfall, the elevator boy and the porter, constitute the decorum of normality against which Miss Collins's folly and desperation become clearly evident. In terms of Williams's hyperbolic design, they are the benchmark that allows us to determine that excess is in fact excess. The two men represent the world from which Miss

Collins has become disconnected, and each step of the way, the contrasts between them and the belle gain in strength. While she denounces any interest in her finances, the elevator boy wants to search her house for hidden riches. While she hysterically cries out to the nonpresent Richard, the porter seeks to calm her down and humor her. Although the two men differ in terms of their attitude toward the faded belle, the porter being compassionate and curious and the elevator boy being condescending and openly disparaging, their combined function in the hyperbolic is as a barometer for dangerous excess. In the metafigurative layout of the play, they are the envoys of the normal and thus make it possible to assess the extent of Miss Collins's pathological detachment.

At the same time, the elevator boy's engagement of Miss Collins's delusion is overtly aggressive. He takes "malicious delight" in her painful confusion, making remarks intended to dismantle her desperate semblance and reveal her folly. His belligerence draws on the natural repulsion between illusion and reality, the antinomic clash that later would become one of the axes of contrast in A Streetcar Named Desire. Thus, the elevator boy openly affirms that Miss Collins's story does not hold water, that she cannot possibly hear the sounds she claims to hear, or that her phantasmal rapist had nowhere to run from the apartment after his assault upon her. He derives condescending satisfaction from debunking her fabrication and revealing the discordant excess in which she is indulging. The porter, in contrast, is more understanding and caring. He seems to be appreciative of her persona, much as Mitch would be considerate of Blanche's in Streetcar. In spite of his pity, however, he has no illusions about her folly and her ultimate fate. Neither mockery nor pity can prevent Miss Collins from ending up in an asylum, from being carried down the "inscrutable dark way" of Williams's "Valediction."

Miss Collins's unhappiness, like the unhappiness of most of Williams's characters, is due to a broken heart and carnal unfulfillment. The music that accompanies the play, Tchaikovsky's "None but the Lonely Heart" (Williams, 27 Wagons 98) brings forth the sense of irreversible loss: "None but the lonely heart / Can know my sadness / Alone and parted / Far from joy and gladness." Miss Collins's fantasies about being raped and bearing Richard's child are a testimony to how upturned her world has become, for the emotional upheaval that accompanies her repetitive assaults by an imaginary beau is one of very few things that can at least hint at the existence of "joy and gladness."

These haunted visitations are paradoxical, insofar as they are both destructive and sanguine. Through them, Miss Collins fabricates a scenario in which

Richard betrays his "Cincinnati girl" (100) and their six children with her—in other words, a scenario in which she constitutes the object of desire, remains in control, and ultimately wins the competition to find a male and bear his progeny, thus repudiating her barrenness. The pull of Miss Collins's folly and excessive longing is so strong that it allows her to reinterpret the morality of the act of rape. In her twisted, hyperbolized world, sexual assault becomes a badge of pride and narcissistic power—it proves her worth. At the same time, regardless of whether the dream of being raped stems from repressed sexual desire or her fear of impending death, it pulls her deeper and deeper into the realm of the unreal.

The letter she leaves for Richard, promising to disclose to him the "secret" about carrying his child, is a message of lost hope. What it reveals is her longing to be an object of imaginary craving that would lead to an imaginary rape and an imaginary conception. But the letter will forever remain unread by its intended addressee, not unlike Bertha's (unwritten) note in *Portrait of a Madonna*. The incomplete act of communication that Miss Collins undertakes testifies to the extent of her detachment. The note she leaves behind for Richard effectively becomes her testament. This being the case, the whole one-act drama reminds one of a wake, of a long wait for the inevitable: the removal of an unfitting element of reality to a "strange" place, a madhouse. With this death-like eviction, the dissolution of Miss Collins's self under the pressure of hyperbolized tensions becomes complete. Throughout the play, Miss Collins has also been waiting, but in her case the waiting began much earlier and has in fact become a manner of being. Just as the drama in *A Streetcar Named Desire* spans life and death, the drama of *Portrait of a Madonna* traverses from an unbearable loss to an unfulfilled restoration that leads to expiration.

Of all the downfalls afflicting Williams's southern belles, the misfortune that overtakes Blanche DuBois is the most spectacular and the most notorious. Blanche perseveres as an engaging, insoluble puzzle of Williams's world—not only because of her intriguing complexity as a character but also because of the canonical status of *A Streetcar Named Desire* in modern American drama. She also is an object of distinctive remorse and regret because of what happens to her at the end of the play. Having been sexually abused and victimized, and having broken down completely, Blanche is famously taken to a mental asylum, resting her arm on the doctor's, declaring her confidence in the "kindness of strangers." Her banishment from the world dominated by the sexual fulfillment of Stella and Stanley, and her subsequent incarceration, are symptomatic of how hyperbolic pressure culminates in Williams's drama.

Williams initiates the pathway to hyperbolic rapture and dissolution by crossing two divergent forces: Blanche DuBois and Stanley Kowalski. Blanche and Stanley are antithetical in all possible respects, expanding on the key figurative duality of Williams's creative process and reminiscent of *Summer and Smoke* (which the playwright authored right after *Streetcar*). Both characters are deposited in a claustrophobic apartment in New Orleans that can hardly contain their excessive confrontation. Psychologically realistic despondency, unrest, and insatiable yearnings are all crammed into an unrealistic "plastic" space, and then, gradually, the tensions are escalated, pushed to the extreme and, ultimately, to the point of complete rupture.

Blanche does not stand a chance of surviving the confrontation between her feeble imaginativeness and Stanley's virulent, earthbound masculinity, and throughout the play she is always at a disadvantage. Williams constructs her as a destitute and despondent person who is effectively devoid of any leverage and who visits her sister's apartment as a last resort, essentially to save herself from homelessness. Having dissipated what was left of the family fortune on medical and funeral bills, Blanche has little choice but to retreat to a shabby hotel, where she gains a questionable reputation as a hard-drinking, neurotic harlot, involuntarily subscribing to the awkward family tradition of "epic fornications" (*Streetcar* 44). Earlier, she was discharged from her job as a teacher because of immoral conduct and an affair with a student. And even before that, Blanche's marriage had a disastrous finale, when her husband committed suicide after being caught red-handed in a homosexual affair and disparaged by his then fastidious wife. So Williams turns all the possible odds against Blanche, and when she arrives at her sister's doorstep, having lost her youth, her partner, her innocence, her job, and her inheritance, she is already completely vanquished and subjugated, hanging by a thread.

The irrevocable flow of time is Blanche's anathema. She loathes its decaying touch and fears its power over her, clinging to the dim light to prevent her wrinkles from being exposed. The whole play is permeated with temporality and is reminiscent of an unfolding process in which the movement of the eponymous streetcar between Desire and Cemeteries provides the symbolic timeline for the unfolding of Blanche's tragedy, culminating in her mental collapse and forceful removal to a mental institution.

Blanche is like a visitor from a cavalier reality that has long since passed away, and everything that remains to represent this world can be fit into her compact suitcase. Everything else has been ravaged by the collapse of her world. Yet, along with the material objects that she managed to salvage from that apocalypse, including furs, pearls, and "bracelets of solid gold" (34), she also carries the stigma of death, the ruination of the Belle Reve plantation that had passed into oblivion. So, as she invades the space of Stella and Stanley's apartment, she brings with her the aura of passing, of unavoidable termination, standing in contrast to the promise of Stanley's progeny. All of these differences of potency and metaphoric directionality—the premonition of death and the potential of life, Blanche's figurative backwardness and Stanley's forwardness—further supplement the strength of the hyperbolic clash.

If Blanche is a hyperbole of a southern belle, driven to the extreme by the flow of time, unfulfilled desire, and the aura of death, then the decorum against which her excess becomes so fully perceptible is the relationship between Stella and Stanley. Their union is based on the very thing Blanche craves and cannot be appeased by. In the marriage of violence and desire, Stanley's animalistic lovemaking seems sufficient to compensate Stella for his aggressive rambunctiousness and brutality. But while their cravings and passions are out in the open, Blanche desperately cultivates her folie de grandeur and hides behind her dilapidated persona as the southern belle. As the masque of propriety is consumed from within by her internal urges, she rapidly diverts from the norm and turns to detached, uncontrollable excess.

Although Blanche loses the duel, at the end of the play one has to admit that she is a determined and persistent fighter. As Williams himself explained, "Was Blanche a 'little person'? Certainly not. She was a demonic creature, the size of her feeling was too great for her to contain without the escape of madness" (*Memoirs* 55). Fighting for survival, the fading southern belle seeks to put up an illusion of becomingness, while Stanley methodically debunks her nostalgic fantasies and provocative stratagems. With each concrete, down-to-earth question about the status of the family heirlooms and his persistent demand to see the "papers" (*Streetcar* 32), he peels away the consecutive layers of illusion constructed by Blanche. The excessive, illusory nature of her detachment cannot withstand this confrontation and Stanley's pseudolegalistic pretensions.

In response, like a moth attracted to a flame that will consume her, Blanche begins a flirtatious game with Stanley, a game in which he refuses to take part. When she asks, "Would you think it possible that I was once considered to be—attractive," he replies, disparagingly, "Your looks are okay." And when she gives him an instructive "I was fishing for a compliment, Stanley," he counters, "I don't go in for that stuff" (38).

Blanche's fundamental failure to engage Stanley in a teasing scheme in which he would be the eager wooer and she the revered lady testifies to the fact that the two speak different languages, and her words lack essential performative power in his "territory" (26). Stanley refuses to be engaged, and he ostensibly ignores her implications, forcing the exchange into another, more uncavalier direction and destroying her attempts at a sentimental uplift. Later, when Blanche tells him to "Possess your soul in patience," he retorts, "It's not my soul, it's my kidneys I am worried about" (124), establishing an almost emblematic Willamesque antagonism between the language of the spiritual and that of the carnal.

Given all the references to the ephemeral, Blanche is not that different from Alma Winemiller, especially as another teacher, a custodian of art. In such a conversational context, Blanche's persona is denigrated and, over time, communicative incongruences escalate, setting the illusory and feeble against the concrete and the carnal and propelling the story to the point of hyperbolic rapture.

When working on an early draft, Williams could not decide about the end of the play, hesitating among three possible endgames: "departure, insanity, or suicide" (*Memoirs* 120). In some ways, however, the finale that he opted for in Blanche's story conjoins all three denouements. Her psychotic collapse and exile into a death-like state of incarceration crown the violent metalogic of contrastive excess that underpins the whole play.

The Doctor and the Matron arrive as harbingers of doom, and as they climb the stairs of the house to take Blanche away, "the gravity of their profession is exaggerated" and they are surrounded by "the unmistakable aura of the state institution with its cynical detachment" (*Streetcar* 171). Blanche overhears Eunice say, "They're waiting in front of the house," and her fearful confusion and the frightened question she asks—"They? Who's 'they'?"—indicate her disengagement (172). She tries to find a referent for the pronoun whose ominous indeterminacy augurs her doom. The sinister collective pronoun "they" stresses the powerlessness of her selfhood, which is collapsing in the face of the rest of society. The question is also symbolic in terms of her fundamental inability to attach signifiers to the signified outside of the excessive realm of her illusions.

Blanche throws a desperate tantrum, like a cornered, imperiled animal that senses its inevitable doom. She has been brutally violated by the animalistic alpha male of the "territory" she has strayed upon and is similarly brutally subdued by the normalizing policies of society. Her uncontrollable, despondent excess becomes curtailed by brute force and the sinister envoys of an institution to which she will be relegated. When Blanche is restrained, the Matron announces that her "fingernails have to be trimmed" (177). Again, like a figurative animal being forcibly tamed, she is deprived of the last means she could use to defend herself—or just to vent her desperate anger. This is the apex of her downfall and the culmination of the hyperbolic tensions that have been escalating throughout the play. She is neutralized and crippled as the last constituents of her selfhood are peeled away and her unwanted, calamitous body is objectified and ferried away. As Eunice coldheartedly expresses it, for Blanche "there wasn't no other place [. . .] to go" (176), except, to once again evoke the image, the "inscrutable dark way" of the mental asylum.

6

HYPERBOLIC EPIPHANY

Flannery O'Connor

In her essay "The Fiction Writer and His Country," Flannery O'Connor stresses that only Christian novelists—among whom she includes herself—are capable of making out the "repugnant" distortions of the modern world to which secular people remain blind. In consequence, a religious artist's goal "will be to make these appear as distortions to an audience, which is used to seeing them as natural" (34). This is exactly the kind of misguided, resistant reader O'Connor assumed she would be confronting through her fiction. Hence, for her, the themes of excessive violence and the grotesque aesthetics became de rigueur, a rhetorical necessity, if she wanted to get her message across successfully and, to draw on one of her most favored tropes, to open her readers' eyes to sempiternal truths. The fiction O'Connor produced remains confrontational and provocative, and the hyperbolic shock and grotesque excess that she deemed indispensable when engaging the contemporary secular world has become her artistic trademark.

In a way, O'Connor's rhetorical agenda bears some resemblance to what revival preachers normally seek to achieve: to agitate and elevate those in the pews and to bring forth their rebirth.[1] A successful revival preacher's rhetorical goal is to devise the most effective ways to reach out to people and to reform them, even if it means unorthodox figuration and strong appeals to pathos. As I noted in chapter 1, while discussing the hyperbolic appeal, within the "rhetoric of the revival," excessive imagery of fire and brimstone is tolerated, or even welcome, if it can scare people into heaven.[2] As a religious writer, O'Connor shares this objective to a certain extent. To her, the robust force of the metahyperbolic shock is more than justified when one seeks to crack the hard shell of the secular mind. In her words, "To the hard of hearing you shout, and for the almost-blind you draw large and startling figures" ("Fiction Writer" 34).

O'Connor's relentless perusal of the contemporary world compels her to organize her narratives around an incessant series of contrasts, adopting hyperbolic metafiguration as the basic rhetorical framework for her fiction. Gradually, she hyperbolizes her characters' defining traits, or she pushes the circumstances of their lives to the extreme, arranging them on a collision course with their own concealed selves and with their environment. All of O'Connor's hallmark narrative strategies, such as doubling, the use of the disproportionate physicality, the mixing of human and animalistic elements, or, more generally, the employment of the grotesque, are offshoots of the hyperbolic mode of comprehension that underpins her thought. And it is in the moment of excessive rapture, when grisly murders are being committed, that her characters abandon all hope, and when they become completely powerless, she submits them to God's will. Thus, the main characteristic that distinguishes Flannery O'Connor's management of the hyperbolic mode from that of other authors is her relentless insistence on its soteriological potency.

The setting of O'Connor's stories is almost exclusively in the rural South and the backwoods of the Bible Belt, and against this dilapidated backdrop she parturiates an emphatically grotesque drama of life. One of O'Connor's most often quoted sentences comes from her essay "Some Aspects of the Grotesque in Southern Fiction" and concerns exactly the entanglement of the southern penchant for the grotesque with the geographic space of the South: "Of course, I have found that anything that comes out of the South is going to be called grotesque by the Northern reader, unless it is grotesque, in which case it is going to be called realistic" ("Fiction Writer" 40). The grotesque resides in the eye of the beholder, and it functions on a double divergent axis—on the one hand, there is the geographic axis, spanning the North and the South, and on the other hand, there is the intellectual or aesthetic scale, spanning mimetic realism and distorted grotesqueness. The geographic is contrastively projected onto the intellectual and aesthetic, binding the mind-set and literary idiom with the physical space and setting North and South, as well as realism and the grotesque, against each other. The space outlined by these two axes constitutes the very stage on which the drama of O'Connor's fiction unfolds.

Kathleen Freeley discusses some of the particular strategies that O'Connor employed to fulfill her artistic agenda and evoke religious revelations in her readers. The writer brings her characters to their knees with blows so powerful that they have no option but to accede to their infirmity and inadequacy. She uproots them and crushes their hopes and dreams—the harder they resist, the more powerful and excessive is the trial O'Connor exposes them to. And, in the end, her characters always give in, because, to her, the submission to God's will is tantamount to the full embrace of one's powerlessness.

O'Connor's persistence in this fictional brutality is the outcome of her dedication to the belief that a distorted, hyperbolic revelation brings her character a moment of grace, a spiritual transformation. In this way, violence and the revelatory experience become intertwined in her fiction, or even mutually dependent. This uncompromising preoccupation with violence as a theme is another feature that distinguishes O'Connor's metahyperbole from that of other authors discussed in this book. John D. Sykes Jr. argues that, in the case of O'Connor, the specific aesthetic of memory that was formed by an entire generation of southern writers and that can be found so abundantly in William Faulkner was replaced with an "aesthetic of revelation."

O'Connor was very open about how her religious agenda is bound to her narrative technique. The imperative for didacticism mingled with her disdain for modern intellectualism and the anxiety that her works could serve any other purpose but the spiritual one. O'Connor particularly shunned secular readings of her fiction and was adamantly against being perused by, for instance, Freudian scholars.[3] In general, she detested the idea of any critical pursuit of a secular framework.

Immobilized by lupus, O'Connor engaged, over the years, in numerous epistolary exchanges with her readers, eagerly discussing the meaning behind her texts. Among her correspondents, Maryat Lee, a playwright from New York, and Hazel Elizabeth "Betty" Hester (referred to as "A" in the letters), a clerk from Atlanta, were the most prolific. The women exchanged hundreds of letters, discussing, among other things, religious symbols, inspirations, and the intended meanings behind O'Connor's stories. This drive to explicate her fiction and to use letters as a bulwark against misinterpretation considerably undermined the independence of her readers. To a certain extent, O'Connor substituted interpretative prescriptivism for their freedom of reading. But the letters, published collectively as *The Habit of Being,* also reveal her religious dedication, the inspiration she took from the thought of Thomas Aquinas, and a surprisingly complex relationship between O'Connor the writer and O'Connor the person.

Two intertwined factors in Flannery O'Connor life come to the fore as the most formative: her struggle with disease and her devout Catholicism. Flannery O'Connor's father passed away from lupus when she was fifteen, and in 1950, when she was living with her friends Sally and Robert Fitzgerald in Ridgefield, Connecticut, seeking to secure for herself the space she needed for her prospective artistic and spiritual endeavors, the first serious symptoms of her own disease appeared. After that episode, her life was marked with an expiry date—just as the life of one of her formidable creations, Hulga from "Good Country People," was a countdown to a premature termination.

It could not have escaped her attention that the very nature of her ailment was inherently uncanny. As an immunological disease, lupus impacted her physicality, but more importantly, it caused her body to recognize itself as an enemy and, ultimately, to turn against itself. Her corporeal self, the most intimate aspect of her identity, was thus subversively beleaguered until the time of her death. It is little wonder, then, that the metaphors of awkward bodily entrapment and identity subjugation became a commonplace figurative framework in a number of her later texts—as in "A Circle in the Fire," where a young protagonist, seeking to liberate herself from the maternal shadow, hisses angrily at her mother, "I ain't you," (*Selected Stories* 190).

As O'Connor writes in one of her letters, "I have never been anywhere but sick. In a sense sickness is a place more instructive than a long trip to Europe, and it's always a place where there's no company, where nobody can follow" (*Habit of Being* 163). The metaphorical representation of pain and ailments as a physical space, a travel destination, is telling of the didacticism she reads into it. Lupus becomes figuratively represented as a stopover in life's journey, a mandatory element of existence that presages the liberation from earthly woes and a blissful rest in life after death. Thus, O'Connor would insist that a precious lesson is to be derived from an ailment, as the negativity of suffering became for her a mandatory prerequisite for the deeper and better understanding of one's existence. As she observed, "Sickness before death is a very appropriate thing and I think those who don't have it miss one of God's mercies" (163). With all her heart, she believed that one has to experience hyperbolic extremes and be exposed to suffering in order to be admitted to grace. To her, nobody but the suffering and the violent could bear the kingdom of heaven away.

The world of O'Connor is thus divided from within, consumed by a violent vortex of conflicting notions, out of which grace emerges as the only available anchor. At the same time, this world barely constitutes a habitable environment, for it is almost exclusively peopled with "freaks." Fugitive murderers roam her southern country roads ("A Good Man Is Hard to Find"), fraud street preachers fake blindness to exploit people (*Wise Blood*), Bible salesmen steal artificial limbs from girls for perverted sport ("Good Country People"), and immigrant workers, who were the victims of war, die under combine harvesters ("The Displaced Person"). There is something particularly apt in Laurence Enjolras's assertion that, as O'Connor's readers go through her stories, "we have an impression that we are moving inside a gallery whose walls have been covered with deforming mirrors" (7).

O'Connor relentlessly conjoins this abnormality with spirituality, as she stresses in a letter to John Hawkes: "Grace, to the Catholic way of thinking, can and does use as its medium the imperfect, purely human and even hypocritical" (*Habit of Being* 389). But the world she devises is also ridden with characters who are morbidly and irreparably miserable. There seems to be no consolation for them in store from any earthly agency. And, as the enticed readers are willing to exhibit sympathy for some of O'Connor's miserable characters, they become subjugated and seized by the narrative, which turns their compassion against them. Promptly, the despondent characters who have caught readers' attention become engaged in the most abysmal and revolting actions. They kill, maim, and repudiate others. The ferocious hyperbolic violence that permeates O'Connor's world is only proportionate to the violence she employs against her readers, whom she feels compelled to shock and shake up. O'Connor considered herself indentured to use any artistic means necessary to deliver her evangelizing message to her readers and to force it into their minds.

The violent realm of O'Connor's fiction is a direct consequence of the way she viewed the world around her. In all her writings, she denigrates contemporary society for its godlessness. As she once explained, "It was a case in which it is easy to see that the moral sense has been bred out of certain sections of the population, like the wings have been bred off certain chickens to produce more white meat on them. This is a generation of wingless chickens, which I suppose is what Nietzsche meant when he said God was dead" (90). Thus, to her, a society in which there was no God had no future, and the fiction that did not fight to elevate such a society had very little to justify its existence. O'Connor's characters, who so desperately seek and search for grace and ultimately fail to embrace it, exhibit this factitious, atheistic winglessness and artificial secularism that ultimately, after a series of brutal trails, becomes their undoing.

These trials, violent and excessive as they are, constitute not an act of sadism on O'Connor's part but an attempt to bring one a step closer to redemption. Her imperative, which she considers the obligation of any artist, is to use the hyperbolic to penetrate matter until spirit is revealed in it. In order to achieve this, O'Connor pointedly distorts the comfortable balance that her characters so strenuously construct and twists and turns the circumstances of their life, exposing to readers, as well as to themselves, the social and psychological tensions that generated them. In her case, figurative distortion is a rhetorical instrument of epiphany, and the hyperbolic metalogic remains O'Connor's defining aesthetic idiom. Every clash of opposites and every violent exaggeration she describes has a communicative purpose, and this purpose is revelation, a new, humbling understanding of who her characters truly are, as we will see here, in the readings of two of O'Connor's short stories and one novel. This glimpse of truth is offered to the characters at their lowest, basest moment, at the culminating moment of hyperbolic excess.

The Woods and the Bull

The compressed form of short story offered Flannery O'Connor just enough narrative space to vehemently pulverize the opposites and to escalate them to the point of a hyperbolic breakage. In the two texts, a dramatic, violent episode marks the climactic moment of the plot: the murder of a child at the hands of her grandfather and the impaling of a woman by a fierce bull. However, what is interesting is the way in which O'Connor constructs the opposites that culminate in these dramatic episodes. The elements she uses to design these opposites, such as the rural landscape or charismatic religious practice, are associated with the South. In such a context, the metatrope of hyperbole serves O'Connor as a framework to demonstrate her characters' powerlessness against the mounting circumstances of life, which, if lived secularly, was to her both hopeless and helpless.

So the violent episodes in the stories here do not grant the protagonists the privilege of a climactic epiphany. They all fall and die in vain, trapped in the midst of Harpham's grotesque "interval," witnessing the deconstruction of their world but not being able to reconstitute it through an epiphanic revelation. In O'Connor's metanarrative design, it is the reader who is to experience a new understanding, out of the wreckage of grotesque distortion, while her characters remain notoriously forlorn, warped, and, ultimately, dead.

Pointing to the scene of the grisly murder, Harold Bloom describes "A View of the Woods" as the "ugliest" of O'Connor's stories ("Introduction" 5). In this text, the figurative path that leads to the divine visitation witnessed by Mr. Fortune, a senile southern landowner who kills his granddaughter, is that of a violent clash and obliteration of identity. The hyperbolic design that O'Connor uses in the story is realized by the strategies of doubling and uncanny mimicry, and the two characters who engage in a ferocious fight at the end of the story seem to blend into one in the heat of violence, constituting one of the most compelling edifices of violent excess in her fiction.

As is often the case with O'Connor, the background for the escalating contrast is a bitter family conflict and a toxic household environment entangled with frustration and hopelessness. Mr. Fortune deplores both his daughter and Pitts, his son-in-law, who lack his business acumen and mind-set. The only person he has any kind feelings for is his granddaughter, Mary Fortune. The affection between them seems to have an uncanny physical underpinning, as Mary's face is a "small replica of the old man's"—she not only manifests a physical resemblance to her grandfather but also seems to have "his intelligence, his strong will, and his push and drive" (*Selected Stories* 336). Because of this affinity, she is the only family member for whom he has any respect. The girl is not the only fixation of the old man; he also seems to be obsessed with progress, declaring, "Any fool that would let a cow pasture interfere with progress is not on my books" (335). He treats his farm as a means to establish power and to exercise control over Pitts, and he threatens to sell the remaining part of the land instead of willing it to them.

Mr. Fortune's only weak point, and the only leverage Pitts has over him, is his use of corporal punishment on Mary. The old man cannot bear to see his granddaughter whipped, and each time it happens he experiences severe mental and physical unrest. In this awkward way, Pitts manages to wreak his revenge on Mr. Fortune for how he manifests his control over the land.

In the story, violence plays an instrumental role in the evocation of the revelatory experience. The old man seems to be a person for whom the epiphany is inaccessible, and he cannot comprehend his granddaughter's objection to the prospective loss of the meadow because, in the land, he sees only an obstacle to progress. "A pine trunk is a pine trunk" (348), he declares, oblivious to the materialist paradox in his words. In a figurative manner that is so vital for O'Connor, his eyes are unable to penetrate the landscape and reach for a deeper understanding beyond. When he attempts to see the view for the third time, the old man gains a glimpse of a mystery and sees as if "someone were wounded behind the woods and the trees were bathed in blood" (348). This vision, however, is fragmentary and inscrutable, a mere indication of the full revelation, which he would not be able to take in because he rejects the Christ figure embodied in the image of the wood and remains blind to all spiritual callings. The only way Mr. Fortune can come close to a revelatory experience is by losing himself in the narcissistic act of violence and by exposing himself to a fundamentally *disintegrative* experience of hyperbolic excess.

As she leads her readers to the climactic apex of the story, O'Connor offers her readers a comprehensive catalog of violent behaviors. The first form of violence is the one Pitts uses to castigate his daughter. Mr. Fortune beholds it from hiding—he "had watched from behind a boulder about a hundred feet away while the child clung to a pine tree and Pitts, as methodically as if he were whacking a bush with a sling blade, beat her around the ankles with his belt. All she had done was jump up and down as if she were standing on a host stove and make a whimpering noise like a dog that was being peppered" (340).

What shocks the old man is his granddaughter's cooperativeness during the castigation. He cannot comprehend her obedience of her father and he takes the corporal punishment as an act against him—just as his granddaughter is his mimicry, the acts of violence directed at her are directed at him. The type of violence visible in this description is neither spontaneous nor instigated by rage—it is a repetitive, premeditated monotony of pain aimed at gaining control. Pitts's practice of corporal punishment is sadistic but, at the same time, obscurely ritualized through its recurrence and the emotionlessness of the castigator, who initiates it "abruptly, for no reason, with no explanation" (340). Both the victim and her pain become objectified, as Pitts declares to the grandfather, "She's mine to whip and I'll whip her every day of the year if it suits me" (341), and turn out to be mere pawns in the awkward game of power between the two men. At the same time, this violence is a source of shame. When the grandfather approaches Mary, she—driven by a sense of pride—denies that the rite of castigation took place at all and declares repetitively, "Nobody's ever beat me in my life and if anybody did, I'd kill him" (341).

A different aspect of violence is visible in Mary Fortune's aggressive reaction to her grandfather's plans to sell to a serpent-like, materialistic salesman, Tilman, the strip of land that allows a view of the woods. The livid girl loses control and, in a tantrum of pure rage, begins to hurl bottles at the two men who have signed the deal. Here, the uncontrollable anger and violence Mary manifests are a spontaneous act of rebellion and a protest aimed at defending both her pride and her beliefs. Mr. Fortune is shocked by her behavior and decides to punish her. The violence he decides to use in response to Mary's outburst is an imitation of Pitts's ritualistic whipping and is intended to castigate the girl: "She respected Pitts because, even with no just cause, he beat her; and if he [Mr. Fortune]—with his just cause—did not beat her now, he would have nobody to blame but himself if she turnout out a hellion" (353).

Mr. Fortune seeks control and reverence, and he wants to experience the same level of obedience from the girl as her father commands. He seeks to uphold the narcissistic harmony with his double, but he fails. It turns out he is unable to complete the ritual of his son-in-law, as Mary does not respond with passive obedience but with hostility. She begins to bite and kick her grandfather in a fit of chaotic rage: "It was as if he were being attacked not by one child but by a pack of small demons all with stout brown school shoes and small rocklike fists" (354). Her violence is no longer an act of protest and defense but an act of excessive, disorderly aggression.

At this point, too, violence manifests its transformative power, and the encounter of the granddaughter and the grandfather becomes a sacrament of excessive transfiguration. As they fall into a whirl of aggression, they undergo a physical change, and their grotesque metamorphosis crowns the story and pushes it toward the epiphanic moment of hyperbole. Unlike the ritualistic whipping from the beginning of the story, the fight between them is not structured—rather, it is chaotic, animalistic, and brutal—and in its escalation, it also becomes grotesquely hyperbolic as the integrity of the body is broken. O'Connor's description figuratively suggests that the girl and the old man fight like wild beasts: "Then with horror he saw her face rise up in front of his, teeth exposed, and he roared like a bull as she bit the side of his jaw. He seemed to see his own face coming to bite him from several sides at once but he could not attend to it for he was being kicked indiscriminately in the stomach and then in the crotch" (355). The macrofigurative, animalistic portrayal distorts the proportions as well as the harmony of their bodies, replacing the controllable rationality with primeval, exorbitant aggression. In the heat of the fight, it also obliterates their identities as, in a frenzied glimpse of his granddaughter's face, Mr. Fortune recognizes his own reflection. In the sacrament of pure rage, their hyperbolic merger becomes complete.

The girl towers over her grandfather physically and seems to have won the grotesque duel: "The old man looked up into his own image. It was triumphant and hostile" (355). Overcome with emotions, the old man no longer perceives Mary as his granddaughter—she becomes more like a distorted image of him, a hyperbolic mimicry incarnate. The substitution of the personal pronoun "she" with the impersonal "it" when referring to Mary signals how her status as a human being with a set identity becomes dramatically distorted in the chaos of excessive violence.

But it is the savage final act of their skirmish that is most obscure and that pushes the excess to its culmination. The old man manages to exchange places with his granddaughter and, having assumed the dominating stance, he chokes her: "With a sudden surge of strength, he managed to roll over and reverse their positions so that he was looking down into the face that was his but had dared to call itself Pitts" (355). With the uncanny resemblance between Mary and her grandfather and the twisting and turning of their bodies, the two figures seem to coalesce further, on the most basic, organic level—they become an exemplary image of a clash of excessive opposites in O'Connor's fiction. A moment ago, the daughter was a double of the old man, a part of his identity upon which he is dependent; now, having been deprived of the human element and having been reduced to a mere image, the girl becomes nothing short of a sacrifice, a scapegoat, killed in a fit of rage by the old man, with his bare hands.

Even when Mary is dead, the old man no longer sees her as his granddaughter: "He continued to stare at his conquered image until he perceived that though it was absolutely silent, there was no look of remorse on it" (355). Having killed his obscure, excessive double, and having sacrificed a shard of his own identity, the man witnesses a glimpse of epiphany that he cannot take in. This torrent of violence causes Mr. Fortune (whose name becomes at this stage deeply ironic) to suffer a heart attack and enables him to have a taste of the revelation that was earlier inaccessible to him. The man has a vision of the view of the woods to which his granddaughter was so attached. He "felt as if he were running as fast as he could with the ugly pines toward the lake. [. . .] He could see [. . .] a little opening where the white sky was reflected in the water. [. . .] On both sides of him he saw that the gaunt trees had thickened into mysterious dark files that were marching across the water" (356). The components of the view of the woods—blood, mentioned earlier, and the image of walking on water—suggest the figure of Christ. But Mr. Fortune dies hopelessly, right in the middle of his agonal vision, without being granted the full revelation or a new comprehension. The dramatic pinnacle of the hyperbolic thus brings only tragic death, whereas it could have brought about new understanding and a constructive religious epiphany.

O'Connor's insistence on how divine grace must penetrate the human heart through an excessive shock is given a literal representation in a second story, "Greenleaf." The text features a number of elements that are emblematic for O'Connor's narratives: a fatherless family living in a rural southern house, a southern lady with a sense of superiority over her "trash" farmhands, a jaded, housebound university intellectual, and a violent event that brings the protagonist to the ground in a brutal clash of opposites that is gradually building throughout the story. The setting of this drama, a shabby farmhouse run by Mrs. May, is permeated with a helpless frustration powerful enough to evoke the O'Connoresque mechanism of violent vision and to create a set of escalating and conflicting tensions that culminate in a violent hyperbolic image.

Mrs. Mary runs the household mostly by herself—her two sons, Wesley and Scofield, have little interest in daily chores. Wesley is busy with his mundane academic duties as a lecturer and Scofield is selling insurance to African Americans—a sly and squalid occupation, from his mother's perspective. The first son bears a studious name that is obviously connotative of John Wesley, the eighteenth-century founder of Methodism who, in his writings, emphasized that through grace, a Christian can be sanctified and allow the love of God to reign supreme in his or her heart. Unlike his famous fellow Methodist, George Whitefield, a theatrical Great Awakening preacher, John Wesley proposed a theology that was essentially sacramental and that did not divorce faith from reason.

In O'Connor's story, Mrs. May's son's methodical academic research is removed from the daily struggles of his mother—as he declares to her, ironically but with a sense of grave acrimony, "I would not milk a cow to save your soul from hell" (Selected Stories 321). Fruitlessly, Mrs. May tries to instill a sense of obligation in her sons, engaging in emotional blackmail and gleefully speculating about how their lives would become miserable when she passed away. In her farmhouse duties, she is forced to rely on the help of Mr. Greenleaf, a lackadaisical laborer, whom she keeps on in spite of his irritating slackness. The farmhand's wife, Mrs. Greenleaf, antagonizes Mrs. May even more. In particular, she is repelled by her habit of "prayer healing," an awkward, excessive practice that consists of burying a heap of the most morbid news articles in the ground and then lying in dirt, engaging in a series of spasmodic jerks, "mumbl[ing] and groan[ing] for an hour or so, moving her huge arms back and forth under her and out again and finally just lying down flat" (316).

Mrs. May had walked in on Mrs. Greenleaf once as she was engaged in such an unorthodox rite. She heard someone calling "Jesus! Jesus!" in the forest "with a terrible urgency," and then she saw Mrs. Greenleaf in the midst of her religious euphoria. "Her face was a patchwork of dirt and tears and her small eyes, the color of two field peas, were red-rimmed and swollen, but her expression was composed as bulldog's" (316). The animalistic simile at the end of the description, so typical for O'Connor, adds to the grotesque effect and throws Mrs. Greenleaf's physicality out of proportion, but it also prefigures the hyperbolic violence, the attack of the ferocious bull, at the end of the text.

Finally, the zealous self-professed healer cries out, "Oh Jesus, stab me in the heart" and falls in the dirt, a "huge human mound, her legs and arms spread out as if she were trying to wrap them around the earth" (317). Her grotesquely enlarged human body, blown out of proportion to tower over the world, becomes as excessive as her awkward, charismatic religiousness, but it is also open for the shocking stroke of faith, so powerful that it may kill. In the story, the piercing and the wrapping are two distinct microfigurative representations of how the human body interacts with the sacred—as if the physique cannot uphold the revelation and, in the process of the climactic epiphany, must be destroyed. The carnal is too fragile a vehicle to sustain the full scale of divinely inspired revelatory excess.

This grotesque practice of prayer healing is shunned by Mrs. May, who, as a nonbeliever respecting religion for its social propriety, maintains that the word "Jesus" ought to be reserved only for the church. The excess of religious zeal is to her inexcusable, and she believes that, in her revival verve, Mrs. Greenleaf has exhibited nothing short of a dementia—although to Mrs. Greenleaf's husband Mrs. May only declares tactfully, "I am afraid your wife has let religion warp her," followed by the conciliatory "Everything in moderation, you know" (332). The figurative "warping," giving in to the hyperbole of irrational religious zeal and suspending decorum, is to her incomprehensible.

Interestingly, as we will discuss in relation to *The Violent Bear It Away*, Rayber, a secular teacher, uses the same metaphorical images with reference to Mason, an old prophet from the backwoods of Powderhead. To O'Connor, the awkward excess of spiritual zeal naturally invites the hyperbolic perversion of orthodoxy and the bending of prescriptive social categories. As a backwoods spiritual thaumaturgist, Mrs. Greenleaf represents to Mrs. May the danger of wild religious excess that cannot be reasoned with, a force that cares neither for the systematic methodological theological study of John Wesley nor for southern social decorum. However, while Mrs. Greenleaf calls out to be pierced by grace, in the end it is Mrs. May that is impaled by the violent Christ-bull.

In the final scene of the story, a stray bull that has been roaming around the farm, and whom Mrs. May commissions Mr. Greenleaf to shoot, attacks Mrs. May, agitated by her honking. It fatally wounds her, piercing her heart "like a wild tormented lover" (333), fulfilling Mrs. Greenleaf's earlier wishful call for stabbing. The picture of the flesh pierced by the horn is O'Connor's figurative image of how grace interacts with the flesh and how a human being is overpowered by the divine. As Robert Brinkmeyer points out, in O'Connor's world, "bodily injury [. . .] signal[s] the penetration of the divine" ("Closer Walk" 83). Thus, the shock and pain generate in Mrs. May a preagonal vision: "The tree line was a dark wound in a world that was nothing but sky—and she had the look of a person whose sight has been suddenly restored but who finds the light unbearable" (O'Connor, *Selected Stories* 333).

When O'Connor was working on "Greenleaf" in January 1956, she wrote in a letter that, as she was planning the violent scene out, she was uncertain whether she was to identify with Mrs. May or with the bull (*Habit of Being* 129). It seems that it is neither the human nor the animal agency that to which she ultimately relates but the very brutal act of piercing itself, the fatal perforation of the human body, and the puncturing of the flesh by an unstoppable, inhuman force that brings about a religious revelation.

The brutal scene of piercing crowns the tensions that escalate throughout the story, conjoining the religious and sexual anxieties of Mrs. May. With all the coital connotations of the piercing, O'Connor pushes the scene to the extreme, putting the emphasis on the transformative power of the violent. And as the metaphoric penetration of the heart transforms into the physical impalement and the abstract language turns into flesh, the sheer ferocious force of O'Connor's Catholic imagery takes full control of the narrative. The hyperbolic power of the impalement pierces the veil of propriety and, upon her death, Mrs. May witnesses the world as the body of Christ, with its side pierced. As the flesh gives in to the violent penetration, the vulnerability of the woman's corporality is exposed, together with the failure of decorum, which offers no protection and no solace from the animalistic violence. Thus, like a host of O'Connor's other characters, Mrs. May, having been hyperbolically "warped" and contrasted with the world around her, has her glimpse of enlightenment, though it tragically comes too late. The full, constructive new meaning and the deeper insight that could emerge from the hyperbolic tensions are taken away from her, and she is left to suffer and die without having been redeemed.

Murderous Baptism and Baptismal Murder

In *The Violent Bear It Away*, O'Connor takes up the eponymous, excessive violence as the adhesive for a book-length narrative. To evangelize her audience, she brings forth three dramatis personae: two prophets (a master and a disciple) and an agnostic schoolteacher—all three of whom remain in a fundamentally conflicted relationship with one another as well as with the world around them. The clashes among their standpoints gradually escalate through a series of violent interludes, ultimately culminating in the murder of a developmentally challenged child.

The excessive resides in the brutal repulsion between intellectual secularism and primordial, prophetic religiousness, visible throughout the novel. The metahyperbolic design of *The Violent Bear It Away* epitomizes this epistemological clash, which escalates beyond proportion, balance, and rationality into fiery violence. In this novel, for O'Connor, hyperbolic violence is both an evangelistic and a heuristic tool, a means to engage the modern, godless world and to impact it by bringing her readers closer to a soteriological epiphany, to push them to, almost literally, bear the kingdom of heaven away.

Simple as this scheme may seem, the copious mechanisms of revelatory violence O'Connor uses in her second novel turn out to be surprisingly complex, and to argue that the violence featured in *The Violent Bear It Away* is merely a divinely sanctioned tool for salvation is actually tantamount to misreading O'Connor's point. In her commentary on O'Connor's reading of Matthew 11:12, from which the book's title is derived ("From the days of John the Baptist until now, the kingdom of heaven suffereth violence, and the violent bear it away"), Susan Srigley ("The Violence of Love") elaborates on the directionality of this violence and makes a compelling case for its inward and self-sacrificial character. The "violence of love" in O'Connor's fiction is a purposeful stratagem, fused with an imperative to overcome the desires of the self. Ultimately, in her fiction, this violence becomes a ritualistic tool to explore the phenomenon of human nature struggling against itself—to O'Connor, in soteriological terms, it emancipates.

In the 1865 edition of the Douay-Rheims Catholic Bible, still popular in O'Connor's time, editor Reverend George Leo Haydock comments, "The kingdom of heaven is to be obtained by mortification, penance, poverty, and those practices of austerity which John, by word and example, pointed out." This inward directionality of violence, which Richard Giannone suggests is reminiscent of ascetic desert fathers, is hardly more visible in O'Connor's fiction than in the network of interlocking antagonistic, mimetic dependences shared by the three characters of her second novel.

The drama of *The Violent Bear It Away* opens with a grotesque death followed by a failed funeral. In an enthralling opening sentence, a hallmark of O'Connor's fiction, she introduces the reader to a fundamentally conflicted and confounded reality:

> Francis Marion Tarwater's uncle had been dead for only half a day when the boy got too drunk to finish digging his grave and a Negro named Buford Muson, who had come to get a jug filler, had to finish it and drag the body from the breakfast table where it was still sitting and bury it in a decent and Christian way, with the sign of its Saviour at the head of the grave and enough dirt on top to keep the dogs from digging it up. (*Three by Flannery O'Connor* 125)

Such a pithy opening, which Jonathan Rogers likens to the "painting of a picture of the fallen world at its ugliest" (133), immediately initiates the sense of grotesque misplacement, engaging the reader like the narrative opening of a sermon. Young Francis Marion Tarwater attempts to bury his old uncle, who had abducted him and raised him to be a prophet. A short time later, the young man abandons the backwoods cabin in Powderhead, Tennessee, where they lived, and sets out to the city to meet Rayber, his cousin, who works as a schoolteacher and who is father to a developmentally challenged child, Bishop.

The old patriarch prophet had had a falling out with Rayber, after Rayber published a quasi-psychological article describing the old man's religious oddities, and so Raber commissions his protégé, Tarwater, to baptize Bishop. After the secular schoolteacher tries, unsuccessfully, to "sivilize" him, Tarwater, swayed by a weird, demonic agency, drowns Bishop in a lake, uttering the rite of baptism, and, in the end, embarks on a sacred journey to "go warn the children of god of the terrible speed of mercy" (267).[4]

A violent contrast of opposites that permeates the desperate world of the novel and every line of dialogue in it can hardly be accepted by the reader with anything but a sense of obscure unease. The microcosm of Powderhead, like the lives of its two prophetic inhabitants, remains in a perpetual state of contrastive antagonism to everything else, framing the hyperbolic metafiguration. Taking the ascetic solitude of the biblical prophets Elijah and Elisha as models for their life, the two prophets set themselves in fundamental opposition to the modern world.

It is hardly surprising, then, that the religious gospel they embrace is quintessentially apocalyptic—Old Tarwater, as skilled in moonshining as in prophesying, spends his days awaiting Judgment Day. And although doomsday did not come, "one morning he saw to his joy a finger of fire coming out of [the sun] and before he could turn, before he could shout, the finger touched him and the destruction he had been waiting for had fallen in his own brain and his own body" (126). It is through this fiery impulse that he received his prophetic epiphany.

At the same time, the old man seeks to prolong his life and to reach out to Bishop from beyond the grave. Through ascetic estrangement, ending in death, his physicality becomes, as it were, cleaved from his will, which endures in his disciple. While his body is finite, mortal, and ultimately frozen behind the table in an awkward caricature of a daily meal, followed by an equally awkward caricature of an unfulfilled funeral rite, his resolve pervades and touches Rayber through a disciple the old man had engineered to continue his legacy.

The prophetic gift is the central element of the hyperbolic in the novel. When Tarwater knocks on Rayber's door and tells him of Mason's death, the schoolteacher says, "Everything he touched, he warped" (176). The old man's behavior, irrational and violent from Rayber's perspective, expressed pure, unpredictable, and unstoppable excess. The micrometaphorical "warping," the pushing and pulling the old man exercised with his will and actions, disturbed the boxed world of the schoolteacher's rationalism. He stresses that Mason had space for only one idea in his head and that the old man was walking and breathing excess, living the Old Testament images of divine retribution. Rayber is repelled by this religious monomania, and he cannot bear the "warping" of reality that gives the old prophet a sense of safety and belonging.

O'Connor needed Mason to be at the same time disturbing and zealous, chaotic and focused on his mission. His obsessive behavior, the screaming and shouting, the ruckus he engaged in, the stalking of his family members, and, ultimately, the child abduction—all of these unruly actions constituted, for him, the means to fulfill his prophetic mission. Tarwater embodies its longevity, as he is reared to be the schoolteacher's nemesis, to provide the old man with a chance to execute his will from beyond the grave. Mason wants to bend the world to match his excessive prophetic fixation. Effectively, he seeks to achieve this by creating his double, another version of himself, and as Frederick Asals points out, this obscure effect of déjà vu may be seen as a key constructive principle of the novel (170).

When he was alive, the old man would occasionally wander into the woods and leave his young disciple alone, and upon his return he would "look the way the boy thought a prophet ought to look." His spiritual wanderings left him rattled and exhausted but full of religious fervor; the patriarch prophet looked "as if he had been wrestling a wildcat, as if his head were still full of the visions he had seen in its eyes, wheels of light and strange beasts with giant wings of fire and four heads turned to the four points of the universe" (*Three by Flannery O'Connor* 127–128). This echoes the experience of the biblical Ezekiel, who witnessed a beast surrounded by fire in his visionary wandering, and the old man's solitary, prophetic roaming allowed him to connect with the very source of his zeal.

Here, O'Connor's fascination with the putative dedication of the desert fathers and their inwardly directed religious intensity comes to the fore. It is in the complete wild, outside the perimeter of Powderhead, that the patriarch prophet could reach out to the spiritual source of his fiery inspiration. Thus, he returns to Powderhead after having fought a battle against the evil forces that sought to divert him from his path. This is not unlike Saint Anthony, who, having given up his property to be donated to the poor, assumed a hermit's life in the desert and confronted a plethora of demons pouring temptations upon him—an image famously portrayed in the grotesque paintings of Hieronymus Bosch, Dorothea Tanning, and Salvador Dali.

Rayber shuns this unruliness, but his animosity toward Mason's religious inspiration is emblematic of his own spiritual and volitional impotency. The old man's unflattering, excessive fixation on the prophetic mission antagonizes Rayber to the point of obsession. The prophetic hyperbole aggravates his rationalist orderliness and challenges his normative vision of how he believes the world should be operating. Old Tarwater cannot be contained, he cannot be reasoned with, and, most importantly, he acknowledges no authority and will violently denigrate anyone who would seek to impose his or her will upon him. Immune to all earthly imperatives, he does not fear any legal consequences of his actions.

Even the prospect of death does not undermine his stance. He plans his own passing, morbidly arranging every detail to make it as easy as possible for Tarwater to carry his body to the grave. Thus, O'Connor presents death not as the sad, nihilistic ending the "devilish" stranger argues for when talking to Tarwater. It is a mandatory part of life, necessary to achieve salvation. The old prophet's ascetic rejection of the modern world and his antisocial gospel of apocalyptic vengefulness may render him a grotesque, but, given O'Connor's appreciation for uncompromising, antimodern religiousness, it also turns him into a truly holy man.

Rayber identifies Mason as a destructive excess and, setting himself in opposition to the old man, he would like to present himself as the champion of the rational, humane decorum of which Mason is the ultimate violation. The schoolteacher aspires to set out the norm, to create a prototype of the modern man, while the old prophet would be cast away beyond the normative perimeter into dangerous intemperance. In metahyperbolic terms, Rayber wants to be the decorum in opposition to Mason's excess.

Ironically, he fails to see that, for all his amalgamative pseudo expertise in sociology, psychology, and history, he is not much wiser than—and surely not very much different from—the one whom he would like to relegate to oblivion. The creed of secularism he proposes as an alternative to the old man's prophetic gospel, for instance, is equally "warped" and flawed with the propensity for violence. After all, it is he who first attempted to murder Bishop, and he only failed due to his lack of decisiveness.

O'Connor emphatically stresses that, driven by the secular and aimless philosophy of the modern world, Rayber fails to incorporate love into his rationalist scheme of things. His secularism is so deeply narcissistic and so narrow-minded that he can hardly be considered more than a type. Rayber himself is guilty of dehumanizing his own offspring. When he depicts Bishop as an "x signifying the general hideousness of fate" (192), he reduces the developmentally challenged child to a nameless letter, a statistical factor, obliterating the boy's identity long before he is actually murdered. It is hardly surprising that his rationalist mind compels him to recognize his love for the child as "horrifying." The powerful sensation of love terrifies him, as it reaches beyond the walls of his rationalist reality.

Rayber is a similar construct to the infamous Hulga, who is likewise pathetically powerless and incurably haunted, but her atheistic malaise is essentially different because of how O'Connor engineers the stories. The metalogical dynamics of "Good Country People" are more uneven, and while, in the face of the terrible truth about Pointer's grisly fetish, Hulga's frustrated, atheistic spitefulness is revealed as naive, she has no counterweight with which to push back the excess. She simply annihilates herself in her miserable, one-note pathway of pseudo intellectualism.

In O'Connor's second novel, Rayber is juxtaposed against the two prophets (who, between themselves, develop ambiguously narcissistic relations), and these two contrasting pulls generate the space for the hyperbolic mode. After young Tarwater arrives at his house, Rayber quickly learns that helping his nephew is beyond his power. In metafigurative terms, he realizes that he cannot be the decorum he wanted to embody, and he fails to normalize what the prophetic hyperbole has generated. The youth's behavior is incorrigible, and despite all Rayber's trying, despite all the educational trips he organizes, the young prophet remains largely unresponsive to what Rayber tries to tell and show him.

The only chance he potentially has to reach the boy is when the confused Tarwater attends a revival meeting, where a young girl, Lucette, preaches about Christ's coming and asks the audience to help her parents financially so that they may carry on with their missionary work. Her message is that of Christian concord, so very different from the "warped" and excessive world of Powderhead prophesying. The offbeat nature of Tarwater's upbringing is also apparent in the fact that, in the seclusion of the backwoods cabin, the young prophet was raised without the company of women. In fact, female characters are conspicuously absent from the text. In the prophetic world of the Tarwaters, the strongest reminder that females even exist is the misogynic labels the patriarch hammers into his disciple's head. All females are "whores," and Bishop's mother is even worse than that—she is much too "ridiculous" to even be given the derogatory label of "whore." This misogynic upbringing has left Tarwater much too damaged to be framed in the rationalist categories Rayber would like him to become a part of and to find solace in. Against the excessive, "warping" magnetism of Mason, there can be no victory.

Yet perhaps one should not blame Rayber for being unable to sway the young prophet to his side, simply because O'Connor does not allow him to do so. As a character, he is both feeble and unconvincing—Harold Bloom dubs him an "aesthetic disaster" ("*Introduction*" 2). The schoolteacher epitomizes all that O'Connor viewed as flawed in the secular mind. Indeed, even for a relatively inattentive reader, his slackness is almost too artificial and too obvious, evident proof of O'Connor's bias in the debate she initiates in her writing.

O'Connor mercilessly strips the secular character to a bare minimum, a strategy that allows her to contrastively bring the two prophets to the forefront of the narrative. But the difference between the characters is not only that of intensity. It is a given that the prophets' fiery religious zeal mercilessly outshines the schoolteacher's hesitant, dim candle of rationalism. A failed teacher, Rayber is also fundamentally incapable of any instructional action, of enlightening objects or phenomena. Afflicted by the paralysis of secular inertia, he can only tentatively prop things up and observe, unable to actually perform meaningful actions. The schoolteacher leaves no disciple, no posterity—and the child he begat is incapable of rational computing and probably cannot even continue his secular legacy. It is little wonder that the old prophet described Rayber's fruit as "dry and seedless, incapable even of rotting, dead from the beginning" (*Three by Flannery O'Connor* 134)—metaphors that are antithetical to how the zealous, living faith is described by the prophet.

Here, O'Connor also emphasizes the contrast between their uses of language. The old man would see his speech as empowered by his faith and dedication, as if it were a living word of Gospel. By contrast, in the magazine article he wrote about his uncle, Rayber surmised that Mason's "fixation of being called by the Lord had its origin in insecurity. He needed the assurance of a call, and so he called himself" (134). These sentences typify the rational, analytical language of the schoolmaster and his secular study of the prophetic phenomenon, seeking to reduce the motivation behind Mason's behavior to an interesting psychological case study.

The old man is persistently enraged by Rayber's words. He indignantly fixates on them in front of Tarwater and hisses irritably, "Called myself. I called myself. I, Mason Tarwater, called myself!" (134). What enrages him so much is that the secular analysis pointed to prophetic agency from within, not from outside. The schoolteacher implied that the old Tarwater was his own prophetic appointer and appointee—in a nutshell, that he was all alone in his Gospel.

Rayber would like to inhabit a postprophetic world in which the old Tarwater is a relic of the past, an artifact that ought to be studied and academically described for posterity, but also one that is irreparably doomed to die out and fall into oblivion. He wishes to be the secular annalist of the extinction and to personally drive the nail into the coffin of prophetic faith. However, he underestimates the longevity of the old man's influence and overestimates his own impact upon Francis Tarwater. Against the haunting presence of the patriarch prophet, his fluttering, secular will can hardly be a match.

O'Connor makes this duel uneven right from the beginning. In terms of the metafiguration, the unruliness of the prophetic trope and the sheer violent power it emanates paralyze the secular and rationalist forces and overwhelm them. Young Tarwater has been bred as an instrument of purgation; his goal is to "burn the eyes [of Rayber] clean" (143). To Rayber's frustration, the prophetic era is far from eclipsed, especially in view of how, at the end of the novel, young Tarwater embraces his prophetic legacy and how, by this acknowledgment, the prophet patriarch, whose awkward demise opened the plot, effectively becomes reborn. Even the old man's death has longevity to it, as he leaves his young protégé with two sacramental assignments: giving Mason a Christian burial and baptizing Bishop. Effectively, he is able to move between death and life, between the demise of the body and the rebirth of the spirituality. The grotesque drama of *The Violent Bear It Away* unfolds between these eschatological signposts and then ends with them, in the grotesque act of Bishop's simultaneous baptism and murder, performed by Tarwater.

Symbolically, the schoolteacher's glasses and hearing aid constantly remind the reader that he remains both blind and deaf to the words of spiritual calling and that his sensory reception of the world remains flawed. The trope of sight, typical for O'Connor, is designed to divulge the fundamental epistemological difference between Rayber and Tarwater. The young prophet sees the schoolteacher's eyes as "shadowed with knowledge," blurred and lacking revelatory precision, "and the knowledge moved like tree reflections in a pond where far below the surface shadows a snake may glide and disappear" (156). In contrast, Tarwater's eyes, at the end of the novel, cease to look hollow and become "scorched" (261), capable of guiding him forward.

Rayber's eyes also fail in another way. The father steers clear of the eyes of his mentally defective child out of fear that he might experience the surge of irresistible love. Viewed by Tarwater as "two pools of light" (136), Bishop's eyes constitute the schoolteacher's parental anathema, testifying to his emotional infecundity. The young prophet's mission to burn the schoolteacher's eyes clean turns out to be a failure because, O'Connor implies, there is nothing to burn out, just a hollow secular space.

In fact, O'Connor systematically designs Rayber's sluggishness to stand in contrast with Tarwater's reckless actions—Tarwater himself keeps stressing that he in fact completed tasks the schoolteacher could not perform. While this evident lack of potency would be one of O'Connor's ploys to castigate secularism, in Rayber there is an equally evident lack of virtue, zeal, and love. This is visible, for instance, in his somewhat desperate definition of the dignity of man: "his ability to say: I am born once and no more. What I can see and do for myself and my fellowman in this life is all of my portion and I'm content with it. It's enough to be a man" (180). His inertia in the wake of the murder of his child is perhaps the most telling proof of secular inactivity that O'Connor could devise. In the "warped" world of the novel, the prophets are strong through the weakness of secular rationalists, who cannot expose the pathological aspects of the excess and who lack the potency to contain the unruliness of the hyperbolic.

In a letter to T. R. Spivey from 1960, O'Connor declared that there are two main symbols in the novel: water and Christ in the form of bread (*Habit of Being* 387). The center of the narrative gravitates around Tarwater's selfish resistance to their call and to the allure that they represent. Thus, the young prophet ultimately genuflects to the will of the patriarch, and the acceptance of the prophetic calling is effectively a renunciation of his narcissistic individuality. He becomes the old man's double, a prolongation of his religious excess, which guides him to perpetuate his master's fiery gospel.

The whole book can actually be seen as a hyperbolized depiction of an ascetic religious struggle, a violent impulse to satisfy a spiritual craving by diminishing carnal thirst and hunger. As O'Connor herself explains, *The Violent Bear It Away* constitutes exactly a "very minor hymn to the Eucharist" (*Habit of Being* 387). If so, it is substantially carnal. The physicality of Tarwater's cravings, of the insatiable thirst and the notorious hunger he experiences throughout the whole story, translates into the authentic presence of the flesh of Christ that O'Connor witnessed in her church every Sunday as a Catholic.

Actually, this framework of death and life propels the book's hyperbolic figuration and allows O'Connor to profile the metalogic of the text in a way that ensures delivery of the most forceful message to readers. It is a matter of interpretation whether the climactic scene of the novel features a baptismal murder or murderous baptism. O'Connor uses this ambivalence to disturb the audience, and as the story reaches its apex, the convoluted forces that pull the novel's grotesque reality in different directions coalesce violently. This is the crux of the metahyperbolic design, the ultimate moment of confrontation between the two excessive opposites she constructs throughout the text. As O'Connor herself admits, it is toward the moment of the grotesque baptism that "I have to bend the whole novel—its language, its structure, its action" ("Novelist and Believer" 162)—it is the climactic moment of her hyperbolic "mode of comprehension," the design she employed in the text. O'Connor's point is critical for the directionality of the tensions that permeate the text, as this bending, just like the warping of the world around old Tarwater, leads to the hyperbolization that, in her view, reveals the fundamental mystery to her readers. The mixing of murder and baptism, death and life, becomes the climax of the hyperbolic metalogic employed by O'Connor.

And so Mason's mission is finally fulfilled by his prophetic protégé, and the young man's potency for action becomes fully revealed, yet in a most grisly manner, callous even by O'Connor's standards. Just as the name of the young prophet, Tarwater, conjoins the antithetical connotations of the clarity of water and the murky, fiery blackness of tar, the confounded nature of the climactic ritual is essential to the novel. Symbolically, water itself has an inherent ambivalence: it may serve to perform the salutary rite of baptism but it also is needed to commit murder by drowning. The confused and twisted nature of the deed is essential for embracing the excessive warping as his way of life. As he drowns Bishop, the young prophet is compelled by a sibilant imperative to utter the words of baptism, effectively turning himself into a passive instrument of the forces that have actually worked through him throughout the whole story. At the same time, immediately after the murder, he seeks to downplay the significance of the rite, undermining the performative potency of his words, calling them "just some words that run out of my mouth and spilled in water" (*Three by Flannery O'Conner* 204), and denying the actual effect of the act upon the reality around him. The young prophet seems to be more inclined to believe that all he did was murder, the completion of an undertaking his uncle could not finalize due to his secular inertia. Yet after that comes the full espousing of the prophetic hyperbole.

The death by water is followed by a catharsis by fire, which functions as the ultimate purifier, framing its figurative structure in the novel. Fire encompasses both the genesis and the apocalyptic revelation of Mason's prophetic gospel. Right at the beginning of the text, Tarwater burns down the Powderhead house, hoping that the old man's body will perish with the building, and at the end of the story he sets fire to the forest that has just been the scene of a rape perpetrated by the lavender-fragranced, satanic stranger. The young prophet-to-be seeks to cremate Mason, and, incidentally, to provide a fiery funeral for him that will live up to the violent, fiery creed he embraced. Obviously, in doing so, he fails to fulfill the old man's last request, for a proper, Christian burial. The blazing forest at the end of the story seems to have more of a purgative function, as the youth seeks to obliterate the space that witnessed his sexual abuse.

Both of Tarwater's incinerating catharses are instigated by the sparks of hyperbolic tension—his arsonous inclinations are the expression of a torrent of excessive pressures that he holds inside. Fire is the only resolution to the conflict, in the wake of the contrasting forces that push and pull the prophet-to-be. In the context of the opening scenes, the fire symbolically springs from the violent severing of the bond with his prophetic master and his leaving the backwoods cuckoo's nest to seek out an atheistic relative, the antithesis of his previous life. In the context of the closing scenes, the ignition is the ultimate encounter with his nemesis, the Luciferian stranger who has been haunting him throughout the story under different disguises. At the same time, the final incendiary purging brings him closer to the ultimate embrace of his prophetic legacy and his mission. After all the warping and pushing and pulling, after all the excessive, extreme acts, including arson and child slaughter, his conflicted, kaleidoscopic chaos is finally set in place.

As the warped gospel of fire is what Tarwater was force-fed by his late prophetic custodian, it would become his prophetic path in the last pages of the book. Yet, at this point, it is a fiery gospel transformed, devoid of the violent egotism of Mason. The young man is given a prophetic mission to preach to the "children of god" about the "terrible speed of mercy" (267), to warp his neighbors and to impact them so strongly that they will abandon the meek secular decorum. The passive voice is iconic of the function Tarwater assumes in the prophetic process—having been the object of sodomitic violence, he now becomes the object of messianic grace acting through him. Figuratively, he assumes the role of the conduit of the epiphany he gained by the ambivalent act of baptismal murder and murderous baptism. And he momentarily identifies the fire that is thus manifest as a prophetic blaze, one that lets him into the legacy of biblical seers, whose mission was to propagate the uncompromising message and to evangelize the timid secularists.

7

TO KILL THE WATCHMAN

Harper Lee

The relationship between the two books by Harper Lee discussed in this chapter, *To Kill a Mockingbird* and *Go Set a Watchman,* is complex and confusing. This is not only because *Watchman* is in fact the first version of *Mockingbird,* with a plot set after the storyline of the earlier text, but also because the relatively recent emergence of Harper Lee's second novel encourages one to revisit some interpretations of Scout's childhood narrative. I will scrutinize the two novels together to demonstrate Harper Lee's employment of the hyperbolic and her representation of various mechanisms that reinforce and defend southern decorum. A joint reading of the two texts seems the most promising way of approaching them, for, when they are considered together, the two books demonstrate the diversity of ritualistic and rhetorical tools the white people of Maycomb use to protect what they believe remains at the core of their regional and communal identity. In essence, the war on the hyperbolic is, for them, a war to protect their southernness and the integrity of the region.

In both novels, the white citizens of Maycomb are afraid of hyperbolic deconstruction, the power of the excessive to dismantle the norms. They fear the realization of what the excess may ultimately reveal about their social fabric. In their haunted and troubled reality, this may mean the subversion of the social order they struggle to maintain and—more importantly—the subversion of their racial and economic status. Any sign of excess or unruliness is viewed as dangerous because it may eventually lead to the reorganization of social semiotics and the collapse of a system whose morally shaky foundations can hardly be sugarcoated or covered up by fabricated myths. Hence, all the efforts of the community members in Lee's novels are aimed at reinforcing decorum and mitigating the unruliness of those elements of the Maycomb world that are deemed excessive and thus potentially disruptive of southern racial divides.

In this sense, one sees a substantial affinity between these two narratives, and it is understandable how *To Kill a Mockingbird* subsequently evolved from *Go Set a Watchman*. Unlike in the case of, for instance, Katherine Anne Porter's short stories or Lillian Smith's autobiography, here, the hyperbolic is not a fraught, metanarrative means for the emancipation of the self from the dictates of regional decorum. As both of Lee's books were written two decades later than Porter's or Smith's, they were propelled by a different artistic drive. In the case of the Maycomb narratives, the hyperbolic becomes the feared Other of the southern norm, which reflects the fears of the community back at them and exposes the region's racial and social prejudices. In the case of Lee, the figures of excess, like the unruly rabid dog or the homecoming protagonist who is "losing her mind," become a means through which she tests the limits of her regional background and its paradoxical coherence.

In Maycomb, the excessive is always a threat that arrives from within, a homely element of the system that was transformed by the unruliness of hyperbole and broke away from the gravitational pull of Dixie. The excess roams free, driven by impulses that cannot be contained by the prescriptive cultural models and social conventions. Its recalcitrant and uncontrolled nature is construed as an aberration of decorum and a communal hazard. Thus, Lee shows how the fear of hyperbolic unruliness mobilizes the people of Maycomb to activate different protective mechanisms of counterattack and reprisal, of both physical violence or rhetorical manipulation. In this sense, the two books, considered as one portrayal of the southern opposition to excess, serve as a metanarrative way to understand the factors that remained instrumental for the establishment of southern identity.

The Threat of Excess

To Kill a Mockingbird is more than just a popular novel. It would be more fitting to view Lee's debut book as a cultural phenomenon that has remained perpetually viral over the past fifty years. The sheer statistics speak volumes about its enduring recognition. The novel's publisher, Harper Collins, boasts that as many as forty million copies of *To Kill a Mockingbird* have been sold over the years, and it has been translated into forty languages (Cavoto 418). Obviously, such phenomenal success is also connected with its equally cult

film version, in which Oscar-winning Gregory Peck gave America the charismatic image of noble Atticus Finch, who intrepidly defends Tom Robinson
against the prejudiced community. The admiration for the Maycomb lawyer
has lasted beyond the generation that grew up with a copy of the book in its
hands and with Peck before their eyes. A 2003 American Film Institute ranking placed Atticus Finch at the top of the list of positive icons of popular cin-
ema—above Indiana Jones, James Bond, and *Casablanca*'s Rick Blaine. What
was belated, however, was the realization that, under all his overt righteousness, Atticus is a southerner and would readily subscribe to the idea that separate could indeed be deemed equal.

Lee's debut novel took some time to mature. In 1957, a tentative version of
the text, first written under the title *Go Set a Watchman,* later changed to *Atticus,* and ultimately becoming *To Kill a Mockingbird,* made its way to J. B. Lip-
pincott and Company, a publishing house that had mainly released medical
publications. There, Tay Hohoff, a slightly eccentric editor whose love for cats
was matched only by her passion for cigarettes, saw some potential in Lee's
text. In order to become publishable, however, the novel needed thorough
changes, if not virtual rewriting. At that stage, in the words of Tay Hohoff, it
resembled more a "series of anecdotes than a fully conceived novel" (quoted
in Shields 87). The editing process was painstaking and turbulent, but once it
was released, *To Kill a Mockingbird* became a national sensation. Overnight,
Harper Lee was elevated to the status of a celebrity, which she hated and which
ultimately drove her to become a recluse.

The initial readings of *To Kill a Mockingbird* viewed it as a constructive
story whose jovial child narrator delivers the text from murky southern apol-
ogetics. Against the backdrop of the turbulent struggle of the civil rights
movement, Frank H. Lyell, in the *New York Times Book Review,* praised Lee
for not succumbing to the "current lust for morbid, grotesque tales of southern depravity" (5). Yet, when one peeks deeper into the convoluted world of
Maycomb, it becomes apparent that the lens of the young protagonist does
not fully mitigate the hyperbolic tensions portrayed by Lee. Michael Manson
points to numerous gothic elements at the beginning of the novel and argues
that they "expose Southern society as driven by gender binaries, patriarchal
abuse, class division, and racial animosity" (310).

In Lee's narrative, a network of normalizing community policies relentlessly ensures that all the gothic constituents of the social fabric remain protected and all the haunted taboos remain undisturbed. To safeguard the segre-

gated status quo and to protect the social code, the white community engages in a series of normative routines that eliminate all the elements that pose a potential threat to it. This defense of racial and social strictures becomes a communal prerogative, and it is only through the eradication of any disruptive and hyperbolic element, or its ritualistic relegation, that what has been accepted as the norm can be perpetuated.

This being the case, the debate about the status of the novel as a bildungsroman ceases to be a mere matter of a label. What the story leads to and the way in which it impacts the young protagonist's coming of age has considerable relevance for the directionality of the figurative tension. Robert Butler observes that *Mockingbird*'s child narrator, constantly doubled by the mature narrator, does not undergo any radical transformation, and her change is certainly insufficient to consider the book to be a novel of development (124–125). To him, it is Jem who grows and ultimately changes with the realization of how Tom Robinson's trial was a lost cause right from the beginning. Similarly, Kathryn Lee Seidel takes issue with the label "bildungsroman" and reads Jem's reaction into Scout's behavior—which, to Jennifer Murray, constitutes an interpretative mistake and one of the ways in which the novel can be "misread" (83). Murray seeks to address this issue by pointing out the discordance in the novel's narration, and she observes that the first-person narration of a child that has an adult voice behind it would naturally suggest that the novel is a bildungsroman, a story of Scout's maturing after witnessing the injustice that turned her world upside down (80). According to Manson, the organization of the book is more complex than one would initially surmise. He stipulates that Lee's novel constitutes a "portrait of Southern maturity" in which the gothic elements are subsumed into the bildungsroman (312), and while the novel opens with the gothic representation of the daily reality of the small-town South, it gradually but distinctly changes into a narrative of personal development.

The straitlaced statement that "It is a sin to kill a mockingbird" seems be one of the main lessons given to the children by Atticus, who seeks to educate them and trigger that personal evolution (99). However, the melodious bird constitutes a meek and a straightforward symbol whose directive borders on blatant moralizing. It epitomizes the righteous norm and the principled morality of balance. Thus, the connection between what the mockingbird represents and Tom Robinson and Boo Radley, two victims of southern society's normalizing policy, is too evident, and the passivity of these two "mockingbirds," who rely on Atticus to save them, takes on an almost demeaning tone.

They are victims deserving compassion, certainly, but the story leaves them little space to fend for themselves, and thus they are mere spectators in their own drama. In this sense, they fit into the decorum.

If one investigates the hyperbolized sources of tensions that impact the world of Maycomb, one comes to realize that it is not the mockingbird that best serves as the symbol of the book. Instead, this distinction ought to be ascribed to the mad dog, and the scene of its killing bears pivotal meaning for the whole story and for Lee's portrayal of the South. The scene is episodic and constitutes a plot fragment that could well be a fine residue of the initially disjointed text of the novel that Tay Hohoff wanted to unify. However fragmented it may be, though, the episode makes a compelling point about the threat of excess in the Maycomb world, and it remains integral to the portrayal of how the hyperbolic extreme engages decorum and the threat it poses to what is construed as a norm.

The liver-colored bird dog known as Tim Johnson, the pet of Maycomb, is spotted behaving erratically on the street, "as if his right legs were shorter than his left legs" (Lee, *To Kill a Mockingbird* 103). Scout's brief description, likening the animal to a "car stuck in a sandbed," stresses how rabies transformed its demeanor, throwing it off balance and rendering it grotesquely uncanny. The strangeness of the dog's changed physicality, as well as its queer movements, fill the children with a sense of anxiety. At the same time, Calpurnia's desperate calls raise the alarm about a disease-ridden, awkwardly behaving dog and put the inhabitants of the neighborhood in a state of nervous suspense. The houses down the whole street are being carefully locked up for fear of the sick animal.

Yet the animal is not an alien invader; it does not come from beyond the town's borders. It is familiar to the neighborhood and has a local history (repetitively stressed by the label "old") and a homey name (sounding, in fact, not dissimilar to "Tom Robinson"). In other words, the animal has been a part of the Maycomb community and is an aberrant, hyperbolized danger from within. The disease, however, has thrown "old Tim Johnson" out of balance, turning what is known and homey into an unnerving danger. The mad dog epitomizes the excess that can disturb the safety of the town and against which a regulatory act of violence needs to be exercised.

When Atticus Finch reluctantly shoots the dog, revealing his stunning marksmanship to the amazed Jem and Scout, he takes on the role of a custodian of the community's safety, capable of alleviating a threat of disarray and fatal illness. The violence he uses against the rabid animal is necessary for the preservation of Maycomb, and thus it has a controlling function of retaining the status quo. When Miss Maudie later explains to Jem and Scout why their father would not boast about his past as "One-Shot Finch," she hypothesizes that "maybe he put his gun down when he realized that God had given him an unfair advantage over most living things" (109). Thus, she evokes the idea of proportion and balance of strength, which legitimizes the use of the gun in Atticus's eyes. Only the disproportion of the hyperbolized threat of an erratic animal calls for picking up a gun, which can figuratively restore the social order and safety.

This scene, however, is not the only instance in which Atticus has to confront the excessive and the erratic. At the end of the story, during the trial of Tom Robinson, he is forced to come up against Mayella Ewell's emotional outburst. Having cornered her during her testimony and pressed the most sensitive sores in her wounded mind, he triggers a reaction that is beyond his control, when she famously cries out, "If you fine fancy gentleman don't wanta do nothin' about it then you're all yellow stinkin' cowards, stinkin' cowards, the lot of you. Your fancy airs don't come to nothin'," before suffering from a fit and turning mute (207). The excessive, unruly behavior, the crying and shouting that she manifests, are indicative of a dangerous loss of control caused by the bending of the normative categories of racial hyperbole. Her desperate exhortation recontextualizes the trial. The ideas of compassion and of the unassailable facts exculpating Tom lose all importance in the wake of the fit and the fact that her testimony is being juxtaposed against the testimony of an African American.

Mayella has absolutely nothing to constitute herself—no social status, no financial or intellectual leverage. Her only prerogative is her skin color, which, in this excessive, decorum-oriented society, grants her the privilege of restitution. In the hierarchy of the four social layers delineated by Jem after the trial, she remains "down at the dump" (249), just above the African American population, and while Scout is reared to be a southern lady, Mayella is fated to never rise above the level of "white trash." In *Go Set a Watchman,* one can see how, for people like Aunt Alexandra, such a low-class stigma remains permanently engraved into a person's status. When Henry Clinton seeks to elevate himself, she appreciates but cannot fully embrace the attempt. In *Mockingbird,* in the discordant, hysterical excess, with the contrasting epithets pitched against each other, Mayella plays for this final and ultimate line of defense—and is successful.

Tom Robinson will be viewed as guilty of this excess and culpable in causing such a tantrum in a white person, however contemptible she may be. Thus, as in the case of the mad dog, the regulatory mechanism of society to subdue the hyperbole will be activated. The code of the community dictates that the racial balance has to be retained, and the score of shame has to be settled, even at the expense of an innocent life—especially if that life belongs to an African American and thus, in Jim Crow's exorbitant racial system, is dispensable. The mechanisms that protect and proliferate the racial excess of segregation cannot tolerate any excess that might potentially throw them off their steady course and disturb the boxed reality of the four "kinds of folk" described by Jem. The society's agenda is to safeguard and propagate the existing social paradigms, which claim Robinson's freedom and, ultimately, his life.

Tom Robinson is shot, not unlike the mad dog. However, the retributive nature of this act of violence becomes evident when Atticus, who managed to put the rabid animal down in one clean shot, tells Aunt Alexandra that Tom, while attempting to escape, was shot seventeen times. While Atticus's violence is protective and regulatory, the violence against Tom is an act of vengeance. Here, Lee vividly presents her readers with a reality framed in the disparity between the rational conception of justice based on legal proceedings and a type of injustice based on prejudice and craving for retaliation—though, on a deeper level, both are similarly prejudiced. The clash between these two realities generates acts of violence throughout the book. It causes Mayella Ewell to accuse Tom in the first place, it causes Bob Ewell to turn violent toward Atticus and his children, and, finally, it causes the guards to gun Tom Robinson down—to employ obviously excessive violence to slaughter and eradicate a threat to the norms of the segregated society.

Clearly, the moral aberration in Harper Lee's novel is that it is an act of compassion that brings about Tom's undoing. Thus, metafiguratively, it is irony that allows us to identify the paradox of the system and the extent to which the members of the community remain pathologically blind to the distortion at the very heart of their moral constitution. It also is the *ironia vitae* of existence in a prejudiced society, in which the categories of empathy and benevolence are paradoxically subverted. In the normative system of the South, in which the issue of race overshadows everything else, Tom's moral empathy for a neighbor undercuts the prescribed relations of power and dependability; it blatantly implies that he is entitled to assume a perspective that would allow him to judge the circumstances of life of a white person. And so, ironically, Atticus loses the trial the moment his client confesses to having felt sorry for Mayella—a declaration that, anywhere outside the excessive reality of the South, would have allowed him to score points with the jury and the judge. Tom's behavior, benevolent and driven by altruistic motives, remains inadmissible in view of the southern racial doctrine and requires a punitive intervention on the part of the community.

To demonstrate this paradox on a metanarrative level, Harper Lee hyperbolizes the setting of Robinson's trial. By stressing the ambiguity of the case through Tom's evident innocence and his benevolent compassion, and by escalating the circumstances to the point of crisis, she manages to juxtapose the sense of morality against the steadfast wall of southern racial prejudice. This metafigurative contrast, exemplified best in the questioning of the witnesses, allows Lee to construct an enduring image of the racial tensions in the South.

At the same time, the community's insistence on the removal of the potentially disruptive element exhibits ritualistic features. Tom Robinson is a necessary scapegoat who needs to be sacrificed for the social balance to be restored and for the negative, "unruly" excess to be erased. Here, Lee's narrative falls into René Girard's anthropological paradigm of communal scapegoat sacrifice. In his works, the French anthropologist points to the violent sacrificial rite as one of the founding characteristics of human social organization. To him, all mounting social conflicts, which are the result of large groups of people craving one and the same thing and succumbing to "mimetic desire," inevitably lead to paroxysms and, sooner or later, threaten the existence of communities. To avoid social turmoil, these conflicts and tensions are placated through the process of scapegoating, in which a member of the society is blamed for the unrest, pronounced aberrant and subversive, and, finally, subjected to ritualistic violence. Having been victimized, the scapegoat is later frequently venerated for the restoration of peace in the community. Girard proves that this pattern has been replicated countless times in different cultural contexts and has had a pivotal impact on the development of mythology and literature.

Girard lists lynching as one of the ways in which this mechanism is enacted. For him, the ritualistic violence of lynching, perpetuating its mythological roots, is an act that is driven by the "spontaneous unanimity" of the participants and becomes the "violence of all" (299). Girard also points to the presence of the truthful in fiction, in fictive stories' ritualistic acts of violence, such as lynching, or even those as absurdly exorbitant as witch trials. Paradoxically, such a trial, even if based on false accusations or inaccurate stereotypes, inevitably leads to a very real and palpable sentence and causes the victim to be subjected to ritualistic scapegoating. This would suggest that there is a need to reevaluate mythology and the accounts of its rituals to look for the ingenuous "signs" of the paradox.

As Girard observes, literature excels at retaining these signs. When one reads the journalistic reports of lynching violence in the South in the 1930s, one may still be able to discern such "telltale signs"; however, the more removed readers are from the times they study, the less they will be able see. Given the passing of time, the "truth will lie only in a novel written by someone named William Faulkner," since "it is only the novel that puts together all the signs" (Jonathan Smith 228). Lee's literary account of the ritualized mechanisms that protect the South's decorum[1] and her use of the metalogic of hyperbole, the clash of opposites, provides the narrative background for such signs of the ritual, allowing us to comprehend and interpret them.

In *To Kill a Mockingbird,* the famous scene of the attempted lynching of Tom Robinson before the trial would be symptomatic of the violent propensity aimed at protecting the social order and eliminating the African American who has allegedly violated the most sacred and sensitive aspect of the southern code. The mob, which is dispersed due to Scout's intervention, approaches the prison with the intention of completing a rite of violence, and when a member of the lynch mob declares to Atticus, who is guarding the prison, "You know what we want" (167), he states the obvious, for they not only want to punish the culprit of an alleged crime but also want to annihilate the threat to their privileged status, to make sure that that the boxed reality of segregation remains undisturbed.

The appearance of Atticus's children, in an almost deus ex machina manner, breaks the rite with a brilliant rhetorical strategy that could well be recommended by psychological manuals on crowd management. Scout addresses individual lynchers, shaming them and unwittingly placing moral responsibility for the act they are about to commit not on the collective shoulders of the mob, where it would be dispersed and lost, but upon the conscience of concrete individuals. The moment the attempted lynching ceases to be Girard's "violence of all," it cannot be executed, for the narrative that served as a collective excuse for the ritual is broken.

The Birth of a Southerner

In *Go Set a Watchman,* readers are given a chance to peek into what they will be tempted to view as the next chapter of Scout's story. In the contemporary age, when each cult novel or movie has to have a sequel, Harper Lee's second book, for better or for worse, inadvertently comes to satisfy the readers' basic curiosity. But this interest in what became of Scout after *To Kill a Mockingbird* does not stem from the need for an intensive artistic experience but from blatant inquisitiveness. A newly discovered novel by J. D. Salinger that presented the rest of Holden Caulfield's life story would undoubtedly be a groundbreaking literary success with astounding readership rates—though the success would be largely redundant. Indeed, in an age of global cultural consumerism, it is hard to accept that not all details need to be revealed and not all cravings for stories need to be satisfied. Thus, it is understandable that, given the canonical status of its predecessor, the publication of *Go Set a Watchman* was surrounded by an air of controversy.

Clearly, the social context of the publication of *Go Set a Watchman* is markedly different from that at the time of *Mockingbird.* Lee's first book came out during the time when Oliver L. Brown was fighting for the right of his daughter to attend an unsegregated school in Topeka, Kansas, while the second one came out during the presidency of Barack Obama, the first African American occupant of the White House. When approached from this perspective, the two texts may seem light-years apart. However, a lot of the demons that haunted Maycomb, where Scout used to live, are still there. Tom Santopietro points out that that *Go Set a Watchman* aligned well with the "new century's zeitgeist, touching as it did upon America's open wound of racial injustice" (210), visible in, for instance, the police violence in Ferguson, Missouri, or the renewed debate over whether the Confederate flag should fly over the state capitol in Columbia, South Carolina. However, *Go Set a Watchman* was not written in the 2000s. It is a book whose genesis actually predates *To Kill a Mockingbird.*

What readers all over the world were told by the press releases was that Tonja Carter, Lee's longtime friend and lawyer, had discovered the manuscript when she was checking on the condition of the original manuscript of the first novel, at Lee's secure archive in the vicinity of her Alabama home. Carter worked with Alice Lee, Harper's lawyer sister and former caretaker, until Alice's death in November of 2014, at the age of 103. The manuscript of *Go Set a Watchman* had allegedly been there all these years.

This in itself evoked some justifiable speculations—it was not easy to believe that a publishable text from Harper Lee, every literary publisher's holy grail, had simply been resting in the archive for more than half a century. Speculations about the dubious authorship of Lee's second novel quickly surfaced, suggesting that it was authored, or coauthored, by either Truman Capote or Tay Hohoff. These concerns about whether it was indeed Harper Lee who wrote the novel have since been dismissed,[2] but the debate about the status of *Go Set a Watchman* continues.

Lee's second book is indeed a hermeneutic conundrum. It is counterintuitive to read the story as anything but a follow-up to Lee's first novel, but it obviously is not. In terms of the plotline, it is set after *To Kill a Mockingbird*—it shows the protagonist not as the tomboy Scout but as the grown-up Jean Louise, returning from New York to her Alabama hometown. This change in the protagonist's name symbolizes a radical change in narration and the appropriation of a markedly different metanarrative means for the portrayal of the region. What joins the two books is the hyperbolic, which is juxtaposed against the prescriptive decorum of the South.

If *To Kill a Mockingbird* is a novel fused with hope, *Go Set a Watchman* is a book of disillusionment. As she declares early in the novel, Jean Louise is upset that her father sold a part of the Finches' land: "I just don't like my world disturbed without some warning" (75). She visibly wishes for the impossible, for the longevity of the childhood narrative. And thus, in the second book, readers are drawn into the powerful clash of the narrator's earnest perspective with the conflicted southern reality.

Of course, the shock of disillusionment is set against a strenuously prepared narrative background. First, Lee makes readers revisit Maycomb along with the protagonist. Side by side with her, the readers are led to grow impatient with Aunt Alexandra's acute sense of southern propriety, verging on prudery. And it is hard to prevent oneself from smiling at the daily paradoxes of the town, such as "Those who Drank Socially were not quite out of the top drawer, and because no one in Maycomb considered himself out of any drawer but the top, there was no Social Drinking" (52). It is mainly because this prudery is so charmingly subverted by Jean Louise that the readers may find it benign and homey. One can almost see here how Lee wanted to realize her ambition to become the Jane Austen of Alabama.

However, the homey stasis Jean Louise encounters turns out to be nothing more than a nostalgic fabrication. The first symptoms of the ailment that lurks beneath the sugarcoated surface of homecoming become visible when

Jean Louise finds a copy of *The Black Plague,* a racist magazine, in one of the rooms. Flabbergasted, she demands an explanation from Aunt Alexandra: "You—Aunty, do you know the stuff in that thing makes Dr. Goebbels look like a naive little country boy?" (102). Disgusted by its content, she throws the magazine into the garbage.

These initial ripples on the surface turn into an emotional tsunami when Jean Louise attends the meeting of the civil council. What she witnesses there is an assembly of steadfast racist activists, among whom her father takes a prominent seat. The speech delivered by Grady O'Hanlon, a local spokesman for Jim Crow, antagonizes and repels her the most. It amalgamates the most obtrusive and insidious racial statements, a defragmented catalog of white supremacy's rhetorical hot buttons: "kinky woolly heads . . . still in the trees . . . greasy smelly . . . marry your daughters . . . mongrelize the race . . . mongrelize . . . *mongrelize*" (108). The disjointed enumeration of racial phrases is iconic of Jean Louise's process of listening in—too shocked to absorb what is in between these phrases, she stumbles upon them, unable to move forward. And hearing such rhetoric employed in the company of her father, and with his permission, violently repulses her. Appalled, she storms out of the building and experiences an attack of nausea.

As with the bodily reactions described by the conflicted narrator of Lillian Smith's *Killers of the Dream,* Jean Louise's very physicality here resists absorbing what she has witnessed. The discord between the idealized image of her father that she has carried from her childhood and the ugly truth reaches so deep into her that her interior convulses, striving to absorb the shock. The South she has suppressed within her resurfaces and demands to be given control, or at least to be acknowledged. Provoked, Jean Louise, in response, becomes unruly and seeks to challenge and defy this southernness.

The physical repulsion is followed by mental revulsion, when she struggles to fight off the racist ideas she discovers are present in the household she had grown to idealize. Jean Louise's encounter with Calpurnia is another pivotal act in the drama, as she notices, to her disbelief, that Cal employs "company manners" (159) when talking with her. The conversation between them is devoid of true communication and turns out to be a mere social formality for Calpurnia, who behaves as she would with any member of the white community. They are worlds apart.

The realization of the implications of Calpurnia's behavior perplexes Jean Louise, as even a desperate "I'm your baby" (159) cannot break Calpurnia's shell. The attempt to evoke the childhood connection is "hopeless," and a moment of demystifying epiphany leads Jean Louise to question whether there had ever been a connection at all. Here, Calpurnia's silence is resounding in the sense that it is the only way she can refuse engagement with a white person without transgressing social decorum—after all, she cannot argue or explicate her grievances. Thus, her lack of conversational engagement is most telling. At this point in the description, Lee twice stresses the "million tiny wrinkles" in Calpurnia's face (160). She is permeated with a sense of old statuesqueness and venerable silence, transformed into a figure that epitomizes quiet, still endurance in the face of oppression.

Having realized the implications of the company manners Calpurnia has assumed, Jean Louise asks her in desperation, "Just one thing before I go— please, I've got to know. Did you hate us?" (160). The question is no longer an expression of disbelief; rather, it is a move to embrace the whole truth, however painful it may turn out to be. Earlier, in Jean Louise's mind, the "us" of the Finch household included Calpurnia; now she acknowledges that she has to rethink whom she can include in the collective pronoun. After a painful moment, in response, Calpurnia "shook her head." Lee does not clarify how Calpurnia did this, and this very ambiguity is pivotal to the conversation. One is left to wonder whether it was a gesture of denial, because she does not wish to admit that she did indeed hate the Finches, or it was an ultimate refusal to continue the conversation with her former "baby," as Jean Louise hoped to see it. Or maybe it was disbelief at the sheer naive absurdity of the question, the answer to which was obvious.

The scene encapsulates the tensions between the world of Scout and the world of Jean Louise, between the idealized reality of childhood and the brutal reality of social divides. As Murray argues, Calpurnia's presence in the Finch household is paradoxical in *To Kill a Mockingbird,* for she is described as a member of the Finch family but, at the same time, neither Scout nor Jem has ever crossed the threshold of her house and virtually nothing is known about her family and background (85). She is close to them only within the fabricated framework of segregated convention, as a surrogate servant-mother. Perhaps the major part of Jean Louise's shock in *Go Set a Watchman* consists of the realization that this veil exists. From this angle, the scene of her confrontation with her old "mammy" seems to confirm Murray's observations.

Through consecutive chapters, Jean Louise participates in a number of conversations that suck her back to the home from which she has alienated herself over the years and expose the true colors of the South to her. Disappointingly, Lee's second book seems to consist of hardly anything but a series of conversations. The main protagonist's reactions are continually filled with disbelief as Jean Louise is forced to accept that her image of the homey South was a mere anamnestic construct and that the members of her family, as well as her childhood acquaintances, hold views she has grown to detest. Unruly and full of confused disbelief, she tosses and turns among her family members and acquaintances, who strive to pull her back into the decorum. All of these exchanges remind one of consecutive onslaughts upon a besieged fortress, and under the pressure of new waves of argumentative assaults, Jean Louise's mind is finally forced to surrender and to accept what she initially wanted to reject. This ultimate triumph of the South's regulatory system, however, comes after a long and tiring war that encompasses numerous rhetorical skirmishes, in which different persuasive appeals to emotion (pathos), logic (Logos), and personal image and integrity (ethos) are used.

Upon hearing that Jean Louise visited Calpurnia, Aunt Alexandra, the custodian of southern propriety, delivers a peroration elucidating the inappropriateness of her niece's actions: "Jean Louise, nobody in Maycomb goes to see Negroes any more, not after what they've been doing to us" (Lee, *Go Set a Watchman* 166). The contrastive juxtaposition of pronouns in her speech makes it clear that the division between the communities is not only physical but also inherently conceptual. To Aunt Alexandra, Jean Louise's failed attempt to connect with her old mammy, and her crossing over to the area inhabited by African Americans, was a faux pas, an act of disloyalty to the community of which she is a part. And with every sentence, the polarized contrast between "them" and "us" becomes escalated: "You do not *realize* what is going on. We've been good to 'em, we've bailed 'em out of jail and out of debt since the beginning of time, we've made work for 'em when there was no work, we've encouraged 'em to better themselves" (166).

The anaphoric enumeration of grievances iconically represents the scale of Aunt Alexandra's boiling resentment. She is seeking to appeal to emotions and to stress her exasperation with how morally dubious the actions of African Americans are, from her perspective. The figurative arrangement of juxtapositions, emphasizing the alleged debt of the African American population to the white people of Maycomb, and their supposed ingratitude, leaves no space for a retort, much less for a constructive reaching out. It entails a one-sided, imbalanced morality of selective judgment, rooted in the concept of racial inequality. Finally, Aunt Alexandra says, "Keeping a nigger happy these days is like catering to a king" (167), thus employing a hyperbolic statement whose argumentative implications about who keeps whom and what one is allowed to expect of life are integral to the hyperbolized racial relations of the South.

All the arguments deployed by Aunt Alexandra turn her, in the eyes of Jean Louise, into a "hostile stranger" (167). And perhaps this is precisely the reason why this initial attempt by the aunt to convince her niece to embrace southernness, with all that it entails, ultimately fails and leads to alienation. Aunt Alexandra does not engage in a dialogue but seeks to force her way into Jean Louise's mind, to reorganize her thoughts, all the time almost surprised that she has to explain all of this to anyone, let alone to her niece—for her, all the corollaries she has explicated are axiomatic.

Aunt Alexandra's words seem uncannily "weird" and "echoing" (168) to her niece, as her mind resists the indoctrination, again to the point of a physical nausea. Or perhaps the nausea Jean Louise experiences, and her desperate attempt at an almost juvenile rebellion, are not directed at the people around her but at herself, as little by little she realizes the truth about Maycomb and the community in which she grew up. Jean Louise feels physically sick because of the sudden epiphany of the implications of her southernness and the shock of balance revealing itself as imbalance—the realization that, deep inside, she may not be much different from those whom she presently detests.

The next onslaught from the southern mind comes with the conversation Jean Louise has with Hester Sinclair during a tea party Aunt Alexandra has thrown for her niece. Hester's longing for a "good nigger trial" makes Jean Louise's "scalp jump," and her concern about "another Nat Turner Uprisin'" as everyone is "sittin' on a keg of dynamite" (172–173) leaves Jean Louise at a loss for words. She even sarcastically blames herself for losing her sense of humor, for being unable to laugh at the jokes the other women are laughing at and for not joining in the racist rhetoric they employ.

After a moment, she tunes in to the conversation and to her interlocutor's network of interlocking ideas, including her opinion about the superiority of the southern countryside to the busy northern city life. However, Jean Louise's attempts to defend New York are doomed to fail, and indeed she does not even try to make her case forcefully. Following Hester's shocked report that, during her trip there, she witnessed a "Negro woman eating her dinner right next to me, right *next* to me," Jean Louise replies, "Did she hurt you in any way?" (181), trying to guide her interlocutor into a constructive realization. But such an elenctic strategy of questioning falls flat, for it is not Logos, it is not reason, that governs Hester's mind, and she cannot be convinced in such a Socratic manner. As a result, Jean Louise realizes that she is "blind" to what other southerners see and that she needs a "watchman" to lead her around and "to draw a line down the middle and say here is this justice and there is that justice and make me understand the difference" (182).

Ultimately, neither Aunt Alexandra nor Jean Louise's childhood acquaintances can really sway her to embrace her southernness. This next battle for her identity is waged by Uncle Jack—aka Dr. Finch—who, with his old cat, Rose Aylmer, on his lap and his peculiar, comic mannerisms, manages to fulfill his role as the spokesman for the South and the advocate of the southern mind. Jean Louise, who, through most of the novel, has bounced back and forth between the known and the unknown, comes to him for assistance and mental anchoring. Indeed, after a lengthy exchange, he contributes greatly to the fostering of her southernness.

At the beginning of their encounter, Jean Louise asks in tears: "What's been happening, Uncle Jack? What *is* the matter with Atticus? I think Hank and Aunty have lost their minds and I know I'm losing mine" (187). Her confused questions presuppose that there has indeed been some kind of change in the people she used to know, that they have somehow metamorphosed into an aberration of what she construes as a homey and romantic myth of the region. Uncle Jack will seek to prove to her that this is not the case, and he sets out to show that it is Jean Louise's perception of things that remains faulty. He proves to her that it is she who is exorbitant, from the perspective of southern decorum, and that it is her unruliness and rebelliousness that is excessive and needs to be rectified.

In Uncle Jack's eristic paradigm, the initial rhetorical battle in the war for Jean Louise's regional identity is all about the exculpation of her father. Having scolded his niece for calling her father a "nigger-hater," Uncle Jack reassures her of his noble intentions, aimed at the protection of the South: "All over the South your father and men like your father are fighting a sort of rearguard, delaying action to preserve a certain kind of philosophy that's almost gone down the drain" (188). Atticus's actions are metaphorically presented as a war waged for the noble cause of regional identity and pride; thus, the actions that repulse Jean Louise to the point of nausea are given a patriotic slant. By doing what he does, her uncle implies, Atticus protects the cultural heritage of Maycomb and of its neighborhood—of which, he stresses, she is a part, whether she likes it or not.

Uncle Jack understands the persuasive task ahead of him, and he looks at Jean Louise as if she were "something under a microscope" (187), a research object of uncanny incomprehensibility, which he needs to illuminate in a careful and meticulous manner. He recognizes the need to explicate to his niece the state of affairs in the South, as he and Atticus view it, and that he must make her understand something that "three-fourths of a nation have failed to this day to understand" (189). But all of this must be done with a proper verbal strategy and with rhetorical elasticity.

Thus, he chooses neither to preach nor to perorate ceaselessly. Instead, he fashions his argument upon a series of premises that he consecutively asks his niece to agree upon. In this way, his Logos-driven rhetorical strategy is much more effective than Aunt Alexandra's one-sided lecture, filled as it is with pathos and emotional appeals based on resentment. With each affirmative answer from Jean Louise, a little skirmish of the rhetorical war is won, and although Jean Louise suspects that she is being "lured slowly and stealthily into Dr. Finch's web" (190), she has little choice but acknowledge the points he is making. The multiple enthymematic premises in his words, strategically positioned throughout the exchange, prove that, in the fight for his niece's southernness, he has thrown as wide a web as he can construct. Her occasional vetoes, such as "It made me sick, Uncle Jack. Plain-out sick" (189), are too general and too subjective to spell an argumentative difference, and thus they mean nothing against his strategic and systematic corollaries.

In response to Jean Louise's general and somewhat desperate remarks, Uncle Jack deploys precise rhetorical commonplaces, local topoi to which she can refer and is obliged to accept. As a persuasive spokesman for the South, Uncle Jack takes Maycomb as a case study, explicating the bonds of kinship among its citizens, each time using people from his niece's childhood as reference points. He asks confidently, "You remember Matthew Arnold, don't you?" or "You remember Dean Stanley, don't you?" (190), using such questions as points of emphatic reassurance.

He builds his argument from the bottom up, with real-life individuals as building blocks of the overall argumentative framework. And when, at the beginning of this listing, Jean Louise fails to see what connects the dots, Uncle Jack bluntly asserts to his doubtful niece, "You've never opened your eyes"

(190). Thus, the trope of sight appears in the book once again, and here it comes to signify Jean Louise's blockade of her inner southernness and her lack of comprehension of the existence of what Uncle Jack would see as a network of pivotal social complexities. Both her idealization of her father and her disconnectedness from her hometown have made her metaphorically blind to how deeply the racial problems are rooted and to the true nature of her own background.

Uncle Jack points out that his niece has failed to see the South for what it is, a separate nation—or, to be more precise, "a nation with its own people, existing within a nation" (196). At this point, his arguments cease to pertain to Maycomb alone, as he embraces his function as the prolocutor of the whole South, defining it, in the antebellum context, as a "society highly paradoxical, with alarming inequities, but with the private honor of thousands of persons winking like lightning bugs through the night" (196). Uncle Jack acknowledges the complexity of the southern identity, of its fundamental individuality, retaining at the same time a distinctly white perspective. His definition is indeed accepting of the premises that serve as the building blocks of racial rhetoric, however docile and learned it may seek to appear.

What follows in their exchange is a rather dense torrent of sociological and economic arguments that overwhelms and confuses Jean Louise. According to Uncle Jack, the complexities of the Civil War and Reconstruction led inevitably to the "ugliest, most shameful aspect of it all—a breed of white man who lived in open economic competition with freed Negroes" (196). His consecutive points successfully drive Jean Louise to small epiphanies—as when she realizes the obvious, that members of her close family were engaged in the Civil War, a conflict that she has relegated as a mere fact of the past, with little relevance for the present moment. "Good Lord, she thought, my own grandfather fought in it" (197). The figurative umbilical cord binding Jean Louise with her regional ancestry is being reattached with every point made by Uncle Jack.

He also stresses the emergence of the "new class" in Maycomb and the danger of excessive government control, without even once focusing fully on the African American population. Impatient, his niece believes that he is purposely beating around the bush and dodging a concrete and precise truth. He, on the other hand, with a sense of a superior understanding of things, seeks to stress the complexity of the South's socioeconomic situation and to prove that, in their debate, there is no one concrete and precise truth. Thus, to him, the shocking council meeting is nothing short of a desperate means for desperate times: "When a man's looking down the double barrel of a shotgun, he picks up the first weapon he can find to defend himself, be it a stone or a stick of stovewood or a citizens' council" (200). Unlike Aunt Alexandra, Uncle Jack neither professes a personal grudge against African Americans nor adopts Aunt Alexandra's thick and ignorant sense of antagonism. Nonetheless, while his take on matters may seem more academic and comprehensive, it is in fact not much less racist.

Finally, in her exchange with Henry at the end of the novel, Jean Louise is given yet another perspective on her burning controversy. Henry explains the motivation behind his action as the need to create an image that will allow him to ascend in the social hierarchy. She is personally hurt by his presence at the city council meeting, and her wounded question, "How could you?," is met with a pragmatic answer: "We have to do a lot of things we don't want to do, Jean Louise" (228). Henry's sole agenda is to liberate himself from the odium of his "white trash" background, so he joins the racist faction not out of a sense of personal grudge or because of the network of socioeconomic factors but simply to elevate himself. His utilitarian motives are repellent to Jean Louise, who disdainfully dubs him a "scared little man" (232) and a "hypocrite" (234). He has no intention of renouncing his engagement with the city council because, as he declares, "This is my life, this town, don't you understand that? God damn it, I'm part of Maycomb County's trash, but I'm part of Maycomb County" (234).

In terms of rhetorical appeals, he centers his argument on his image, on ethos—the overcoming of the "white trash" stigma and respectable identification with the local community. The premise behind his reasoning is that in order to be a part of Maycomb, one unequivocally needs to attend the city council meetings and one needs to subscribe to racist views. The rhetorical ethos he would like to project is that of a uncompromising local activist who embraces and follows the dictates of the community's calling. In gaining the appreciation of the community, however, Henry loses Jean Louise's respect, for she can only see his actions as meekly opportunistic, remaining blind to the aspirational motivation behind them.

The threat of the hyperbolic for the normative decorum of the region's metalogic, and its clashing opposites, are visible in all of these conversations. In *Go Set a Watchman*, Lee most vividly exemplifies the ways in which the South fends for itself and protectively preserves its idiosyncratic, segregated norm. To contain Jean Louise's unruliness, the envoys of the community employ a diversity of rhetorical mechanisms that, at a certain level, coalesce into one compelling voice. And the metalogic of the hyperbolic contrast figuratively frames all of these conversations, as her rebellious, searching spirit clashes with the steadfast views of her aunt, her uncle, her partner, and, ultimately, her father. The bringing together of opposites, their violent encounter, and their gradual escalation leads to mental and physical violence, to fits and excess.

Understandably, Jean Louise resists the indoctrination, but the gravitational pull of her hometown and of her family, even with their true colors exposed, cannot be resisted. Her ultimate fierce argument with her father, and her calling him names, like the unforgivable "son of a bitch" (253), is the final act of desperation, the last painful contraction before her birth as a "seeing" southerner. Out of the violence of repulsion and verbal skirmishes emerges a new understanding, through which Jean Louise gives up her excessive unruliness and starts to accept the region's paradoxical idiom. All the hyperbolic tribulations she has experienced were intended, in the words of her uncle, "to soften your coming into this world" (263).

The carnal metaphor of birth is recurrent in the text. Earlier, during their momentous conversation, Uncle Jack stated, "Human birth is most unpleasant. It's messy, it's extremely painful, sometimes it's a risky thing. It is always bloody" (199–200). While these words refer to the political emergence of the New South, they also aptly describe the troubled mental parturition of the South's citizenry. Likewise, Uncle Jack's description of Jean Louise's falling out and prospective making up with her father reminds one of the cutting of the umbilical cord, of a painful separation of one body from another: "You had to kill yourself, or he had to kill you to get you functioning as a separate entity" (265). (This is the trope that is so pivotal in Lillian Smith's autobiography, as discussed in chapter 4.) All of these macrofigurative images, consistent in their emphasis on carnal pain, represent the mental turmoil of the hyperbolic confrontation between the inflated perspectives of Jean Louise and the people of Maycomb, of the mental and rhetorical raptures that lead to the inevitable conclusion and the triumph of southernness.

At the very end of the novel, Atticus, having been temporarily castigated and rejected by Jean Louise, is picked up from work by his prodigious daughter, to whom he declares, "I am proud of you" (277). This appreciation celebrates both her step into true adulthood and her acceptance of the community of which she is a part—as well as of its prerogatives. As a southerner, she belongs in Maycomb, for good or ill, and her visit to her hometown, which she initially swore would be only temporary, has transformed her permanently.

Tom Santopietro likens Jean Louise's process of demystification to what the readers can find in Thomas Wolfe's *You Can't Go Home Again*. There, George Webber realizes that he cannot return to "the old forms and systems of things which once seemed everlasting but which are changing all the time" (Wolfe, quoted in Santopietro 204). In *Go Set a Watchman*, it is hardly surprising that Jean Louise bends her mind-set enough to be able to move back to Alabama for good. Indeed, her uncle hints at this right before her final encounter with Atticus: "Jean Louise, have you ever thought about coming home?" (271), implying that her birth as a southerner should be followed up by the actual physical homecoming and that "her kind" is needed by her homeland. And although she declares, "I can't live in a place that I don't agree with and that doesn't agree with me" (272), there is little doubt by now that her views are evolving, as they have over the past few chapters, and that her very understanding of the South is changing as well. As her uncle explains approvingly, she has "a shadow of the beginnings" (273) of the maturity required to live in the South now. In terms of the hyperbolic, she ceases to be a dangerous, unruly excess and is reborn as a southerner who gravitates toward the acceptance of the decorum.

In this interpretation, in which the hyperbolic is represented as an antinormalizing threat, Harper Lee's second novel does not seem to be so remote from her first book. One can criticize the occasional fragmentariness of *To Kill a Mockingbird* and the conversational prolixity of *Go Set a Watchman*, yet, on a certain level, the anecdotal narration and the series of conversations share a common denominator—the South exercising diverse means to protect and perpetuate itself. If we experimentally consider the two novels as one, not on the basis of plotline but in terms of the prevalence of the regulatory mechanisms that guard southern racial excess, Harper Lee's narrations reveal themselves as the story of the main protagonist's gradual reimmersion in the South.

Thus, the initial question about the status of *To Kill a Mockingbird* as a bildungsroman has a rather convoluted and ambiguously affirmative answer. Lee's narration, understood as the conjunction of her two books, tells the story of the birth of a southerner, of the protagonist's development into an inhabitant of Jim Crow Alabama. Jean Louise's conversations with her father, her uncle, her aunt, and Henry might remind one of a soft police interrogation or an interview for admission to a religious sect, in which a future neophyte is progressively drawn into the new orthodoxy. As Jean Louise's consecutive defenses run up white flags in response to her relatives' arguments, she slowly becomes transformed and embraces her southernness. The dialectics of the advocates for the South prevail over anything she has learned during her stay in New York. In this sense, the publication of *Go Set a Watchman* necessitates a rereading of *To Kill a Mockingbird* because, taken together, the two books reveal how the segregated South perseveres and how it recaptures those who attempt to escape from it.

CODA

In "Existence and Hermeneutics," Paul Ricoeur comments on how symbolic language relates to self-understanding. The French philosopher argues that "the purpose of all interpretation is to conquer a remoteness, a distance between the past cultural epoch [. . .] and the interpreter himself." The interpreter has the potential to render the foreign familiar by making it his own and, as a result, it is "the growth of his own understanding of himself that he pursues through his understanding of the other" (16). Despite the circumstantial resemblance between certain aspects of southern culture and my own cultural background, which I implied in the introduction, my personal encounter with the literature of the South is all about overcoming such remoteness—the kind of complex remoteness that is fashioned not only by the medium of a language that is not my native tongue, or by the obvious geographic and cultural distance, but also by the flow of time. Although we continually remain preoccupied by the writings of the authors studied in this book, teaching, studying, and reading them, it may easily escape one's attention that they belong to an increasingly remote epoch, removed from us by almost a century.

Four of the authors studied in *Southern Hyperboles* were born on the eve of the twentieth century (curiously, Faulkner, Smith, and Lumpkin were born in the very same year—1897). It is a period whose circumstances contemporary readers, especially from outside the South (or, even more, from outside the United States), will find increasingly difficult to comprehend. The study of metafiguration may become a helpful hermeneutic tool to overcome this remoteness, to render the "modes of comprehension" that formed these writings more approachable, and to explain the complex dialectical engagement of readers with the works I have studied here.

Through my discussions of short stories, novels, and dramas in *Southern*

Hyperboles, I have sought to demonstrate that the hyperbolic mode of comprehension in southern fiction can manifest in a wide range of forms. All of this variety, however, springs from a uniform source of tension and ambivalence, pertaining mostly to white writers. Thus, what comes out of all the figurative "warpings" and "twistings" of the southern mind discussed in the book is an insight into the dynamic artistic processes within a unique culture engineered by a powerful sense of decorum, one that is framed by a tense network of gender, social, racial, and intellectual prerogatives of the region. It is against this backdrop of the "old order," perpetuated through notorious mythmaking, prescriptive social and gender constructs, and historical whitewashing during the first decades of the twentieth century, that southern fiction could develop the rebellious violence of the hyperbolic mode, and it is due to these pressures that a distinct aesthetics of the grotesque managed to develop and flourish.

In this sense, the hyperbolic metalogic of violent contrast and the transgression of the decorum it involved became the zeitgeist of the troubled times in Dixie. In the period from the 1930s to the late 1950s, when the works studied here were set down, the mind of the South remained, as it were, in motion, straddling two realities, looking simultaneously backward and forward. This exotropia of thought contextualized the artistic use of excessive aesthetics, which had the strength to push cultural decorum to the breaking point and form narratives that could overcome it. This creative process required exactly the metafigurative strength of hyperbole to generate meaning through a rapid process of conceptual breakage, through the clashes of bloated, contrasting extremes, to confront the oppressive sense of prescriptive norms.

In the texts discussed here, these processes take place in a variety of forms. In Katherine Anne Porter's stories, the metafiguration serves as the principle organizing the representation of her protagonist's emancipation from norms. The "architecture" of Porter's artistic design relies on the pseudo-autobiographical character of Miranda crossing the consecutive thresholds of revelation, slowly reaching the point of maturity. In order to grow, Miranda needs to confront the old order decorum, which has dictated the behavioral patterns of her family. In particular, Porter pays a significant amount of attention to the gender prescriptivism of the culture with which she seemed so well acquainted and which she simultaneously embraced, through her fabrication of the southern belle image, and rebelled against, in her complicated private life. Via the fictional character of Miranda, Porter confronts these gender stereotypes and challenges the decorum of the "old order," setting it in a hyperbolic contrast and blowing it out of proportion in a series of trials that are reminiscent of a pilgrimage.

Next, my discussion focuses on the rhetorical and figurative aspects of William Faulkner's texts. In his case, I seek out the hyperbolic mode in his linguistic contrasts, both in the sense of divergent modes of eristic predication and in the micro- and macrofigures used by Faulkner to describe the paradoxical entanglements in "A Rose for Emily." Both the impenetrable, monolithic arguments of the debate that ensues at the barbershop in "Dry September" and the metaphors of spatial and existential disparity between Miss Emily and the people of Jefferson allow Faulkner to portray the tensions his characters are subjected to and to draw the image of the metanarrative conflicts that permeate the world of Yoknapatawpha County.

For the authors of two social autobiographies, Lillian Smith and Katharine Du Pre Lumpkin, the hyperbolic metalogic expresses not the external but the internal tensions of a mind in flux. The narrators of both memoirs discussed here sought to confront what they respectively label as "intellectual deafness" and the "twilight zone"—the veiled and muzzled areas in their minds into which the selective mode of thinking had been instilled during their childhoods. The metanarrative rapture in the narratives, and their attempts to regain their voices and come up with a new vocabulary to revisit the identity, inevitably rely on the violence of hyperbolic metalogic. While, for Smith, the reclaiming and reinventing of her own voice amounts to metafigurative operations of metaphoric breakage and departure, in the case of Lumpkin, it is more about an attempt to deconstruct the Lost Cause plantation mythology as proselytized by the narrator's father. Through the hyperbolic clash of the mythologized space with a distraught reality, the narrator of *The Making of a Southerner* seeks to reverse the eponymous process of "making" that she underwent and to repossess the power to construe the narrative without the ideological semiotics of the Lost Cause.

For Tennessee Williams, the drama of the personal and moral collapse of his female characters springs from their disintegration under the various pressures of southern social decorum. The hyperbolic dissolution his belles experience is both figurative and physical. The figurative becomes visible through the contrasts the playwright consistently selects to escalate the divide between his characters and the surrounding world. Figuratively, the content is set against the container, cold is antagonized by warmth, and the tangible vies with the ephemeral, to name just a few of the plentiful metaphoric binaries.

The figurative castigation of the body is expressed in the concluding episodes involving the abandoned figures of the belles (or pseudo belles, in the case of Bertha). They become relegated to a state of oblivion, forcefully institutionalized, and they wither away under the force of social pressures, gender models, and overwhelming, heartbroken loneliness. In my discussion of this dramatic scheme, the tragic story of Williams's sister is, for me, the obvious blueprint for the tragic downfall he replicates in his plays, but certainly his drama goes beyond the mere mirroring of a real-life trauma. The despondency of his banished belles, who become excessive, exiled grotesques, is unveiled against the backdrop of social decorum, rendering them, in essence, hyperbolic. And at the end of this process, as in *A Streetcar Named Desire,* the terminus of their journey is always the stop tellingly named Cemeteries.

For Flannery O'Connor, hyperbolic metalogic constitutes the basis for the violent aesthetics of her stories and for the grotesque debasement that befalls the characters that populate them. At the consummative point of the hyperbolic escalation, which comes at the moment of either the brutal death of the body or the demise of hope, O'Connor always brings her characters a revelation from without—an epiphanic shock that is meant to startle, terrorize, and evangelize her readers, luring the secular world into a debate that she believed it was bound to lose when it was confronted with religious truth.

In the two books by Harper Lee, the hyperbolic mode demarcates the perimeters of "insiderhood" and "outsiderhood," to borrow the terms Scott Romine uses in reference to the southern narrative community ("Framing Southern Rhetoric" 4). Lee's stories also demonstrate the power of the southern mind-set over a maturing individual who seeks to come to terms with her Dixie upbringing. What I sought to stress in my discussion is the way in which Lee testifies to how the southern mind defends its prerogatives and seeks to retain control over a person raised as a southerner. The ritualistic and dialectic mechanisms to protect the link between an individual and the southern community, as well as a fierce eristic defense of the South's integrity, derive their magnetic strength from the decorum of social and racial propriety. By reorganizing one's attitude toward decorum, or by confronting the powerful mechanisms protecting it, an individual can define himself or herself anew in the context of southernness.

Obviously, a literary historian's work is never done. The pursuit of any research project inevitably leads to the discovery of a wide network of contiguous ideas and topics, each of which is often worthy of another book, or at least of an article of its own. Such is the case with *Southern Hyperboles*. In the course of my work, I stumbled upon a number of other subjects to which one could apply the method of inquiry used in this book. Some of these topics involve looking into the use of figurative hyperbole in the context of southern public oratory, seeking the manner in which it underpins the speeches and pamphlets that were part of the ongoing vitriolic debates about the racial, social, and political status of the South. The extent to which the hyperbolic mode of comprehension permeates southern religious discourse would be another potent idea. Or perhaps a comparative discussion of more contemporary literature, paired with the writings of the authors studied here, would be of interest—to check the extent to which the hyperbolic metalogic has evolved with the metamorphosis of the mind of the South over recent decades.

Of course, different authors might have been selected for discussion in this book—perhaps some whose oeuvre lends itself more felicitously to figurative analysis or those who are more diverse in terms of ethnicity. This last element, in particular, deserves further attention. As I indicated in the introduction, a comprehensive study of black writers' management of metafiguration calls for a substantial study of its own, especially in the context of the figures that writers of color employ to negotiate their identity within the hyperbolic "mind of the South" discussed in this book.

However, this book has spatial limitations, and the temptation to indulge in digression had to be overcome. As a result, these additional ideas, as promising as they seem, had to be left out, and they await possible follow-up research projects. That being the case, *Southern Hyperboles* makes no claim about the completeness of the interpretation presented here. A more reasonable final assertion would be that I hope this book will serve to inspire further studies oriented toward rhetoric and figuration in southern fiction.

NOTES

3.
The Polyphony of the Past:
William Faulkner

1. All the changes to William Faulkner's short story are discussed extensively by John K. Crane in "But the Days Grow Short."

2. A full summary of the existing critical research on "A Rose for Emily" is beyond the scope of this study. Yet there are some influential publications concerning the chronology of the story and the narration that simply must be indicated in this context. These include William Going, "Chronology in Teaching 'A Rose for Emily'"; Robert H. Woodward, "The Chronology of 'A Rose for Emily'"; Paul D. McGlynn, "The Chronology of 'A Rose for Emily'"; Helen E. Nebeker, "Chronology Revised"; Ruth Sullivan, "The Narrator in 'A Rose for Emily'"; and, more recently, Thomas Klein, "The Ghostly Voice of Gossip in Faulkner's 'A Rose for Emily.'"

4.
Breaking out of Hyperbole:
Lillian Smith and Katharine Du Pre Lumpkin

1. Anne Loveland's biography of Lillian Smith, *A Southerner Confronting the South,* explores Smith's embattled public life and how she tackled not only Jim Crow but also the National Association for the Advancement of Colored People, which she scolded for gradualism. Likewise, she did not spare other southern liberal thinkers, such as Ralph McGill or Hodding Carter, excoriating them for what she saw as an inefficient fight against segregation. Smith is presented as courageous and relentless in the political reality following *Brown v. Board of Education,* which shrank the space for the moderate white liberalism that advocated patience and flexibility and in which even a popular politician with moderate views, like the gubernatorial candidate James "Big Jim" Folsom, could hardly compete with James Patterson, who was backed by Ku Klux Klan (see Sims).

2. One such attempt was Robert Brinkmeyer's *The Fourth Ghost,* in which the author proposes to extend the study of the southern trauma beyond the haunted trinity and to

consider it in the context of European Fascism between the 1930s and 1950s. Brinkmeyer outlines how white southern writers such as William Alexander Percy, Thomas Wolfe, Robert Penn Warren, and Katherine Anne Porter used the nightmare of Fascist Europe to draw images, build analogies, and create metaphors to study the clash between cultures that they were witnessing all around them in the South.

3. It is beyond the scope of this book to provide an account of the numerous studies of the Lost Cause myth in American literature. Some earlier publications focus on the Lost Cause as "civil religion" (*Wilson*) or survey its relationship to the drama of individual Civil War figures (Connelly and Bellows). More recently, scholars have investigated the falsifications of historiography within the Lost Cause paradigm (Nolan and Gallagher) or have endeavored to reconstruct the "Native South" through the prism of the Lost Cause nostalgia (Melanie Benson Taylor). The perspective assumed in this study, however, is limited to the hyperbolic aspects of the myth and its relevance for the change that takes place in the narrator of *The Making of a Southerner.*

5.
Hyperbolic Dissolution:
Tennessee Williams

1. For a more comprehensive discussion of the metadramatic function of the reverse figuration in *Summer and Smoke,* see Michał Choiński, "Figures of Contrast in Tennessee Williams's *Summer and Smoke.*"

2. For a detailed analysis of figurative representation of prostitutes in Williams's early works, see Michał Choiński, "Hyperbolic Bodies for Sale."

6.
Hyperbolic Epiphany:
Flannery O'Connor

1. A number of critics have pointed out this analogy. In his early analysis of Flannery O'Connor's writings, "A Closer Walk with Thee" (1986), Robert Brinkmeyer observes that her didactic and communicative religious tone draws on the rhetoric of Christian fundamentalists. Similarly, L. B. Kennelly argues that O'Connor's *The Violent Bear It Away* is rhetorically "exhortative" and is inspired by a type of sermonic communication that centers on the persuasive formation of beliefs rather than on an appeal to reason.

2. In *Rhetoric of the Revival,* I study the persuasive and manipulative strategies adopted by revival preachers to appeal to large colonial audiences. Among the most effective rhetorical ploys are the use of dialogic interludes and figurative appeals to unity.

3. James Mellard comments on O'Connor's notorious reservations about psychoanalysis, stressing that her skepticism is so far-reaching that, paradoxically, Freud becomes her feared Other. He argues that what antagonized O'Connor so much was the postulate of the power of the unconscious, and its secular implications. She would much rather attribute all human imperatives to the workings of divine grace.

4. In his brief comment on the book, Harold Bloom describes the young Tarwater as a "Gnostic version of Huckleberry Finn" ("Introduction" 2).

7.
To Kill the Watchman:
Harper Lee

1. There are numerous studies on the ritualistic and quasireligious implications of lynching, though their survey is beyond the scope of this book. See the landmark studies by Brundage and by Tolnay and Beck or, more recently, the discussions of Markovitz, Bernstein, or Matthews.

2. Among other techniques, stylometry, a computer-aided method of authorship attribution, was used to juxtapose the "authorial fingerprints" of Harper Lee, Tay Hohoff, and Truman Capote with *To Kill a Mockingbird* and *Go Set a Watchman*. The results of this experiment were published by Gamerman and by Choiński, Eder, and Rybicki.

WORKS CITED

Anderson, Eric Gary. "Environed Blood: Ecology and Violence in *The Sound and the Fury* and *Sanctuary*." *Faulkner and the Ecology of the South,* edited by Joseph R. Urgo and Ann J. Abadie. Jackson: UP of Mississippi, 2005, pp. 5–46.

Anderson, Eric Gary, Taylor Hagood, and Daniel Cross Turner, editors. *Undead Souths: The Gothic and Beyond in Southern Literature and Culture.* Baton Rouge: Louisiana State UP, 2015.

Ankersmit, F. R. *Historical Representation.* Stanford, CA: Stanford UP, 2001.

Applebome, Peter. *Dixie Rising: How the South Is Shaping American Values, Politics and Culture.* New York: Random House, 1997.

Aristotle. *Nicomachean Ethics.* Translated by W. D. Ross. Kitchener: Batoche, 1999.

———. *On Rhetoric: A Theory of Civic Discourse.* Translated by George A. Kennedy. New York: Oxford UP, 1991.

Asals, Frederick. *Flannery O'Connor: The Imagination of Extremity.* Athens: U of Georgia P, 1982.

Asylum Projects. "Farmington State Hospital," www.asylumprojects.org/index.php?title=Farmington_State_Hospital.

Ayers, Edward L. "What We Talk About When We Talk About the South." *All Over the Map: Rethinking American Regions,* edited by Edward L. Ayers, Patricia Nelson Limerick, Stephen Nissenbaum, and Peter S. Onuf. Baltimore: Johns Hopkins UP, 1996, pp. 62–82.

Bak, John S. *Tennessee Williams: A Literary Life.* New York: Palgrave Macmillan, 2013.

Bakhtin, Mikhail. "The Epic and the Novel: Towards a Methodology for the Study in the Novel." *The Dialogic Imagination,* edited by Michael Holquist. Austin: U of Texas P, 1981.

———. *Rabelais and His World.* Translated by Hélène Iswolsky. Cambridge, MA: MIT Press, 1968.

Bernstein, Patricia. *The First Waco Horror: The Lynching of Jesse Washington and the Rise of the NAACP.* College Station: Texas A&M UP, 2005.

Bhaya Nair, Rukmini, Ronald Carter, and Michael Toolan. "Clines of Metaphoricity, and Creative Metaphors as Situated Risk Taking." *Journal of Literary Semantics,* vol. 17, no. 1, 1988, pp. 20–40.

Bloom, Harold. *Agon: Towards a Theory of Revisionism.* New York: Oxford UP, 1983.

———. *The Anxiety of Influence: A Theory of Poetry.* New York: Oxford UP, 1973.

———. "Introduction." *Flannery O'Connor,* edited by Harold Bloom. New York: Infobase, 2009, pp. 1–9.

Blotner, Joseph. *Faulkner: A Biography.* Jackson: UP of Mississippi, 2005.

Bone, Martyn Richard. *The Postsouthern Sense of Place in Contemporary Fiction.* Baton Rouge: Louisiana State UP, 2005.

Bride, Mary, and Arthur L. Clements. "Faulkner's 'A Rose for Emily.'" *Explicator,* vol. 20, June 1962, p. 78.

Brinkmeyer, Robert H., Jr. *The Art and Vision of Flannery O'Connor.* Baton Rouge: Louisiana State UP, 1989.

———. "A Closer Walk with Thee: Flannery O'Connor and Southern Fundamentalists." *Southern Literary Journal,* vol. 18, no. 2, 1986, pp. 3–13.

———. *The Fourth Ghost: White Southern Writers and European Fascism, 1930–1950.* Baton Rouge: Louisiana State UP, 2009.

———. "'Jesus, Stab Me in the Heart!': *Wise Blood,* Wounding, and Sacramental Aesthetics." *New Essays on Wise Blood,* edited by Michael Kreyling. Cambridge UP, 1995, pp. 71–90.

———. *Katherine Anne Porter's Artistic Development: Primitivism, Traditionalism, and Totalitarianism.* Baton Rouge: Louisiana State UP, 1993.

Brundage, W. Fitzhugh. "White Women and the Politics of Historical Memory in the New South, 1880–1920." *Jumpin' Jim Crow: Southern Politics from Civil War to Civil Rights,* edited by Jane Dailey, Glenda Elizabeth Gilmore, and Bryant Simon. Princeton, NJ: Princeton UP, 2000, pp. 115–140.

Burke, Kenneth. *A Grammar of Motives.* Cleveland: World Publishing, 1962.

———. *A Rhetoric of Motives.* Berkeley: U of California P, 1969.

Butler, Robert. "*The Religious Vision of To Kill a Mockingbird.*" *On Harper Lee: Essays and Reflections,* edited by Alice Hall Petry. Knoxville: U of Tennessee P, 2008, pp. 121–134.

Caron, Timothy P. "'He Doth Bestride the Narrow World Like a Colossus': Faulkner's Critical Reception." *A Companion to William Faulkner,* edited by Richard C. Moreland. Hoboken, NJ: Wiley-Blackwell, 2007, pp. 479–499.

Cash, W. J. *The Mind of the South.* New York: Vintage, 1991.

Cason, Clarence. *90° in the Shade.* Chapel Hill: U of North Carolina P, 1935.

Cavoto, Janice E. "Harper Lee's *To Kill A Mockingbird.*" *The Oxford Encyclopedia of American Literature,* edited by Jay Parini and Philip W. Leininger. Oxford UP, 2004, pp. 418–421.

Cheatham, George. "Death and Repetition in Porter's Miranda Stories." *American Literature,* vol. 61, no. 4, 1989, pp. 610–624.

Choiński, Michał. "Figures of Contrast in Tennessee Williams's *Summer and Smoke.*" *Polish Journal of American Studies,* vol. 13, 2019, pp. 321–330.

———. "Hyperbolic Bodies for Sale: The Figurative Representations of Prostitutes in Tennessee Williams's Early Works." *Polish Journal of American Studies,* vol. 12, 2018, pp. 129–143.

———. *Rhetoric of the Revival.* Berlin: Vandenhoeck and Ruprecht, 2016.

Choiński, Michał, Maciej Eder, and Jan Rybicki. "Harper Lee and Other People: A Stylometry Diagnosis." *Mississippi Quarterly.* Forthcoming.

Chrzanowska-Kluczewska, Elżbieta. *Much More than Metaphor: Master Tropes of Artistic Language and Imagination.* Frankfurt: Peter Lang, 2013.

———. "Philosophical Underpinnings of Metaphors: Is Vico's Tropological Circe a Vicious Circle?" *In Search of (Non)Sense,* edited by Elżbieta Chrzanowska-Kluczewska and Grzegorz Szpila. Newcastle upon Tyne: Cambridge Scholars, 2009, pp. 102–114.

———. "Tropological Space: The Imaginary Space of Figuration." *Studia Linguistica Universitatis Iagellonicae Cracoviensis.* vol. 127, 2010, 25–37.

[Cicero]. *Ad C. Herennium, libri IV: De Ratione Dicendi.* Translated by Harry Caplan. Cambridge, MA: Harvard UP, 1954.

Ciuba, Gary M. *Desire, Violence, and Divinity in Modern Southern Fiction: Katherine Anne Porter, Flannery O'Connor, Cormac McCarthy, Walker Percy.* Baton Rouge: Louisiana State UP, 2011.

Claridge, Claudia. *Hyperbole in English: A Corpus-Based Study of Exaggeration.* Cambridge: Cambridge UP, 2011.

Clayton, Bruce. "W. J. Cash: A Native Son Confronts the Past." *Reading Southern History: Essays on Interpreters and Interpretations,* edited by Glenn Feldman. Tuscaloosa: U of Alabama P, 2001, pp. 112–123.

Cobb, James C. *Away Down South: A History of Southern Identity.* New York: Oxford UP, 2005.

Connelly, Thomas Lawrence, and Barbara L. Bellows. *God and General Longstreet: The Lost Cause and the Southern Mind.* Baton Rouge: Louisiana State UP, 1982.

Crane, John K. "But the Days Grow Short: A Reinterpretation of Faulkner's 'Dry September.'" *Twentieth-Century Literature,* vol. 31, no. 4, 1985, pp. 410–420.

Davis, Barbara Thompson. "Katherine Anne Porter, The Art of Fiction No. 29." *Paris Review,* no. 29, Winter-Spring 1963,www.theparisreview.org/interviews/4569/katherine-anne-porter-the-art-of-fiction-no-29-katherine-anne-porter.

Davis, David A. "The Forgotten Apocalypse: Katherine Anne Porter's *Pale Horse, Pale Rider,* Traumatic Memory, and the Influenza Pandemic of 1918." *Southern Literary Journal,* vol. 43, no. 2, 2011, pp. 55–74.

DeMouy, Jane Krause. *Katherine Anne Porter's Women: The Eye of Her Fiction.* Austin: U of Texas P, 1983.

Derrida, Jacques. "Racism's Last Word." *Critical Inquiry,* vol. 12, no. 1, 1985, pp. 290–299.

———. *Writing and Difference.* Translated by Alan Bass. Chicago: U of Chicago P, 1978.

DiCicco, Lorraine. "The Dis-Ease of Katherine Anne Porter's Greensick Girls in 'Old Mortality.'" *Southern Literary Journal,* vol. 33, no. 2, 2001, pp. 80–98.

Dixon, Peter. *Rhetoric.* New York: Routledge, 1990.

The Douay-Rheims Bible. Edited by George Leo Haydock. New York: Johnson, Fry, 1865.

Duck, Leigh Anne. *The Nation's Region: Southern Modernism, Segregation, and U.S. Nationalism.* Athens: U of Georgia P, 2006.

Eagleton, Terry. *Literary Theory: An Introduction.* London: Routledge, 1983.

Egerton, John. *The Americanization of Dixie: The Southernization of America.* New York: Harper's Magazine Press, 1974.

Enjolras, Laurence. *Flannery O'Connor's Characters.* Lanham, MD: UP of America, 1998.

Ettenhuber, Katrin. "Hyperbole: Exceeding Similitude." *Renaissance Figures of Speech,* edited by Sylvia Adamson, Gavin Alexander, and Katrin Ettenhuber. Cambridge UP, 2008, pp. 197–214.

Falk, Signi Lenea. *Tennessee Williams.* New York: Twayne, 1978.

Faulkner, William. *Absalom, Absalom!* New York: Vintage, 1990.

———. *Essays, Speeches and Public Letters.* Edited by James B. Meriwether. New York: Modern Library, 2004.

———. "An Introduction to *The Sound and the Fury.*" *Mississippi Quarterly,* vol. 26, 1973, pp. 410–415.

———. *Light in August.* New York: Vintage, 1990.

———. *Lion in the Garden: Interviews with William Faulkner, 1926–1962.* Edited by James B. Meriwether and Michael Millgate. New York: Random House, 1968.

———. *The Portable Faulkner.* Edited by Malcolm Cowley. New York: Viking, 1946.

———. *Selected Letters of William Faulkner.* Edited by Joseph Blotner. New York: Random House, 1977.

———. *Selected Short Stories.* New York: Modern Library, 2012.

Fiedler, Leslie A. *Love and Death in the American Novel.* Champaign, IL: Dalkey Archive Press, 1960.

Fogelin, Robert J. "Some Figures of Speech." *Argumentation: Across the Lines of Discipline,* edited by Frans H. van Eemeren, Rob Grootendorst, Anthony Blair, and Charles A. Willard. Dordrecht: Foris, 1987, pp. 263–272.

Foucault, Michel. *The Order of Things: An Archaeology of the Human Sciences.* London: Routledge, 2009.

Fox, Heather. "Resurrecting Truth in Katherine Anne Porter's 'The Fig Tree.'" *The Explicator,* vol. 72, no. 3, 2014, pp. 219–223.

Freeley, Kathleen. *Flannery O'Connor: Voice of the Peacock*. New Brunswick, NJ: Rutgers UP, 1982.

Freeman, Margaret H. "Poetry and the Scope of Metaphor: Toward a Cognitive Theory of Literature." *Metaphor and Metonymy at the Crossroads*, edited by Antonio Barcelona. Berlin: De Gruyter Mouton, 2006, pp. 253–281.

Gamerman, Ellen. "Data Miners Dig into 'Go Set a Watchman.'" *Wall Street Journal*, 17 July 2015, p. D5.

Gaston, Paul M. *The New South Creed: A Study in Southern Mythmaking*. New York: Knopf, 1970.

Genette, Gérard. *Figures of Literary Discourse*. Translated by Alan Sheridan. Oxford: Basil Blackwell, 1982.

Giannone, Richard. *Flannery O'Connor: Hermit Novelist*. Urbana: U of Illinois P, 2000.

Gibbons, Kaye. "Planes of Language and Time: The Surfaces of the Miranda Stories." *Kenyon Review*, vol. 10, 1988, pp. 74–79.

Gibbs, Raymond W., Jr. *Poetics of Mind: Figurative Thought, Language, and Understanding*. Cambridge UP, 1994.

Girard, René. *Violence and the Sacred*. Baltimore: Johns Hopkins UP, 1977.

Givner, Joan. *Katherine Anne Porter: A Life*. Athens: U of Georgia P, 1991.

Gladney, Margaret Rose, and Lisa Hodgens, editors. *A Lillian Smith Reader*. Athens: U of Georgia P, 2016.

Going, William T. "Chronology in Teaching 'A Rose for Emily.'" *Exercise Exchange*, vol. 5, 1958, pp. 8–11.

Gray, Richard. *The Life of William Faulkner*. Oxford: Wiley-Blackwell, 1994.

———. *A Web of Words: The Great Dialogue of Southern Literature*. Athens: U of Georgia P, 2007.

Greeson, Jennifer Rae. *Our South: Geographic Fantasy and the Rise of National Literature*. Cambridge, MA: Harvard UP, 2010.

Gretlund, Jan Nordby. *Frames of Southern Mind: Reflections on the Stoic, Bi-racial & Existential South*. Odense UP, 1998.

Griffin, Alice. *Understanding Tennessee Williams*. Columbia: U of South Carolina P, 1995.

Hagopian, John, and Martin Dolch. "Faulkner's 'A Rose for Emily.'" *Explicator*, vol. 22, April 1964, p. 68.

Hall, Jacquelyn Dowd. "'You Must Remember This': Autobiography as Social Critique." *Journal of American History*, vol. 85, no. 2, pp. 439–465.

Hannon, Charles. *Faulkner and the Discourses of Culture*. Baton Rouge: Louisiana State UP, 2005.

Harpham, Geoffrey Galt. *On the Grotesque: Strategies of Contradiction in Art and Literature*. Princeton, NJ: Princeton UP, 1982.

Hawhee, Debra. *Bodily Arts: Rhetoric and Athletics in Ancient Greece.* Austin: U of Texas P, 2004.

Hinrichsen, Lisa. *Possessing the Past: Trauma, Imagination, and Memory in Post-Plantation Southern Literature.* Baton Rouge: Louisiana State UP, 2015.

Hobson, Fred. *But Now I See: The White Southern Racial Conversion Narrative.* Baton Rouge: Louisiana State UP, 1999.

———. Foreword. *Strange Fruit,* by Lillian Smith. Athens: U of Georgia P, 1985, pp. vii–xviii.

———. *Tell about the South: The Southern Rage to Explain.* Baton Rouge: Louisiana State UP, 1983.

Holman, C. Hugh. "The Southerner as American Writer." *The Roots of Southern Writing,* edited by C. Hugh Holman. Athens: U of Georgia P, 1972, pp. 1–16.

Howell, Elmo. "Faulkner's 'A Rose for Emily.'" *Explicator,* vol. 19, January 1961, p. 26.

Jakobson, Roman. "*The Metaphoric and Metonymic Poles.*" *Selected Writings.* Vol. 2: *Word and Language,* edited by Roman Jakobson. The Hague: Mouton, 1971, pp. 254–259.

Johnson, Christopher D. *Hyperboles: The Rhetoric of Excess in Baroque Literature and Thought.* Cambridge, MA: Harvard UP, 2010.

Kayser, Wolfgang. *The Grotesque in Art and Literature.* Translated by Ulrich Weisstein. New York: Columbia UP, 1957.

Kendrick, Benjamin Burks, and Alex Mathews Arnett. *The South Looks at Its Past.* Chapel Hill: U of North Carolina P, 1935.

Kennelly, L. B. "Exhortation in *Wise Blood:* Rhetorical Theory as an Approach to Flannery O'Connor." *South Central Review,* vol. 4, no. 1, pp. 92–105.

King, Larry L. *Confessions of a White Racist.* New York: Viking, 1971.

Klein, Thomas. "The Ghostly Voice of Gossip in Faulkner's 'A Rose for Emily.'" *Explicator,* vol. 65, no. 4, 2007, pp. 229–232.

Kreuz, Roger J., and Richard Roberts. "Two Cues for Verbal Irony: Hyperbole and the Ironic Tone of Voice." *Metaphor and Symbolic Activity,* vol. 10, no. 1, 1995, pp. 21–31.

Kreyling, Michael. *Inventing Southern Literature.* Jackson: UP of Mississippi, 1998.

———. *The South That Wasn't There: Postsouthern Memory and History.* Baton Rouge: Louisiana State UP, 2010.

Ladd, Barbara. "Race as Fact and Fiction in William Faulkner." *Companion to Faulkner Studies,* edited by Richard C. Moreland. Hoboken, NJ: Wiley-Blackwell, 2007, pp. 133–148.

Lakoff, George, and Mark Johnson. *Metaphors We Live By.* Chicago: U of Chicago P, 1980.

Lakoff, George, and Mark Turner. *More than Cool Reason: A Field Guide to Poetic Metaphor.* Chicago: U of Chicago P, 1989.

Lahr, John. *Tennessee Williams: Mad Pilgrimage of the Flesh*. New York: Norton, 2014.

Lee, Harper. *Go Set a Watchman*. London: Arrow, 2015.

———. *To Kill a Mockingbird*. London: Arrow, 2015.

Leverich, Lyle. *Tom: The Unknown Tennessee Williams*. New York: Crown, 1995.

Levy, Helen Fiddyment. *Fiction of the Home Place: Jewett, Cather, Glasgow, Porter, Welty, and Naylor*. Jackson: UP of Mississippi, 1992.

Lodge, David. *The Modes of Modern Writing: Metaphor, Metonymy, and the Typology of Modern Literature*. London: Edward Arnold, 1977.

Loewenberg, Ina. "Labels and Hedges: The Metalinguistic Turn." *Language and Style*, vol. 15, no. 3, 1982, pp. 193–207.

Loveland, Anne C. *Lillian Smith, a Southerner Confronting the South*. Baton Rouge: Louisiana State UP, 1986.

Lumpkin, Katharine Du Pre. *The Making of a Southerner*. 1946; Athens: U of Georgia P, 1992.

Lyell, Frank H. "One-Taxi Town: *To Kill a Mockingbird*." *New York Times Book Review*, 10 July 1960, www.nytimes.com/1960/07/10/archives/onetaxi-town-to-kill-a-mockingbird-by-harper-lee-294-pp.html.

Manson, Michael L. "*To Kill a Mockingbird* and the Turn from the Gothic to Southern Liberalism." *The Palgrave Handbook of the Southern Gothic*, edited by Susan Castillo Street and Charles L. Crow. New York: Palgrave Macmillan, 2016, pp. 309–321.

Markovitz, Jonathan. *Legacies of Lynching: Racial Violence and Memory*. Minneapolis: U of Minnesota P, 2004.

Matthews, Donald G. "The Southern Rite of Human Sacrifice: Lynching in the American South." *Mississippi Quarterly*, vol. 1–2, 2008, pp. 28–70.

McCarthy, Michael, and Ronald Carter. "'There's Millions of Them': Hyperbole in Everyday Conversation." *Journal of Pragmatics*, vol. 36, 2004, pp. 149–184.

McElroy, Bernard. *Fiction and the Modern Grotesque*. London: Palgrave Macmillan, 1989.

McGlynn, Paul D. "The Chronology of 'A Rose for Emily.'" *Studies in Short Fiction*, vol. 6, no. 4, Summer 1969, pp. 461–462.

McPherson, Tara. *Reconstructing Dixie: Race, Gender, and Nostalgia in the Imagined South*. Durham, NC: Duke UP, 2003.

Mellard, James M. "Flannery O'Connor's Others: Freud, Lacan, and the Unconscious." *American Literature*, vol. 61, no. 4, 1989, pp. 625–643.

Millgate, Michael. *The Achievement of William Faulkner*. New York: Vintage, 1971.

Mitchell, Broadus. *The Rise of Cotton Mills in the South*. Baltimore: Johns Hopkins UP, 1921.

Mitchell, Broadus, and George Sinclair Mitchell. *The Industrial Revolution in the South*. Baltimore: Johns Hopkins UP, 1968.

Morris, Willie. *North Towards Home.* Boston, MA: Houghton Mifflin Harcourt, 1967.

Murray, Jennifer. "More Than One Way to (Mis)Read a *Mockingbird.*" *Southern Literary Journal,* vol. 43, no. 1, 2010, pp. 75–91.

Nebeker, Helen E. "Chronology Revised." *Studies in Short Fiction,* vol. 8, Summer 1971, pp. 471–473.

Nolan, Allan T., and Gary W. Gallagher. *The Myth of the Lost Cause and Civil War History.* Bloomington: Indiana UP, 2010.

Norrick, Neal R. "On the Semantics of Overstatement." *Sprache erkennen und verstehen,* edited by Klaus Detering, Jürgen Schmidt-Radefeldt, and Wolfgang Sucharowski. Tübingen: Halle/Salle, Max Niemeyer, 1982, pp. 168–176.

O'Connor, Flannery. "The Fiction Writer and His Country." *Mystery and Manners.* New York: Farrar, Straus and Giroux, 1969, pp. 25–36.

———. *The Habit of Being.* Edited by Sally Fitzgerald. New York: Vintage, 1979.

———. "Novelist and Believer." *Mystery and Manners.* New York: Farrar, Straus and Giroux, 1969, pp. 154–168.

———. *The Presence of Grace and Other Book Reviews by Flannery O'Connor.* Edited by Martin W. Carter and Leo J. Zuber. Athens: U of Georgia P, 1983.

———. *Selected Stories.* New York: Farrar, Straus and Giroux, 1971.

———. *Three by Flannery O'Connor: Wise Blood, The Violent Bear It Away, Everything That Rises Must Converge.* New York: New American Library, 1983.

O'Connor, Flannery, and Richard Giannone. *Spiritual Writings.* Edited by Robert Ellsberg. Maryknoll, NY: Orbis, 2003.

O'Dell, Darlene. *Sites of Southern Memory: The Autobiographies of Katharine Du Pre Lumpkin, Lillian Smith, and Pauli Murray.* Charlottesville: UP of Virginia, 2001.

Oesterreich, Peter L. "Irony," translated by Andreas Quintus. *Encyclopedia of Rhetoric,* edited by Thomas O. Sloane. New York: Oxford UP, 2001, pp. 404–406.

Osterweis, Rollin Gustav. *The Myth of the Lost Cause, 1965–1900.* Hampden, CT: Archon, 1973.

Ostrowski, Donald. "A Metahistorical Analysis: Hayden White and Four Narratives of 'Russian' History." *Clio,* vol. 19, no. 3, 1990, pp. 215–236.

Perelman, Chaïm, and Lucie Olbrechts-Tyteca. *The New Rhetoric: A Treatise on Argumentation.* Translated by John Wilkinson and Purcell Weaver. U of Notre Dame P, 1969.

Pimentel, Luz Aurora. *Metaphoric Narration: Paranarrative Dimensions in "A la recherché du temps perdu."* Toronto: U of Toronto P, 1990.

Poole, W. Scott. "Religion, Gender, and the Lost Cause in South Carolina's 1987 Governor's Race: 'Hampton or Hell!'" *Journal of Southern History,* vol. 68, no. 3, 2002, pp. 573–598.

Porter, Katherine Anne. *The Collected Essays and Occasional Writings of Katherine Anne Porter.* New York: Delacorte, 1970.

———. *The Collected Stories of Katherine Anne Porter.* New York: Harvest/Harcourt, 1979.

———. *Letters of Katherine Anne Porter.* Edited by Isabel Bayley. New York: Atlantic Monthly Press, 1990.

———. *Selected Stories.* New York: Harcourt Brace Jovanovich, 1969.

Poss, S. H. "Variations on a Theme in Four Stories of Katherine Anne Porter." *Twentieth Century Literature,* vol. 4, no. 1/2, 1958, 23–24.

Puttenham, George. *The Arte of English Poesie.* London: Richard Field, 1589. www .gutenberg.org/ebooks/16420.

Quintilian. *Institutio Oratoria.* Translated by Harold Edgeworth Butler. Cambridge, MA: Harvard UP, 1980.

Radavich, David. "The Midwestern Plays of Tennessee Williams." *Tennessee Williams Annual Review,* vol. 8, 2006, www.tennesseewilliamsstudies.org/journal/work. php?ID=67.

Rampton, David. *William Faulkner: A Literary Life.* New York: Palgrave Macmillan, 2008.

Richards, I. A. *The Philosophy of Rhetoric.* New York: Oxford UP, 1936.

Ricoeur, Paul. "Existence and Hermeneutics." *The Conflict of Interpretations: Essays in Hermeneutics,* edited by Don Ihde. Evanston, IL: Northwestern UP, 1974, pp. 3–27.

———. *The Rule of Metaphor: The Creation of Meaning in Language.* Translated by Robert Czerny. London: Routledge, 2003.

Ritter, Joshua. "Recovering Hyperbole: Rethinking the Limits of Rhetoric for an Age of Excess." *Philosophy & Rhetoric,* vol. 45, no. 4, 2012, pp. 406–428.

Robertson, Ben. *Red Hills and Cotton: An Upcountry Memory.* New York: Knopf, 1941.

Rogers, Jonathan. *The Terrible Speed of Mercy: A Spiritual Biography of Flannery O'Connor.* Nashville: Thomas Nelson, 2012.

Romine, Scott. "Framing Southern Rhetoric: Lillian Smith's Narrative Persona in 'Killers of the Dream.'" *South Atlantic Review,* vol. 59, no. 2, 1994, pp. 95–111.

———. *The Narrative Forms of Southern Community.* Baton Rouge: Louisiana State UP, 1999.

———. *The Real South: Southern Narrative in the Age of Cultural Reproduction.* Baton Rouge: Louisiana State UP, 2008.

Rooke, Constance, and Bruce Wallis. "Myth and Epiphany in Porter's 'The Grave.'" *Katherine Anne Porter,* edited by Harold Bloom. New York: Chelsea House, 1986, pp. 61–68.

Ruskin, John. *The Stones of Venice.* Memphis, TN: General Books, 2009.

Saddik, Annette J. *Tennessee Williams and the Theatre of Excess: The Strange, the Crazed, the Queer.* Cambridge UP, 2015.

Santopietro, Tom. *Why "To Kill a Mockingbird" Matters.* New York: St. Martin's, 2018.

Seidel, Kathryn Lee. "Growing Up Southern: Resisting the Code for Southerners in *To Kill a Mockingbird.*" *On Harper Lee: Essays and Reflections,* edited by Alice Petry. Knoxville: U of Tennessee P, 2007, pp. 79–92.

Seneca the Younger. *De Beneficiis.* Edited by Carl Hosius. Los Altos, CA: Packard Humanities Institute, 1982.

Shapiro, Michael, and Marianne Shapiro. *Figuration in Verbal Art.* Princeton, NJ: Princeton UP, 1988.

———. *Hierarchy and the Structure of Tropes.* Bloomington: Indiana UP, 1976.

Shields, Charles. *I Am Scout: The Biography of Harper Lee.* New York: Henry Holt, 2008.

Siegel, Robert. "The Metaphysics of Tennessee Williams." *Magical Muse: Millennial Essays on Tennessee Williams,* edited by Ralph F. Voss. Tuscaloosa: U of Alabama P, 2002, pp. 111–130.

Sims, George E. *The Little Man's Big Friend: James E. Folsom in Alabama Politics, 1946–1958.* Tuscaloosa: U of Alabama P, 1985.

Smith, Jonathan Z. "The Domestication of Sacrifice: Discussion." *Violent Origins: Walter Burkert, René Girard, and Jonathan Z. Smith on Ritual Killings and Cultural Formation,* edited by Robert G. Hamerton-Kelly. Stanford, CA: Stanford UP, 1987, pp. 206–238.

Smith, Lillian. *Killers of the Dream.* New York: W. W. Norton, 1994.

Snead, James A. *Figures of Division: William Faulkner's Major Novels.* New York: Methuen, 1986.

Sperber, Dan, and Deirdre Wilson. "Irony and the Use-Mention Distinction." *Radical Pragmatics,* edited by Peter Cole. New York: Academic Press, 1981, pp. 295–318.

Spitzbardt, Harry. "Overstatement and Understatement in British and American English." *Philologica Pragensia,* vol. 6, 1963, pp. 277–286.

Srigley, Susan. "The Violence of Love: Reflections on Self-Sacrifice through Flannery O'Connor and René Girard." *Religion and Literature,* vol. 39, no. 3, 2007, pp. 31–45.

Stafford, T. J. "Tobe's Significance in 'A Rose for Emily.'" *Modern Fiction Studies,* vol. 14, 1969, pp. 451–453.

Stanivukovic, Goran V. "'Mounting above the Truthe': On Hyperbole in English Renaissance Literature." *Forum for Modern Language Studies,* vol. 43, no. 1, 2007, pp. 9–33.

Stockwell, Peter. *Cognitive Poetics: An Introduction.* London: Routledge, 2002.

Stout, Janis P. *Katherine Anne Porter: A Sense of the Times.* Charlottesville: U of Virginia P, 1995.

Styron, William. *Sophie's Choice.* New York: Random House, 1979.

Sullivan, Ceri. *The Rhetoric of the Conscience in Donne, Herbert, and Vaughan.* New York: Oxford UP, 2008.

Sullivan, Ruth. "The Narrator in 'A Rose for Emily.'" *Journal of Narrative Technique*, vol. 1, September 1971, pp. 159–178.

Sykes, John D., Jr. *Flannery O'Connor, Walker Percy, and the Aesthetic of Revelation.* Columbia: U of Missouri P, 2007.

Taylor, Melanie Benson. *Reconstructing the Native South: American Indian Literature and the Lost Cause,* Athens: U of Georgia P, 2011.

Taylor, Walter. *Faulkner's Search for a South.* Urbana: U of Illinois P, 1983.

Thomson, Philip John. *The Grotesque.* London: Methuen, 1972.

Thompson, Tracy. *The New Mind of the South.* New York: Free Press, 2013.

Tillman, Nathaniel. "*Strange Fruit* in Retrospect." *Phylon,* vol. 5, no. 3, 1944, pp. 288–289.

Titus, Mary. *The Ambivalent Art of Katherine Anne Porter.* Athens: U of Georgia P, 2005.

Tolnay, Stewart Emory, and E. M. Beck. *A Festival of Violence: An Analysis of Southern Lynchings, 1882–1930.* Urbana: U of Illinois P, 1995.

Vann, Richard T. "The Reception of Hayden White." *History and Theory,* vol. 37, no. 2, 1998, pp. 143–161.

Vico, Giambattista. *The New Science.* Translated by Thomas Goddard Bergin and Max Harold Fisch. Ithaca, NY: Cornell UP, 1948.

Vitruvius [Marcus Vitruvius Pollio]. *The Ten Books on Architecture* [De architectura]. Translated by Morris Hicky Morgan. Cambridge, MA: Harvard University Press, 1914. http://www.gutenberg.org/ebooks/20239.

Volpe, Edmond L. *A Reader's Guide to William Faulkner: The Short Stories.* Syracuse, NY: Syracuse UP, 2004.

Warren, Robert Penn. "Cowley's Faulkner." *William Faulkner: The Critical Heritage,* edited by John Bassett. London: Routledge, 1975, pp. 314–328.

———. "John Crowe Ransom: A Study in Irony." *Virginia Quarterly Review,* vol. 11, no. 1, 1935, www.vqronline.org/essay/john-crowe-ransom-study-irony.

Wasser, Audrey. "Hyperbole in Proust." *Modern Language Notes,* vol. 129, no. 4, 2014, pp. 829–854.

Watters, Pat. *Down to Now: Reflections on the Southern Civil Rights Movement.* Athens: U of Georgia P, 1993.

Weinstein, Philip M. *Faulkner's Subject: A Cosmos No One Owns.* New York: Cambridge UP, 2008.

Welty, Eudora. *Occasions: Selected Writings.* Edited by Pearl Amelia McHaney. Jackson: U of Mississippi P, 2009.

White, Hayden. *Metahistory: The Historical Imagination in 19th-Century Europe*. Baltimore: Johns Hopkins UP, 1973.

———. *Tropics of Discourse: Essays in Cultural Criticism*. Baltimore: Johns Hopkins UP, 1978.

White, Walter F. "I Investigate Lynchings (*American Mercury*, January 1929)." *The Making of African American Identity*, vol. 3, 1917–1968, National Humanities Center Research Toolbox, nationalhumanitiescenter.org/pds/maai3/segregation/text2/investigatelynchings.pdf.

Williams, Tennessee. *27 Wagons Full of Cotton and Other One-Act Plays*. New York: New Directions, 1953.

———. *The Glass Menagerie*. London: Bloomsbury, 2009.

———. *Memoirs*. New York: New Directions, 2006.

———. *New Selected Essays: Where I Live*. Edited by John S. Bak. New York: New Directions, 2009.

———. *Notebooks*. Edited by Margaret Bradham Thornton. New Haven, CT: Yale UP, 2006.

———. *A Streetcar Named Desire*. New York: New Directions, 2004.

———. *The Theatre of Tennessee Williams*. Vol. 2. New York: New Directions, 1971.

Wilson, Charles Reagan. *Baptized in Blood: The Religion of the Lost Cause*. Athens: U of Georgia P, 1980.

Woodward, C. Vann. *American Counterpoint: Slavery and Racism in the North-South Dialogue*. Boston, MA: Little, Brown, 1971.

———. *The Burden of Southern History*. Baton Rouge: Louisiana State UP, 1960.

Woodward, Robert H. "The Chronology of 'A Rose for Emily.'" *Exercise Exchange*, vol. 13 (March 1966), pp. 17–19.

Yaeger, Patricia. *Dirt and Desire: Reconstructing Southern Women's Writing, 1930–1990*. Chicago: U of Chicago P, 2000.

INDEX